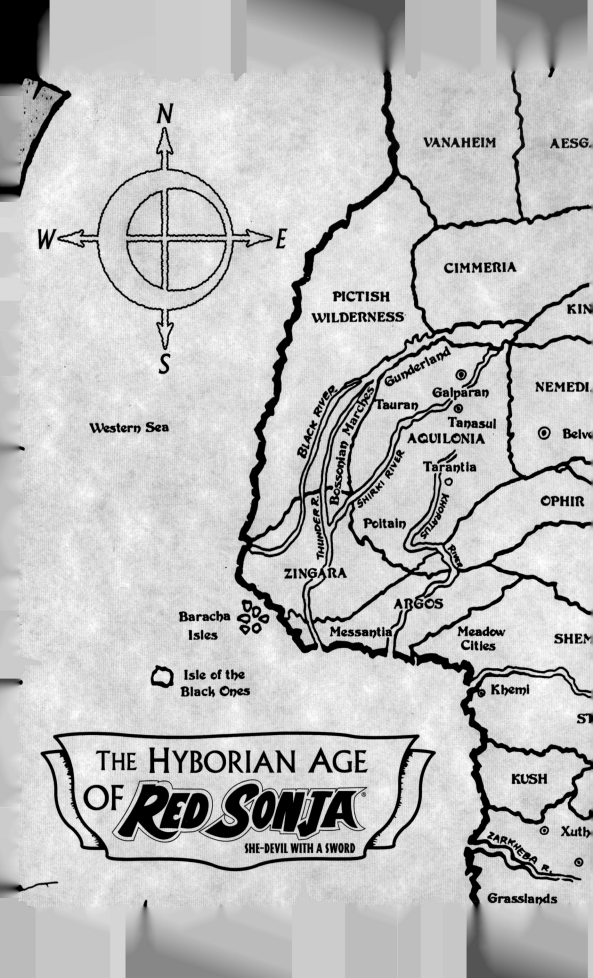

N

W   E

S

VANAHEIM   AESGA

CIMMERIA

KIN

PICTISH
WILDERNESS

NEMEDI.

Gunderland

Galparan

Tauran   Tanasul

BLACK RIVER

Bossonian Marches

AQUILONIA

Belve

Western Sea

SHIRKI RIVER

Tarantia

OPHIR

THUNDER R.

KHOROTUS

Poitain

ZINGARA

River

Baracha
Isles

ARGOS

Messantia

Meadow
Cities

SHEM

Isle of the
Black Ones

Khemi

THE HYBORIAN AGE
OF **RED SONJA**®
SHE-DEVIL WITH A SWORD

KUSH

ST

Xuth

ZARKHEBA R.

Grasslands

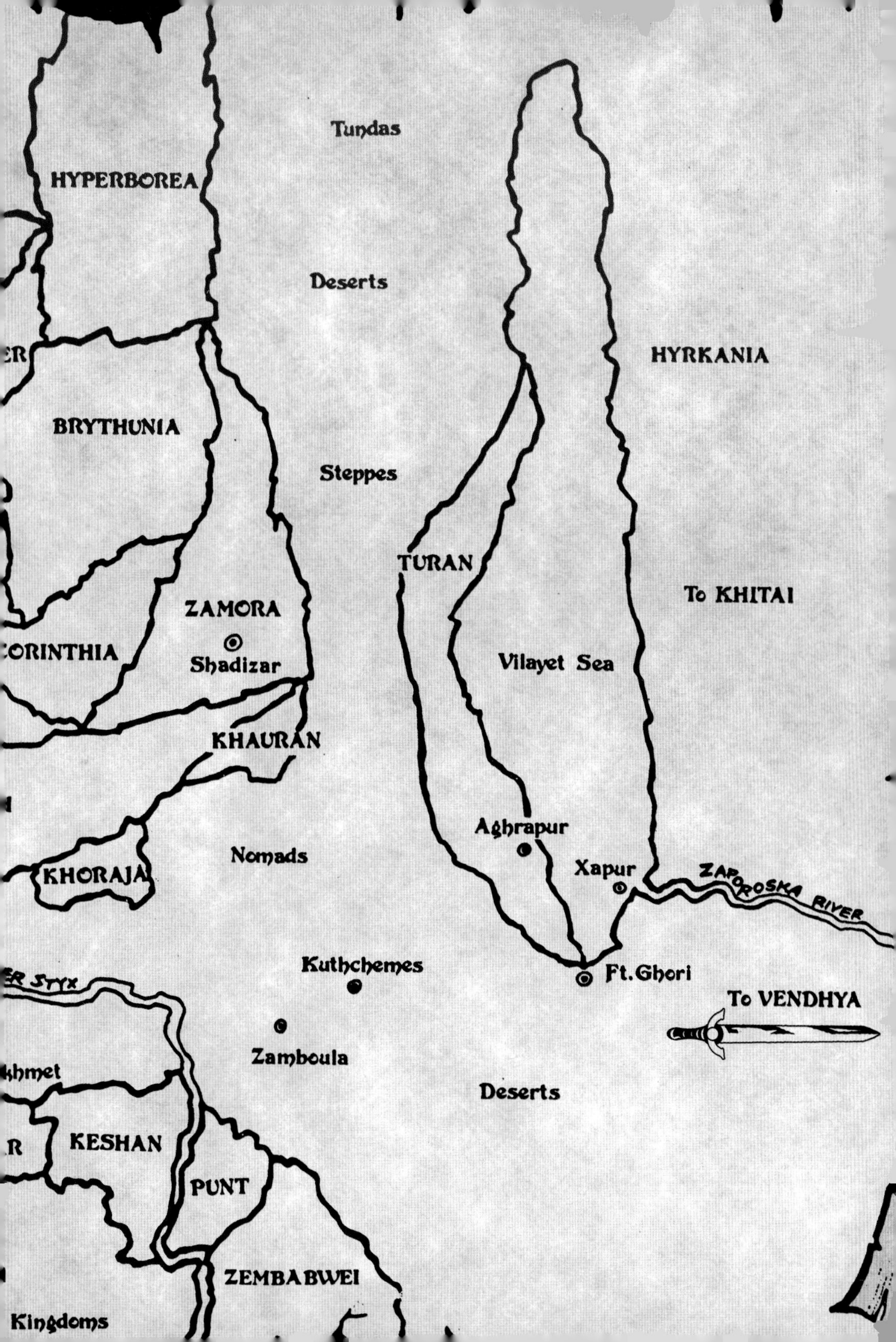

Tundas
HYPERBOREA
Deserts
HYRKANIA
BRYTHUNIA
Steppes
TURAN
To KHITAI
ZAMORA
Shadizar
CORINTHIA
Vilayet Sea
KHAURAN
Aghrapur
Nomads
KHORAJA
Xapur
ZAPOROSKA RIVER
Kuthchemes
Ft. Ghori
To VENDHYA
Zamboula
Deserts
KESHAN
PUNT
ZEMBABWEI
Kingdoms

Dynamite Entertainment Presents

SAVAGE RED SONJA®

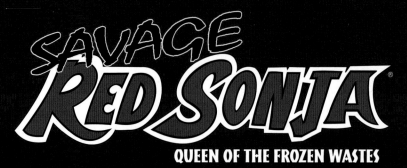

QUEEN OF THE FROZEN WASTES

Dedicated to **Robert E. Howard**

- WRITERS
  Frank Cho & Doug Murray
- ART
  Homs
- Color
  Will Murai
- Lettering
  Simon Bowland

THIS VOLUME COLLECTS ISSUES ONE THROUGH FOUR OF SAVAGE RED SONJA: QUEEN OF THE FROZEN WASTES.

BASED ON THE HEROINE CREATED BY
ROBERT E. HOWARD

EXECUTIVE EDITOR / RED SONJA
LUKE LIEBERMAN

IN MEMORY OF ARTHUR LIEBERMAN

FOR MORE ON RED SONJA VISIT: WWW.DYNAMITE.COM OR WWW.REDSONJA.COM.

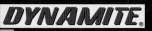

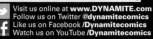

DYNAMITE®
Visit us online at **www.DYNAMITE.com**
Follow us on Twitter **@dynamitecomics**
Like us on Facebook **/Dynamitecomics**
Watch us on YouTube **/Dynamitecomics**

Nick Barrucci, CEO / Publisher
Juan Collado, President / COO
Joe Rybandt, Senior Editor
Josh Johnson, Art Director
Rich Young, Director Business Development
Jason Ullmeyer, Senior Graphic Designer
Keith Davidsen, Marketing Manager
Josh Green, Traffic Coordinator
Chris Caniano, Production Assistant

COMIC SHOP LOCATOR SERVICE
888-COMIC-BOOK
comicshoplocator.com

Second Printing
ISBN-10: 1-93305-38-X
ISBN-13: 978-1-93330-538-7
10 9 8 7 6 5 4 3 2

For information regarding press, media rights, foreign rights, licensing, promotions, and advertising e-mail: marketing@dynamite.com

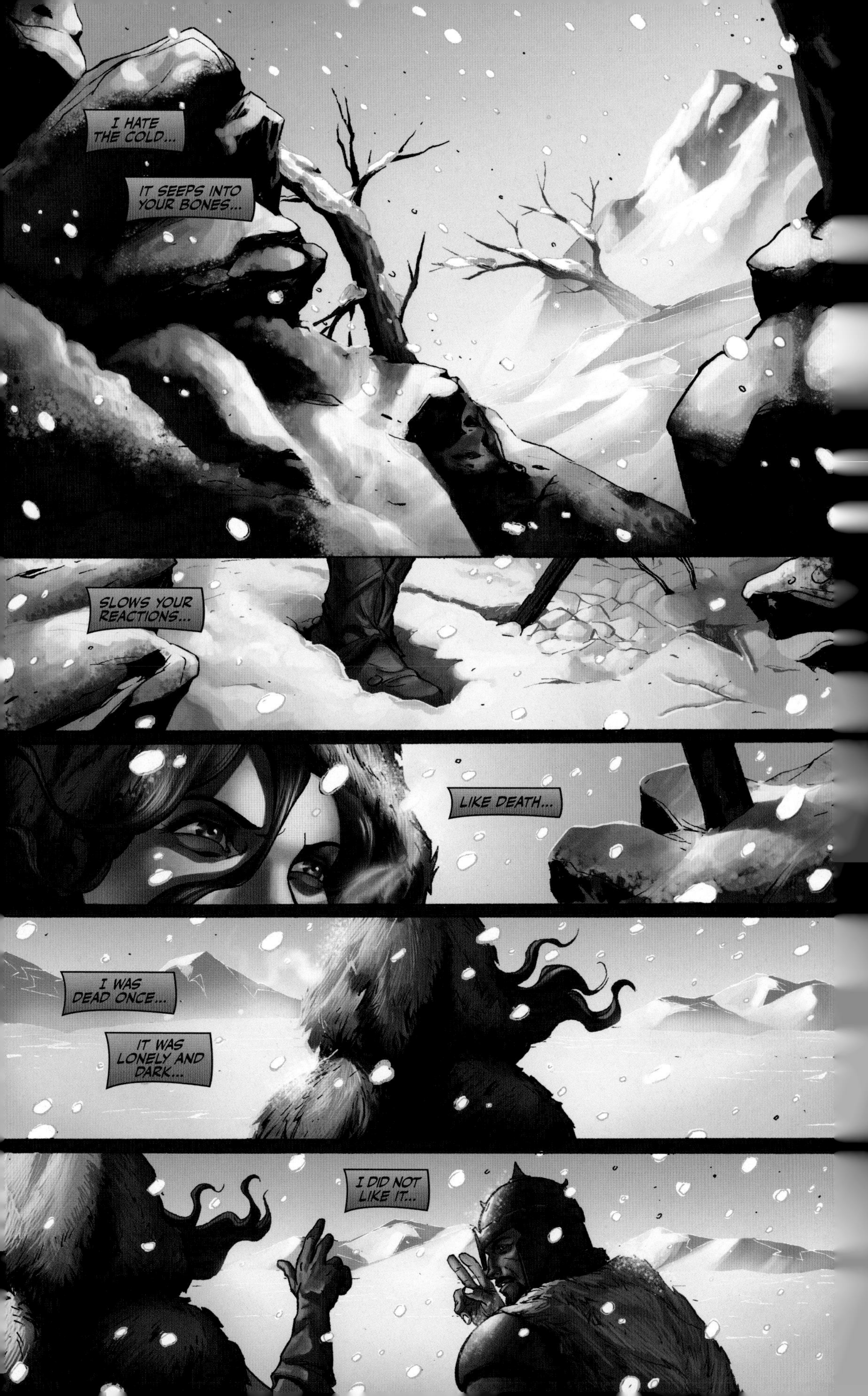
I HATE THE COLD...
IT SEEPS INTO YOUR BONES...
SLOWS YOUR REACTIONS...
LIKE DEATH...
I WAS DEAD ONCE...
IT WAS LONELY AND DARK...
I DID NOT LIKE IT...

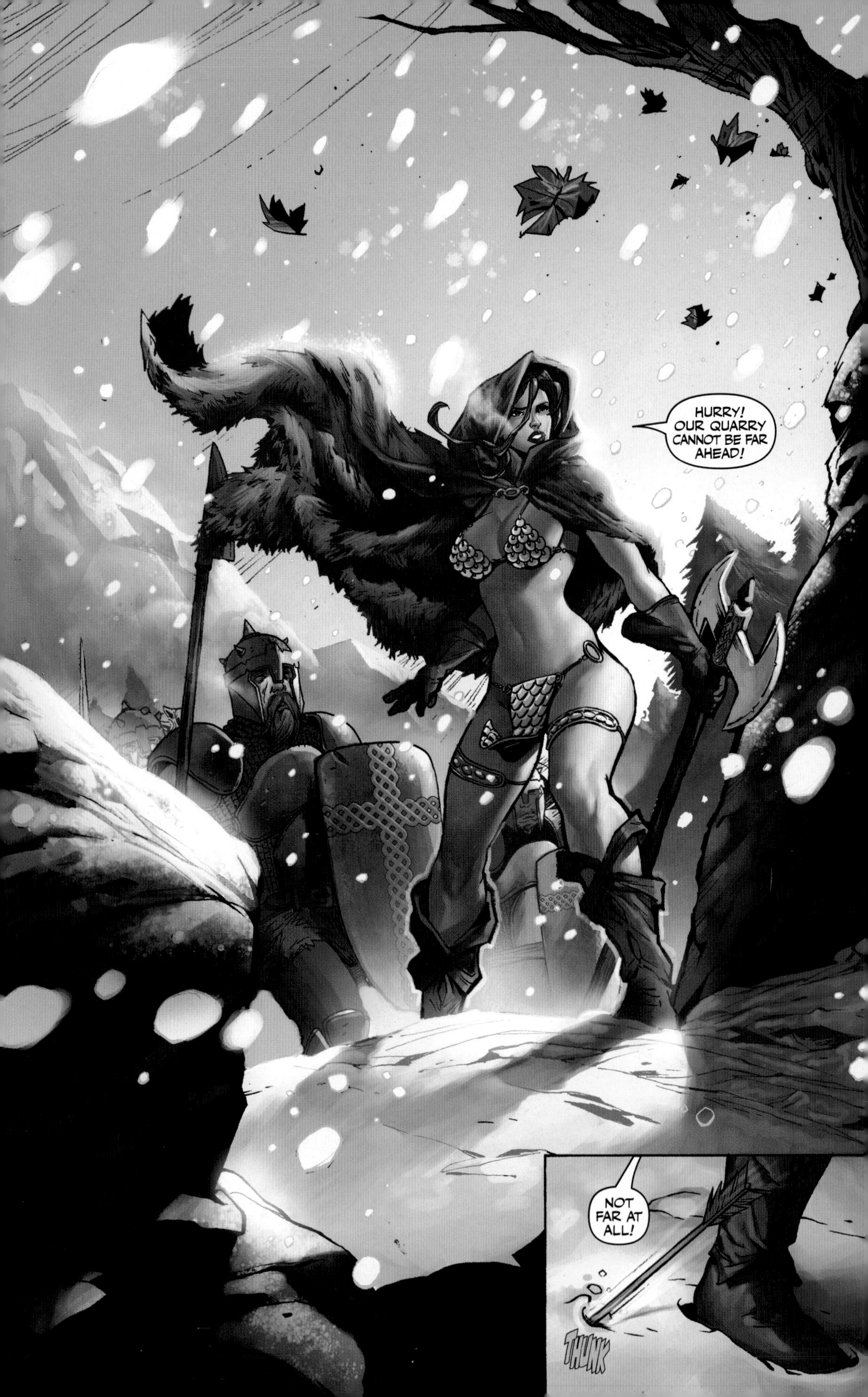
HURRY! OUR QUARRY CANNOT BE FAR AHEAD!
NOT FAR AT ALL!
THUNK

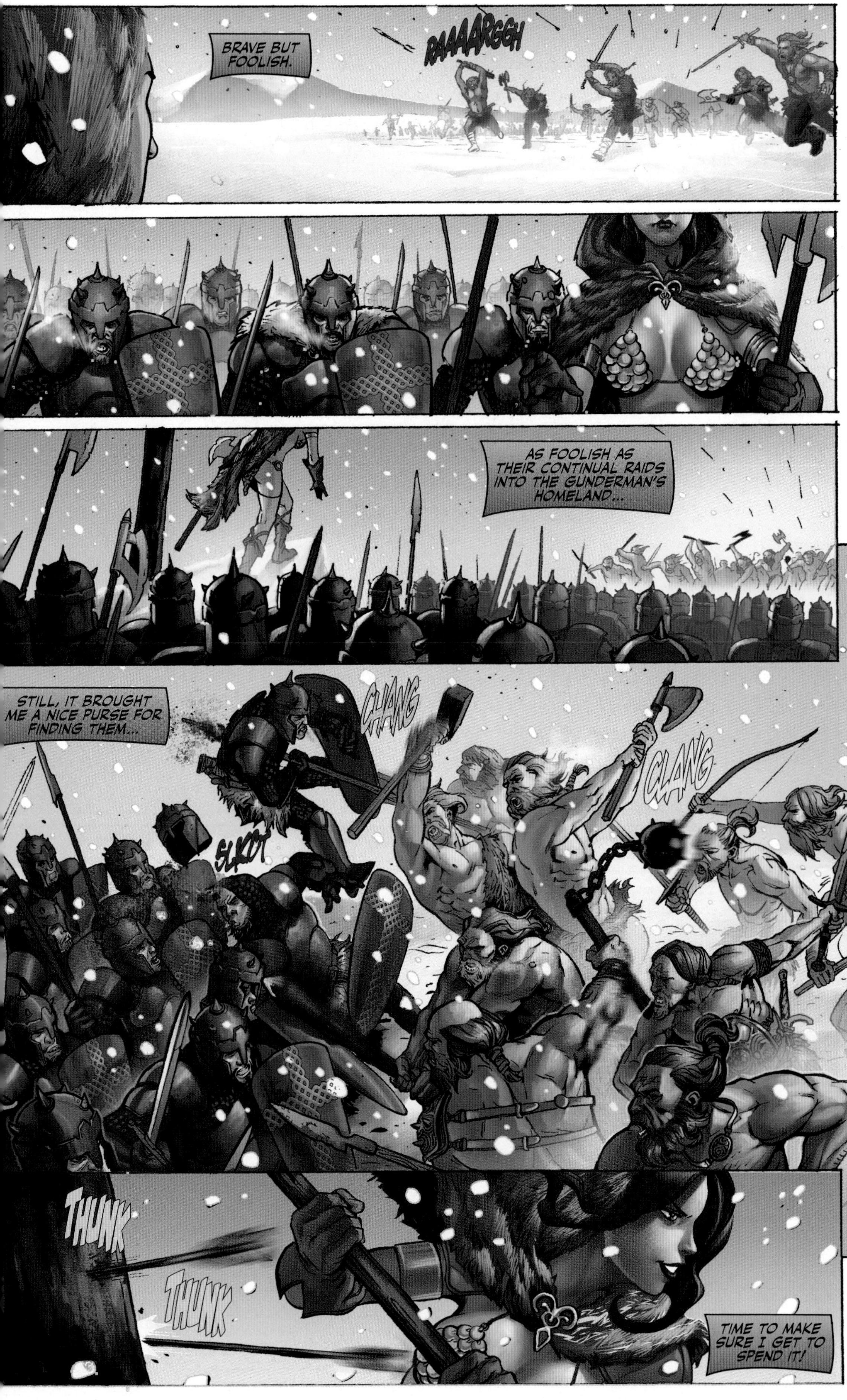
BRAVE BUT FOOLISH.
RAAAARGGH
AS FOOLISH AS THEIR CONTINUAL RAIDS INTO THE GUNDERMAN'S HOMELAND...
STILL, IT BROUGHT ME A NICE PURSE FOR FINDING THEM...
CHANG
CLANG
SLKDT
THUNK
THUNK
TIME TO MAKE SURE I GET TO SPEND IT!

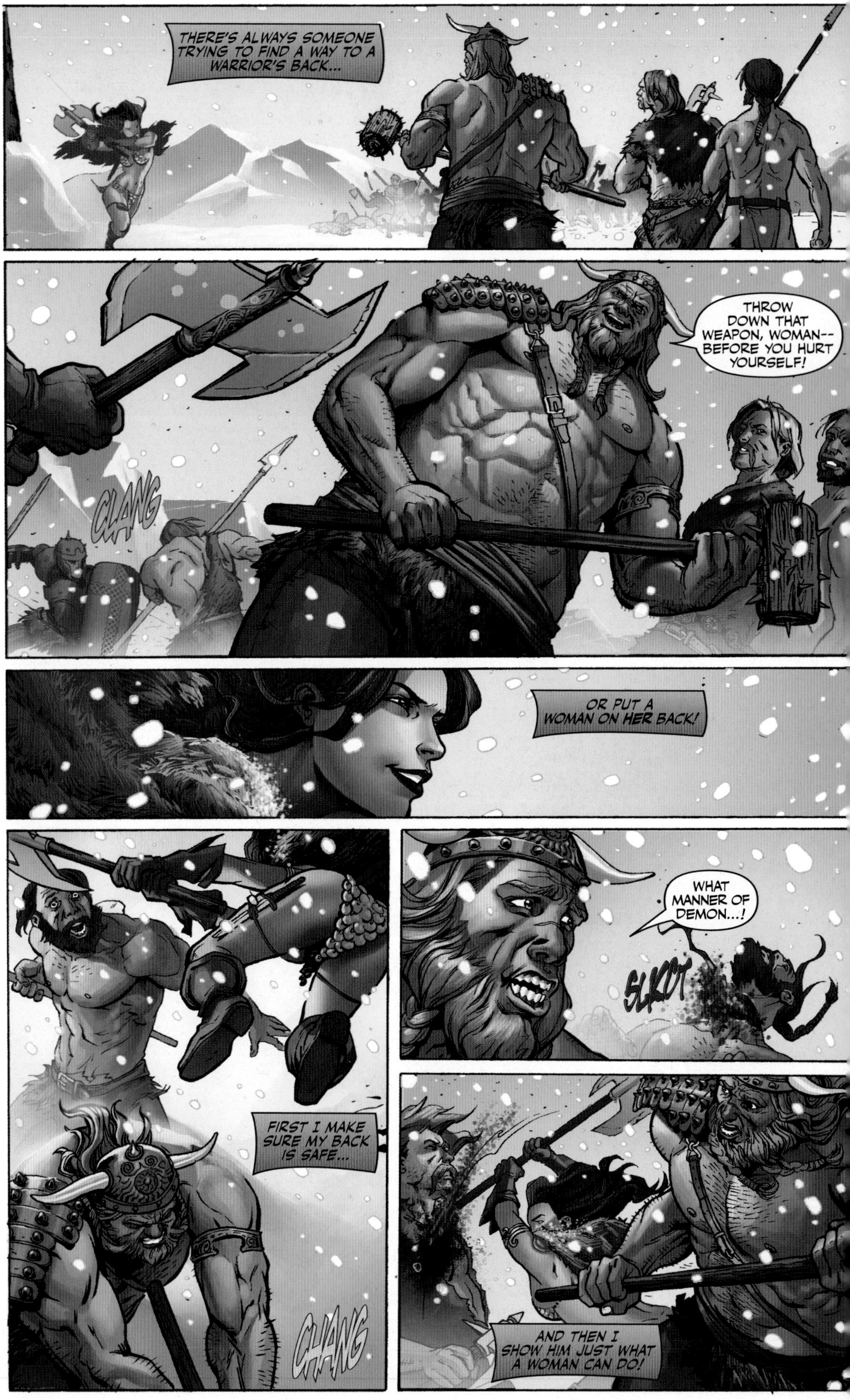
THERE'S ALWAYS SOMEONE TRYING TO FIND A WAY TO A WARRIOR'S BACK...
THROW DOWN THAT WEAPON, WOMAN-- BEFORE YOU HURT YOURSELF!
CLANG
OR PUT A WOMAN ON HER BACK!
FIRST I MAKE SURE MY BACK IS SAFE...
CHANG
WHAT MANNER OF DEMON...!
SLKOT
AND THEN I SHOW HIM JUST WHAT A WOMAN CAN DO!

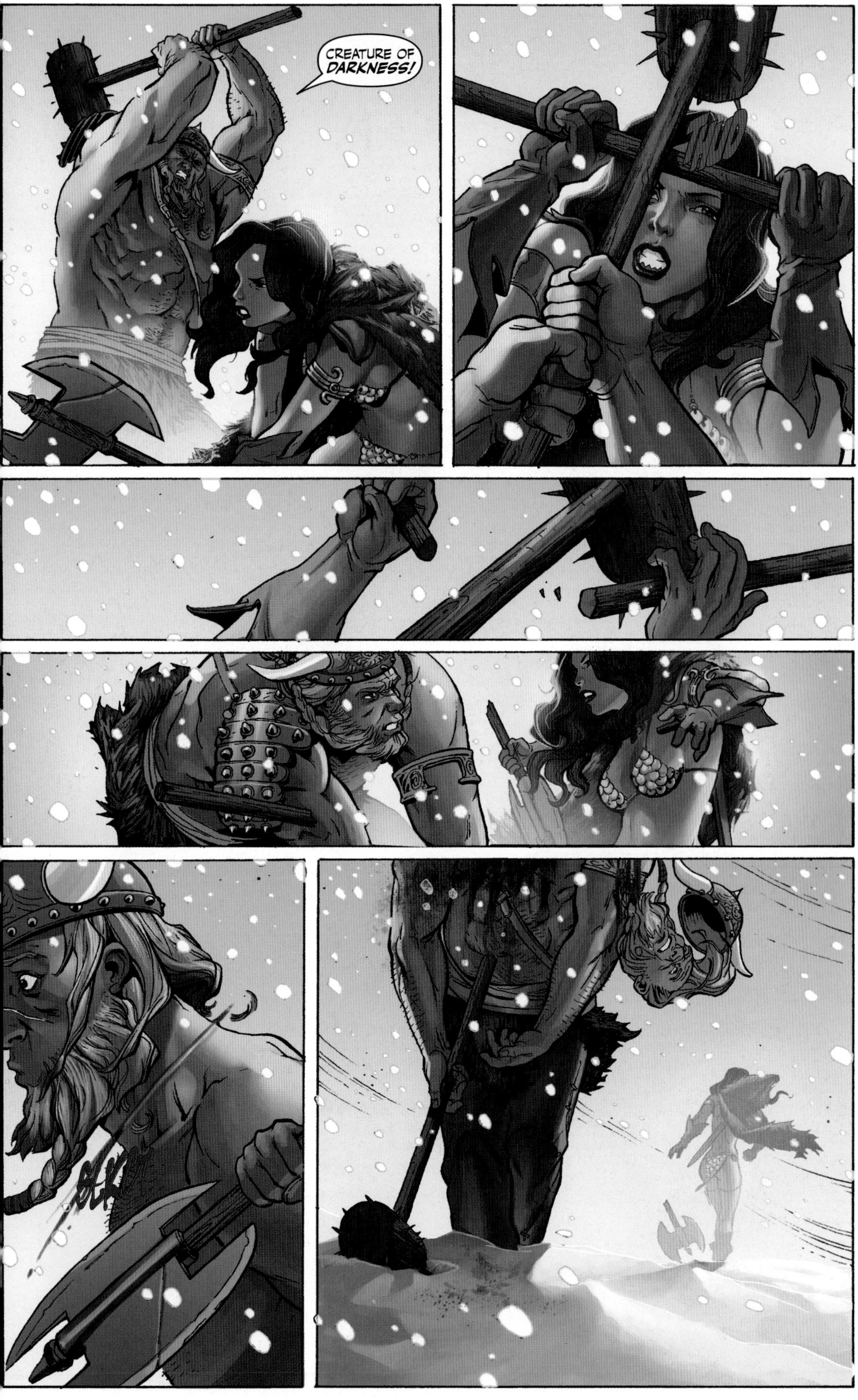
CREATURE OF DARKNESS!
THUD

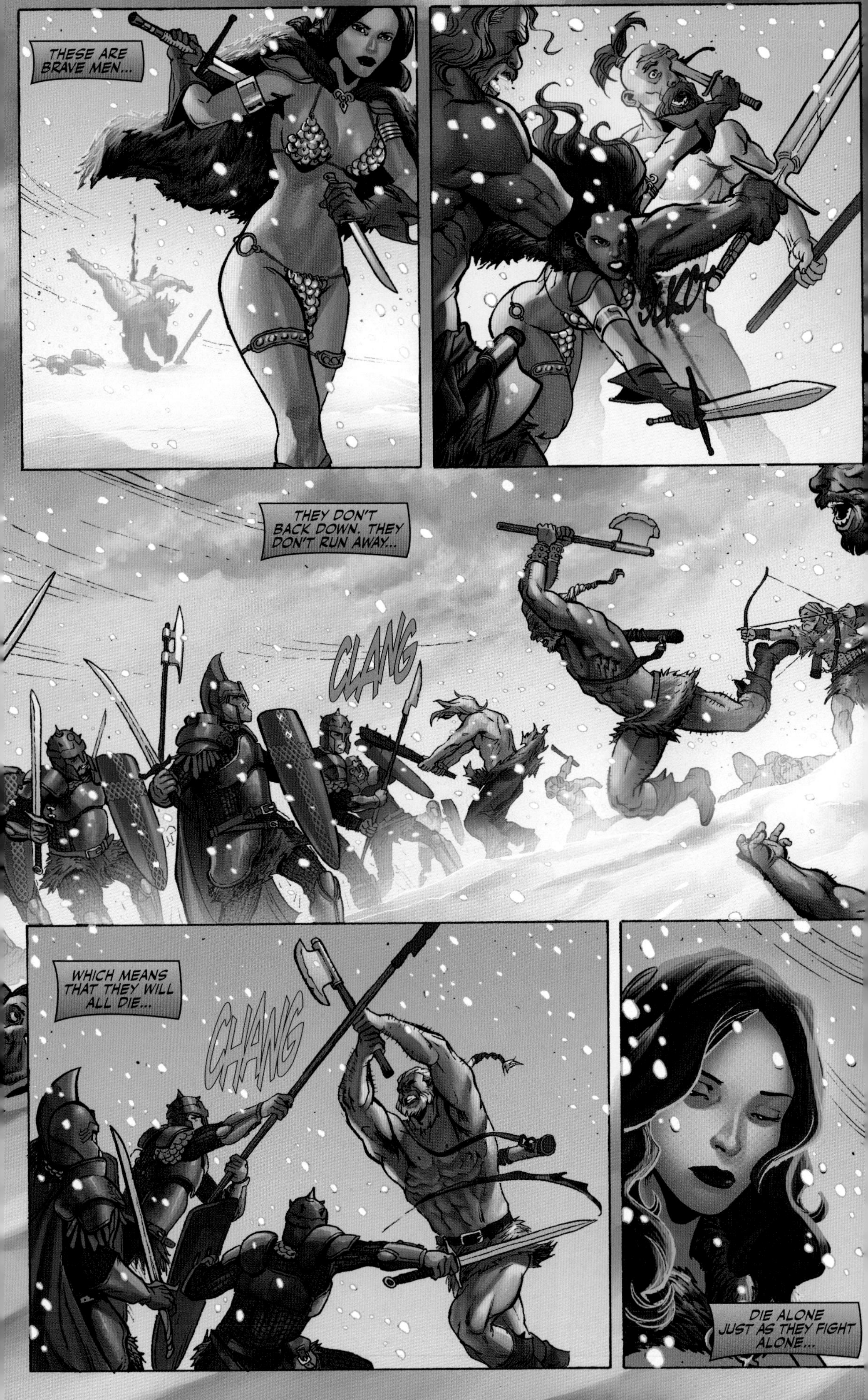
THESE ARE BRAVE MEN...
THEY DON'T BACK DOWN. THEY DON'T RUN AWAY...
CLANG
WHICH MEANS THAT THEY WILL ALL DIE...
CHANG
DIE ALONE JUST AS THEY FIGHT ALONE...

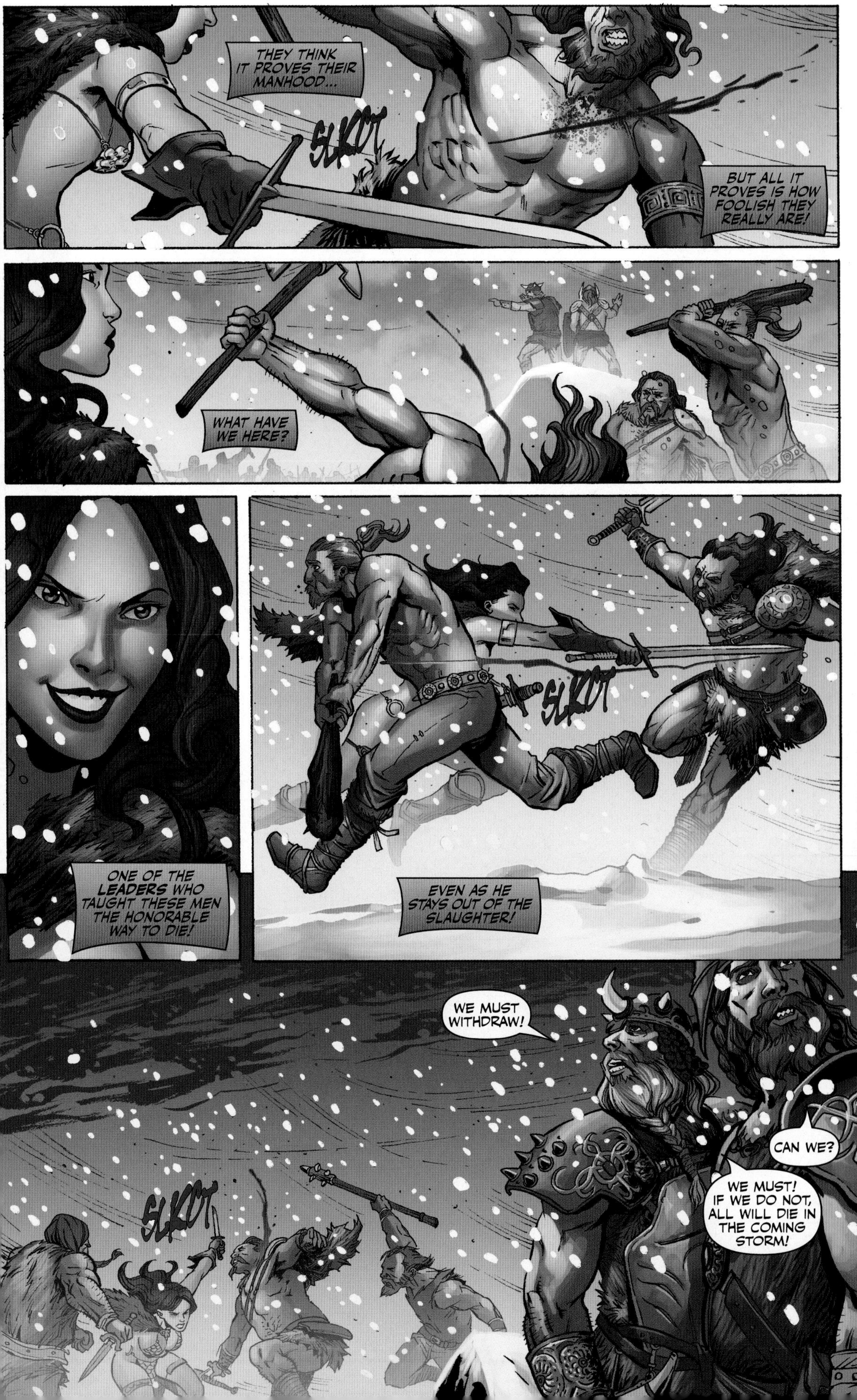
THEY THINK IT PROVES THEIR MANHOOD...
SLKDT
BUT ALL IT PROVES IS HOW FOOLISH THEY REALLY ARE!
WHAT HAVE WE HERE?
ONE OF THE LEADERS WHO TAUGHT THESE MEN THE HONORABLE WAY TO DIE!
SLKDT
EVEN AS HE STAYS OUT OF THE SLAUGHTER!
WE MUST WITHDRAW!
CAN WE?
WE MUST! IF WE DO NOT, ALL WILL DIE IN THE COMING STORM!
SLKDT

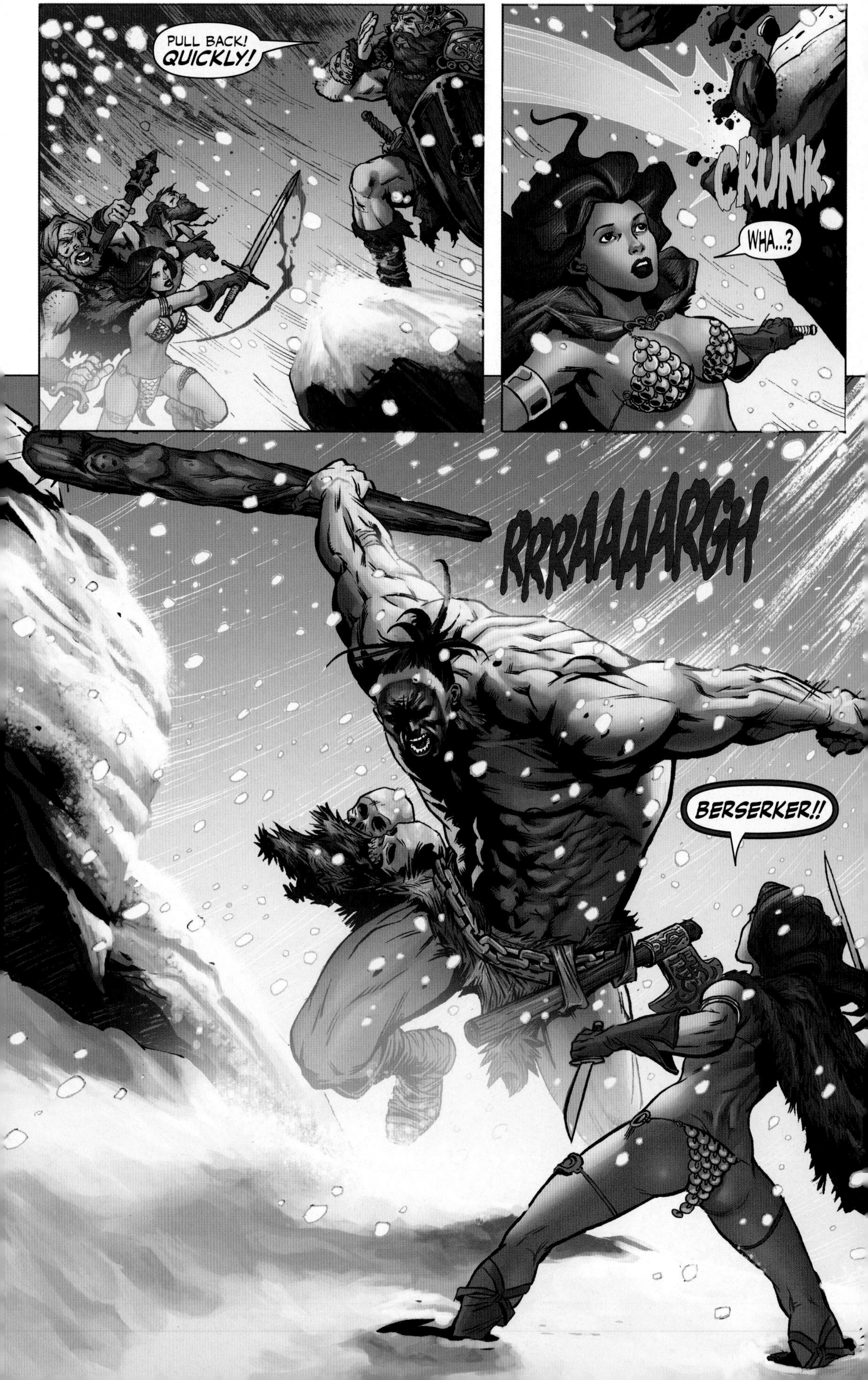
PULL BACK!
QUICKLY!
CRUNK
WHA...?
RRRAAAAARGH
BERSERKER!!

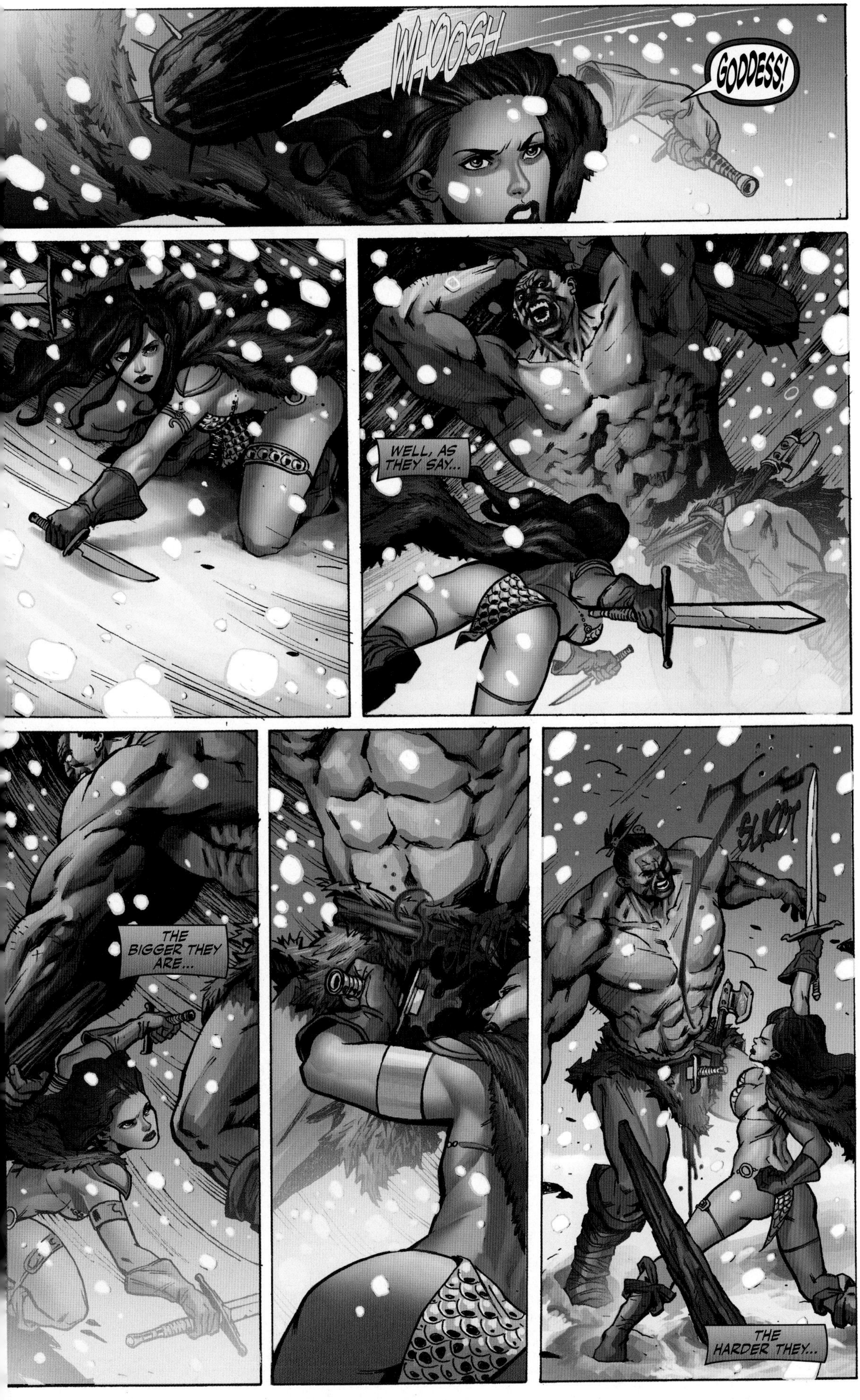
WHOOSH
GODDESS!
WELL, AS THEY SAY...
THE BIGGER THEY ARE...
THE HARDER THEY...

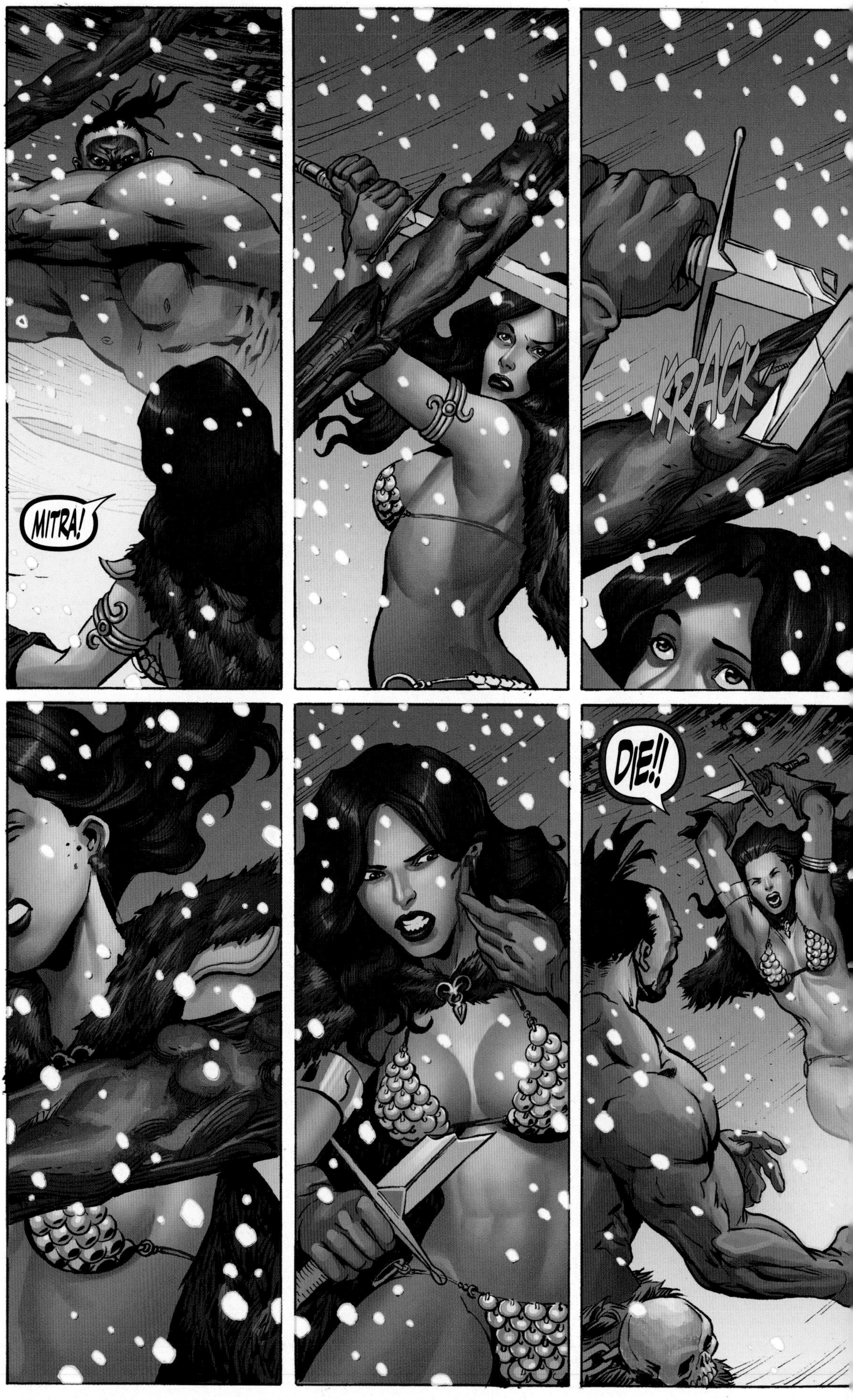
MITRA!
KRACK
DIE!!

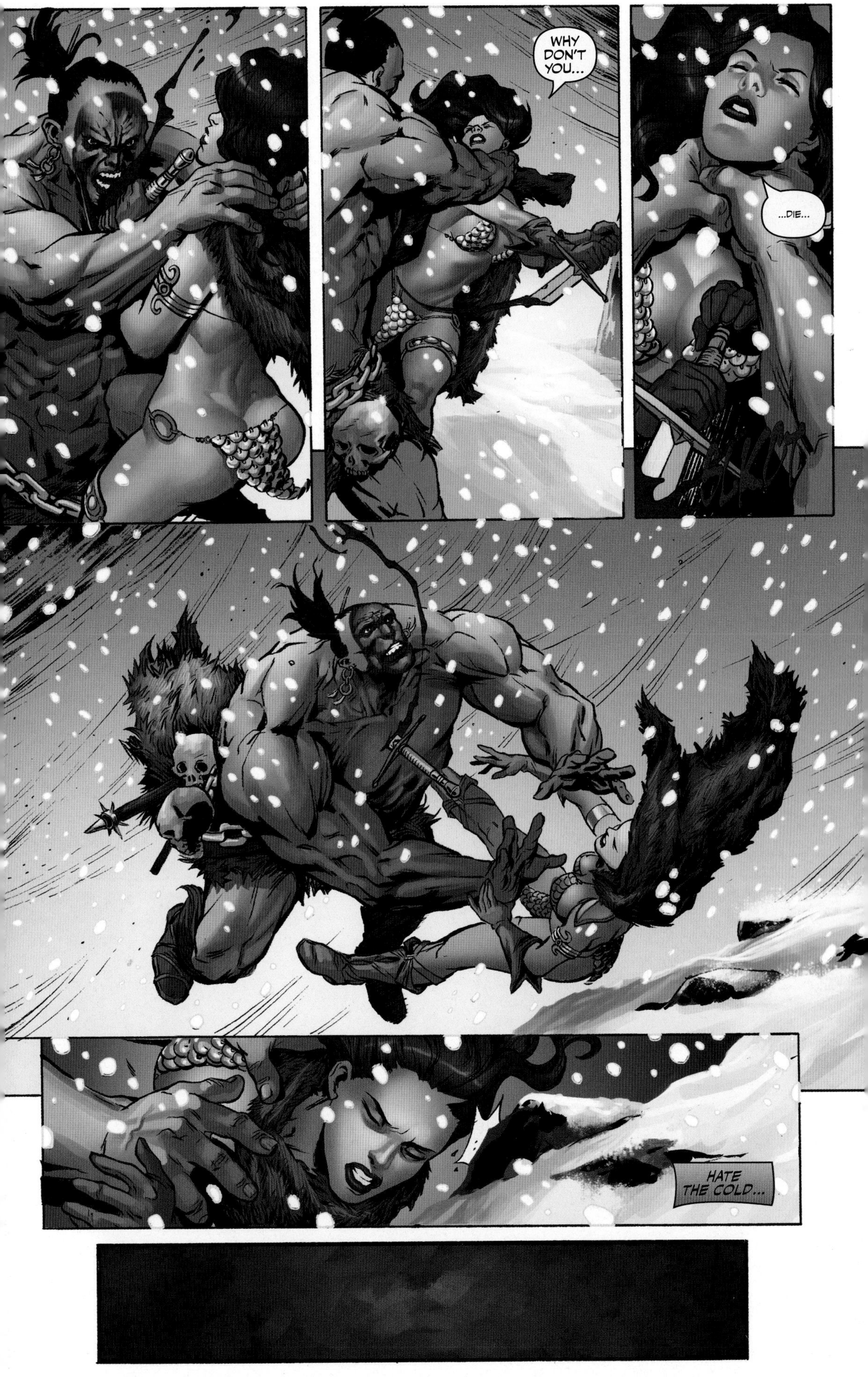
WHY DON'T YOU...
...DIE...
HATE THE COLD...

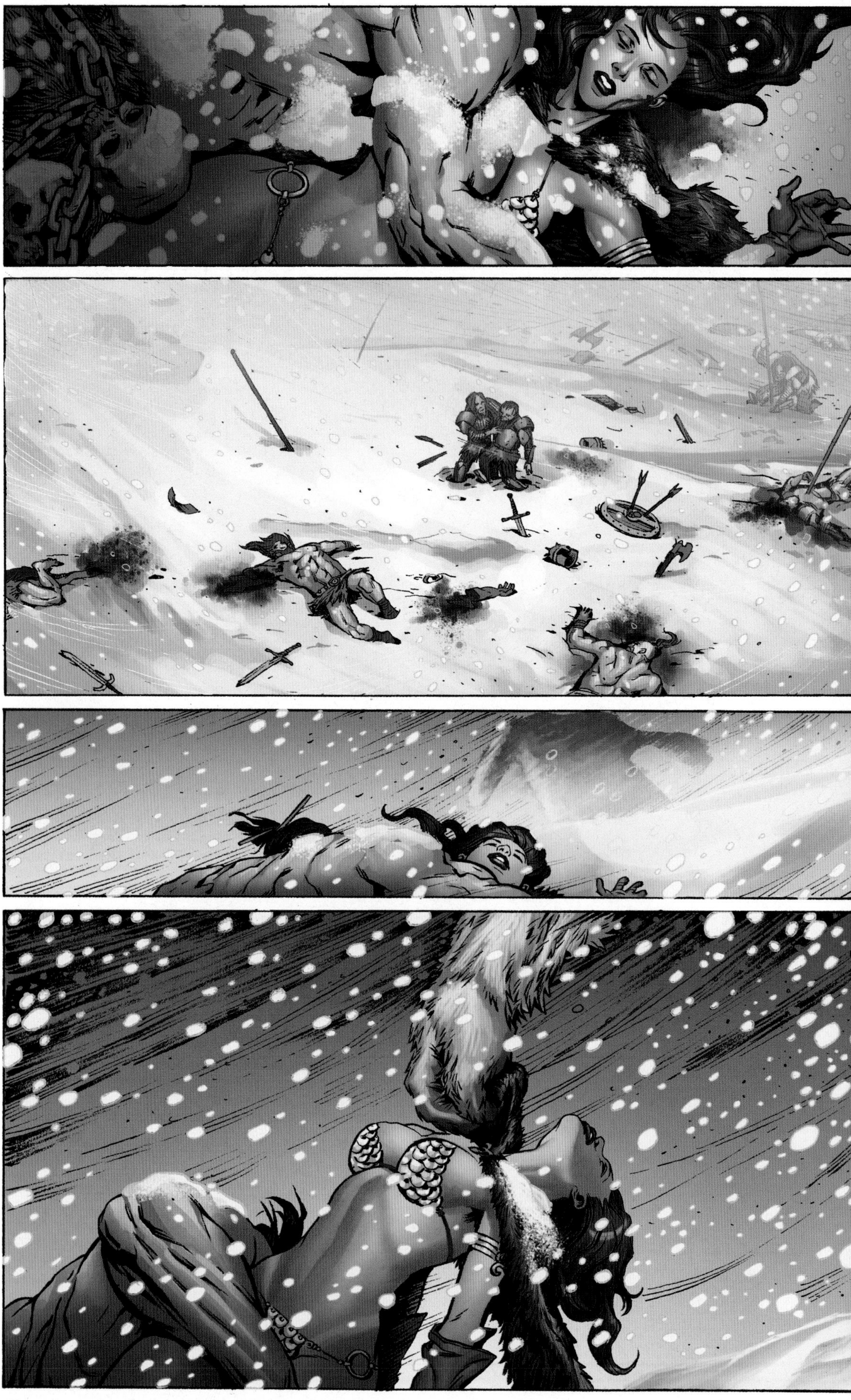

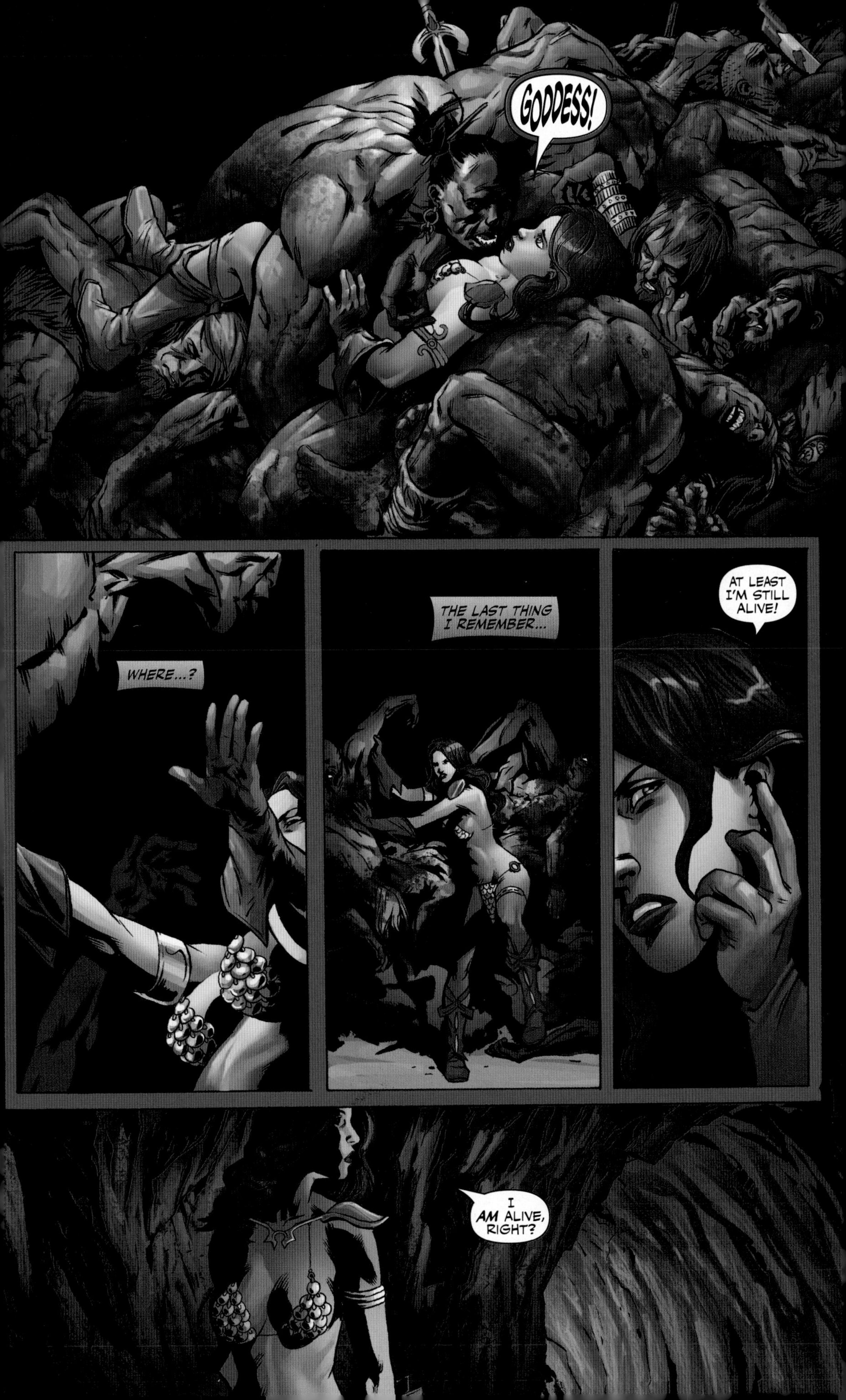
GODDESS!
WHERE...?
THE LAST THING I REMEMBER...
AT LEAST I'M STILL ALIVE!
I AM ALIVE, RIGHT?

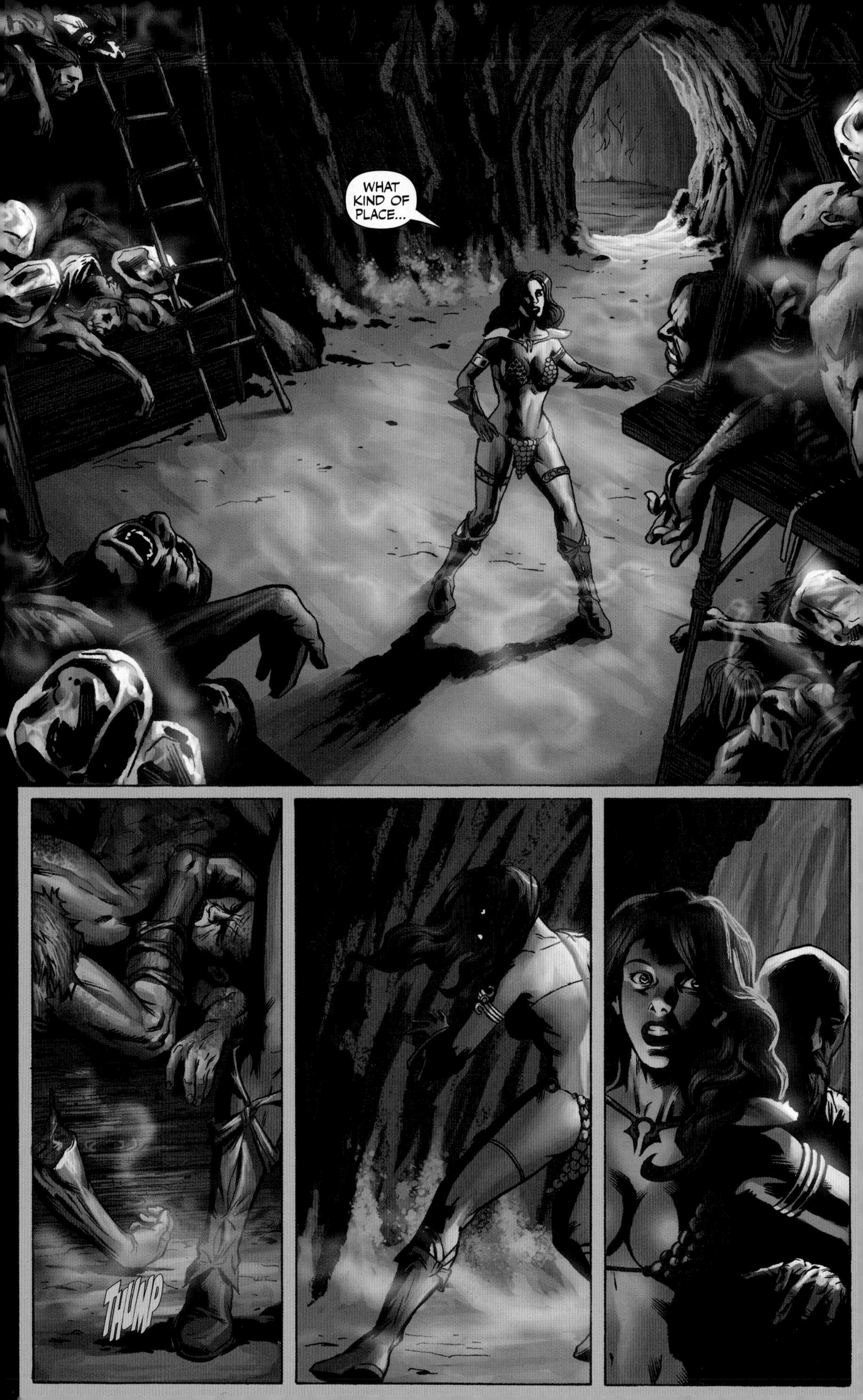
WHAT KIND OF PLACE...
THUMP

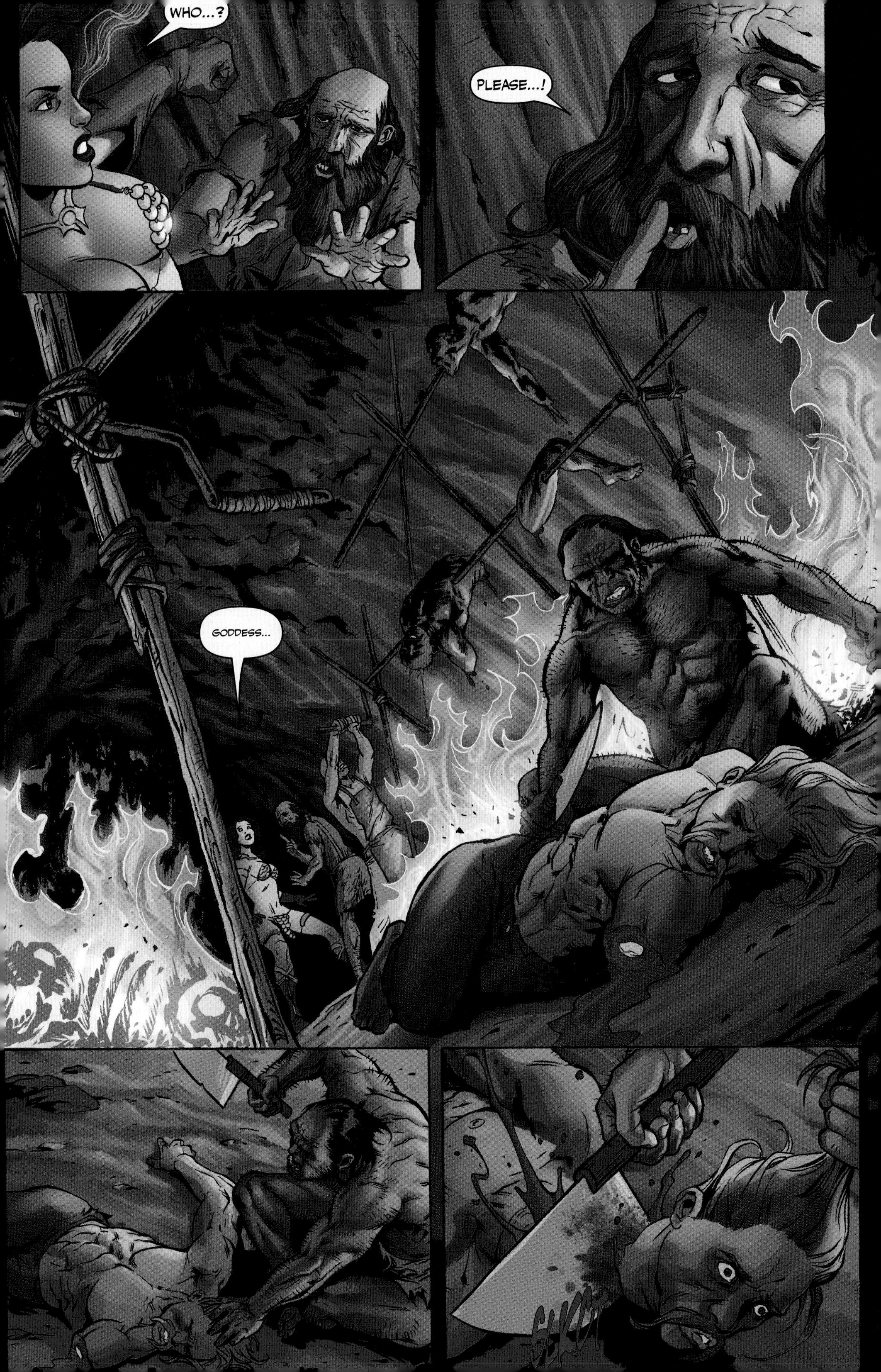
WHO...?
PLEASE...!
GODDESS...

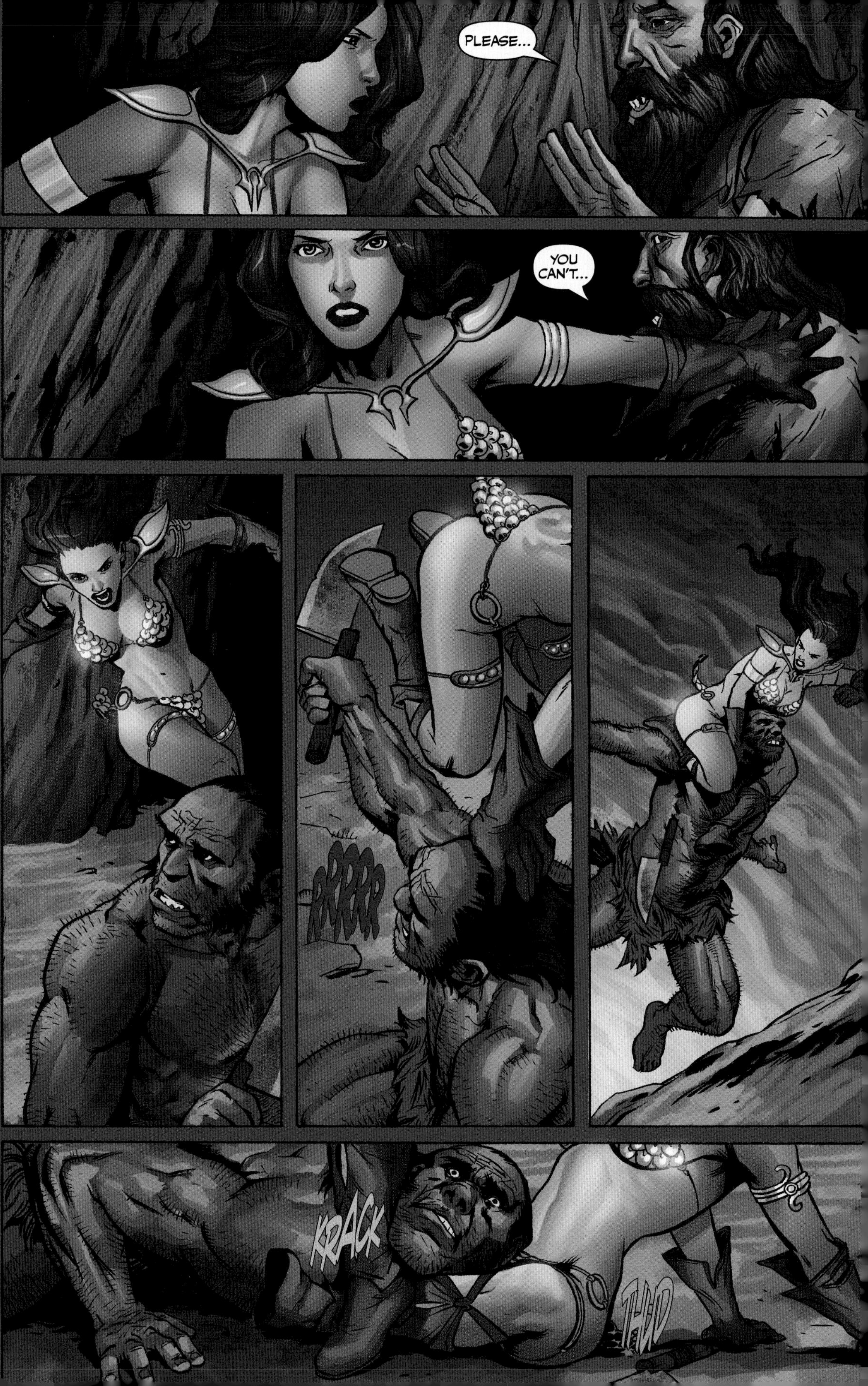
PLEASE...
YOU CAN'T...
RRRRRR
KRACK
THUD

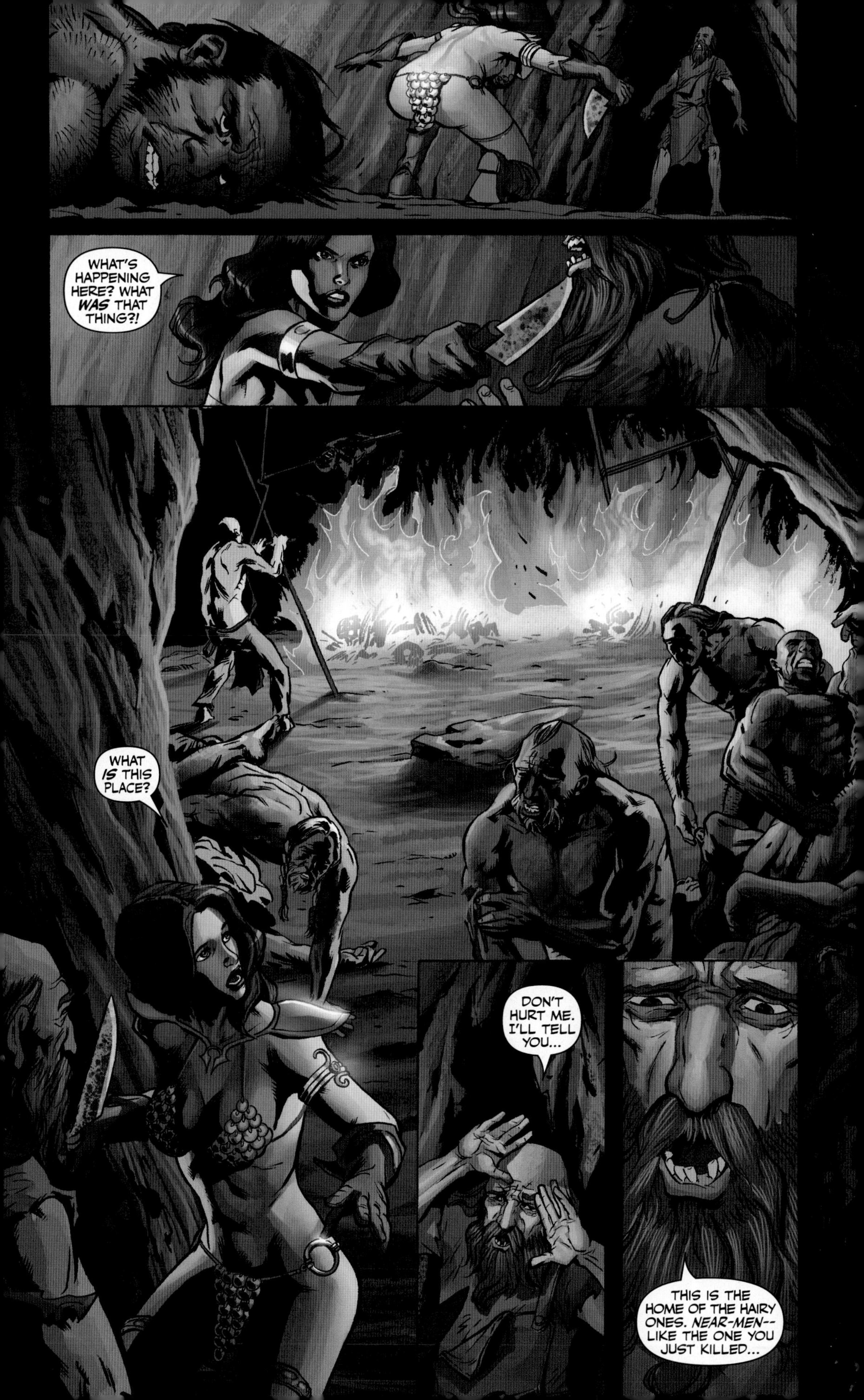
WHAT'S HAPPENING HERE? WHAT *WAS* THAT THING?!
WHAT *IS* THIS PLACE?
DON'T HURT ME. I'LL TELL YOU...
THIS IS THE HOME OF THE HAIRY ONES. *NEAR-MEN*-- LIKE THE ONE YOU JUST KILLED...

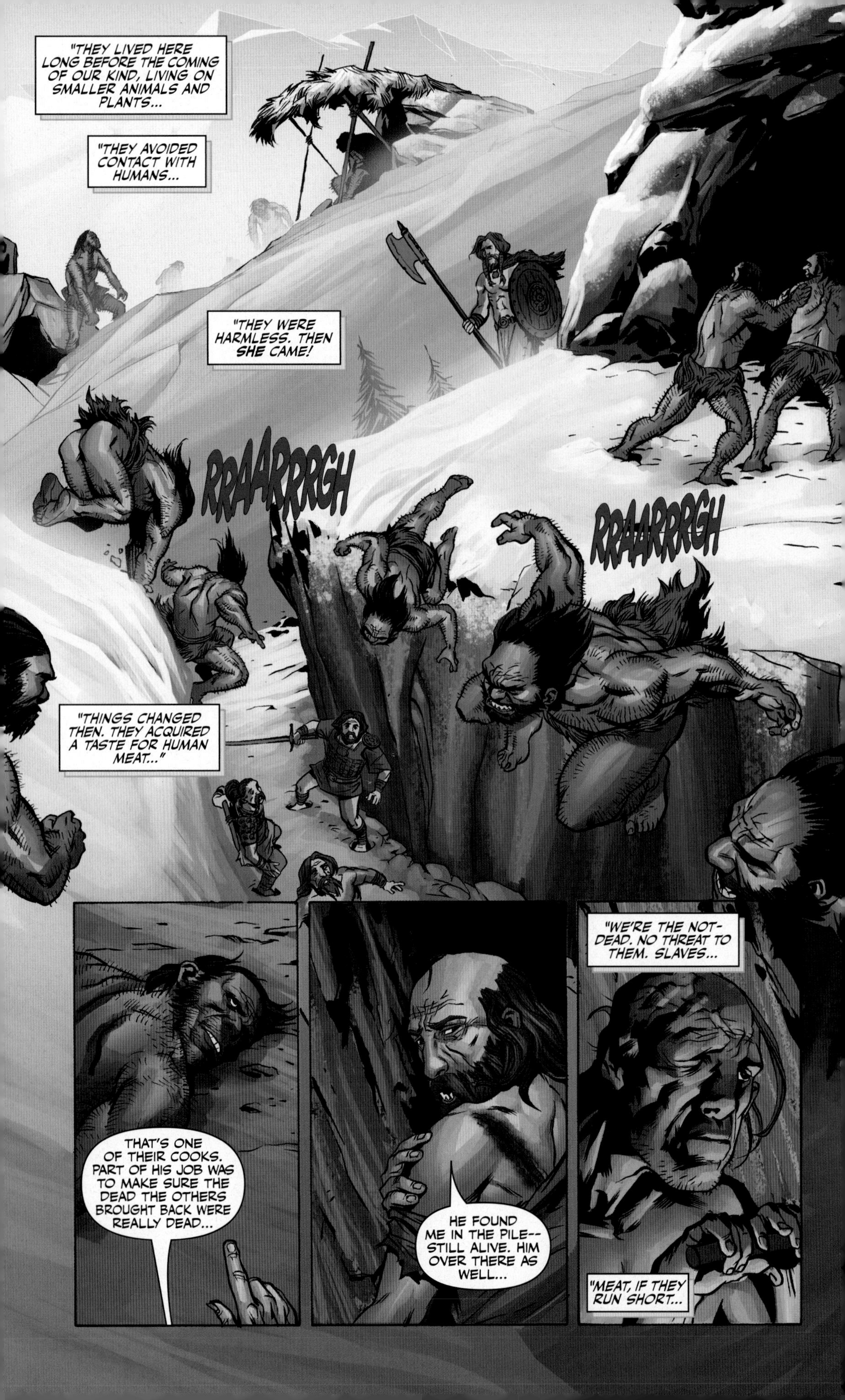
"THEY LIVED HERE LONG BEFORE THE COMING OF OUR KIND, LIVING ON SMALLER ANIMALS AND PLANTS...
"THEY AVOIDED CONTACT WITH HUMANS...
"THEY WERE HARMLESS. THEN SHE CAME!
RRAARRRGH
RRAARRRGH
"THINGS CHANGED THEN. THEY ACQUIRED A TASTE FOR HUMAN MEAT..."
THAT'S ONE OF THEIR COOKS. PART OF HIS JOB WAS TO MAKE SURE THE DEAD THE OTHERS BROUGHT BACK WERE REALLY DEAD...
HE FOUND ME IN THE PILE-- STILL ALIVE. HIM OVER THERE AS WELL...
"WE'RE THE NOT-DEAD. NO THREAT TO THEM. SLAVES...
"MEAT, IF THEY RUN SHORT...

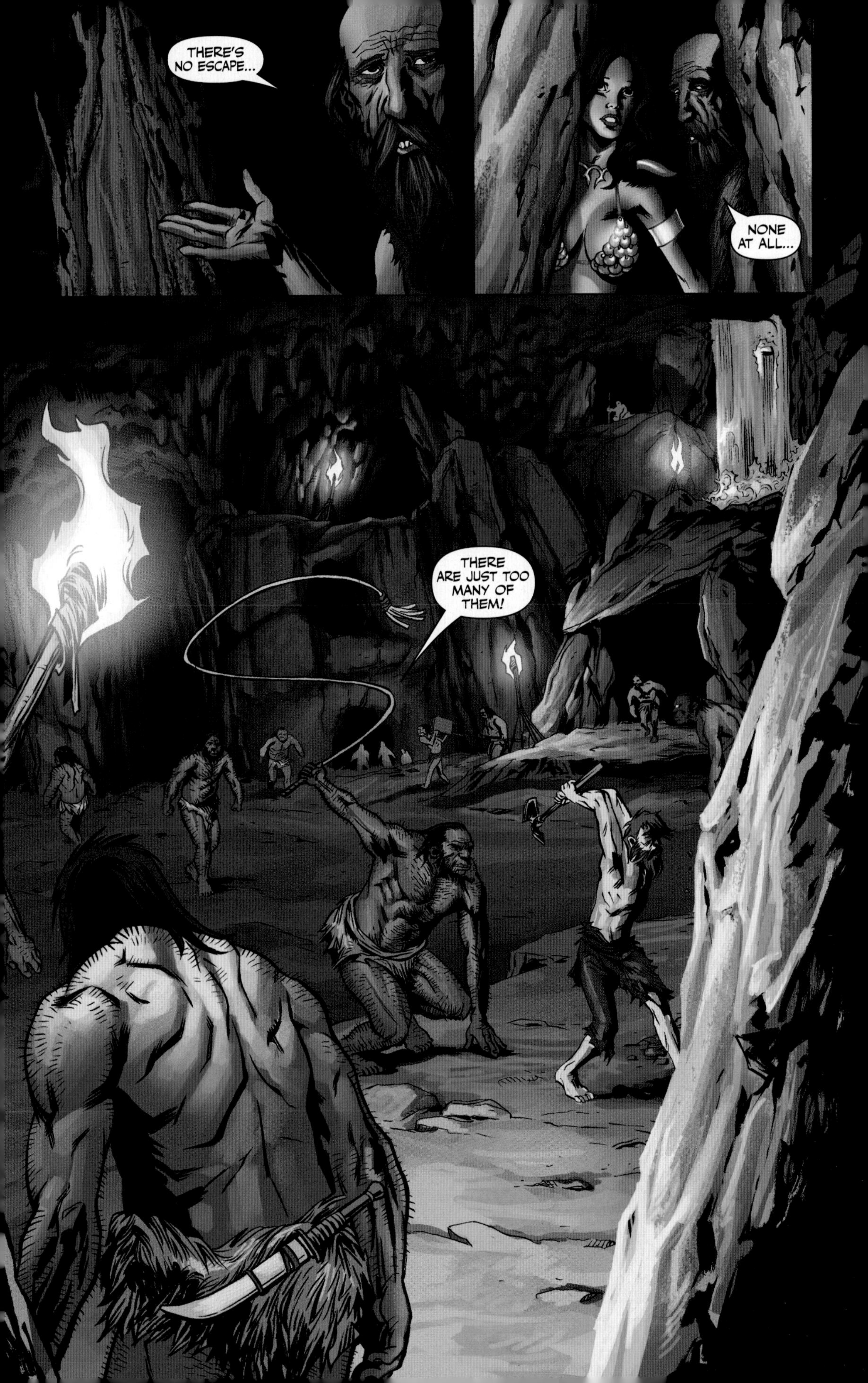
THERE'S NO ESCAPE...
NONE AT ALL...
THERE ARE JUST TOO MANY OF THEM!

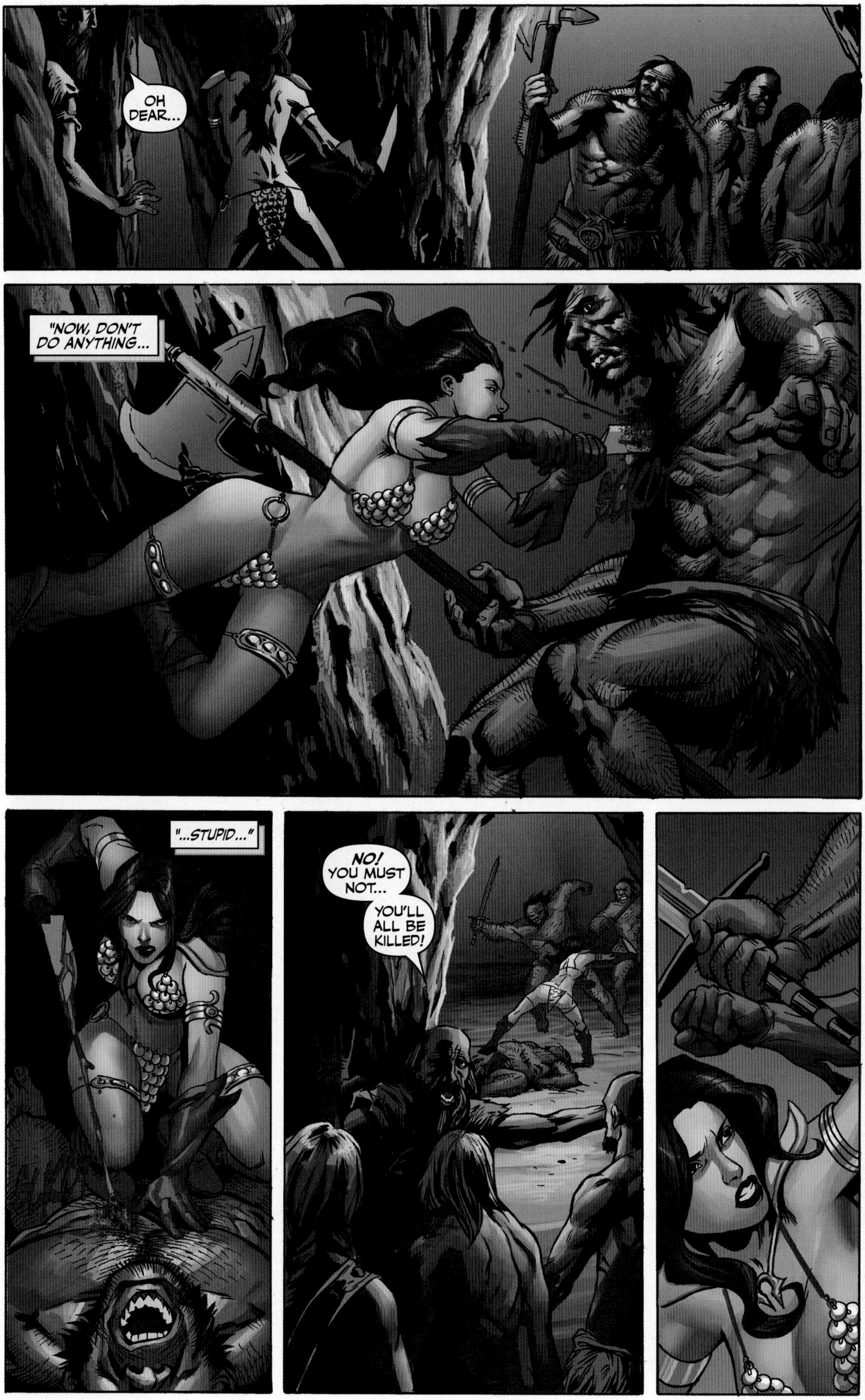

OH DEAR...
"NOW, DON'T DO ANYTHING...
"...STUPID..."
NO! YOU MUST NOT...
YOU'LL ALL BE KILLED!

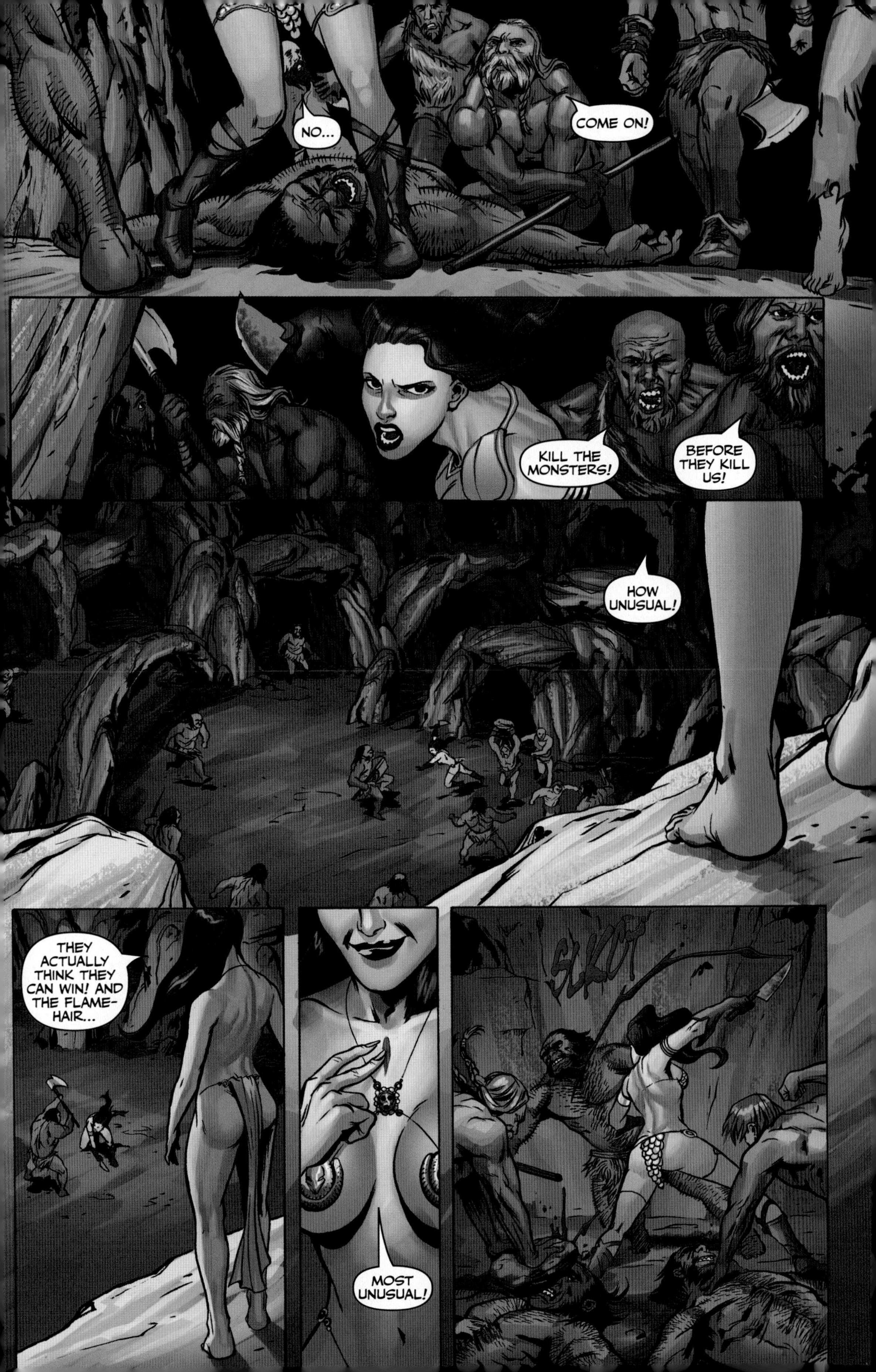
NO...
COME ON!
KILL THE MONSTERS!
BEFORE THEY KILL US!
HOW UNUSUAL!
THEY ACTUALLY THINK THEY CAN WIN! AND THE FLAME-HAIR...
MOST UNUSUAL!
SLKOT

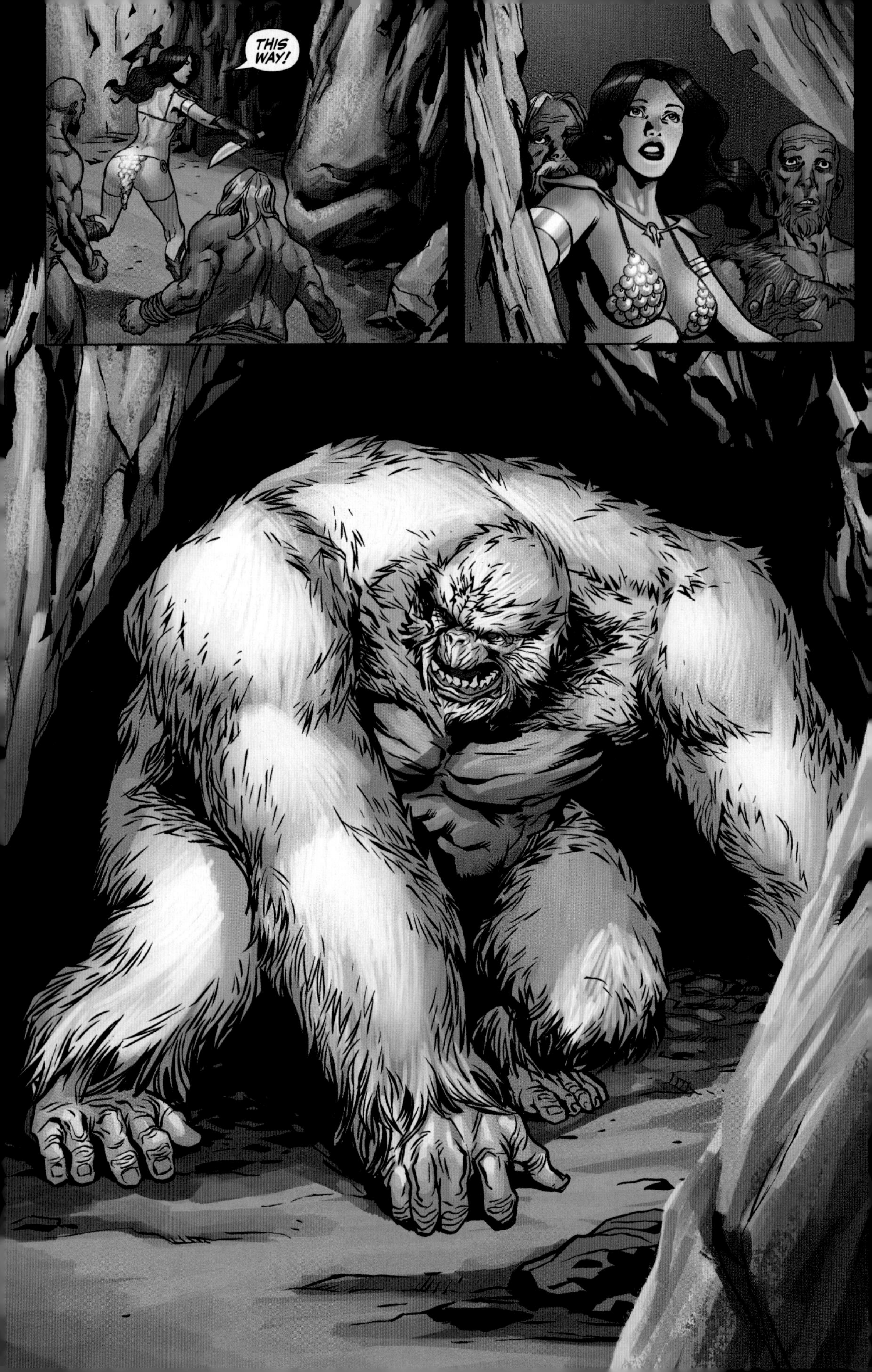
THIS WAY!

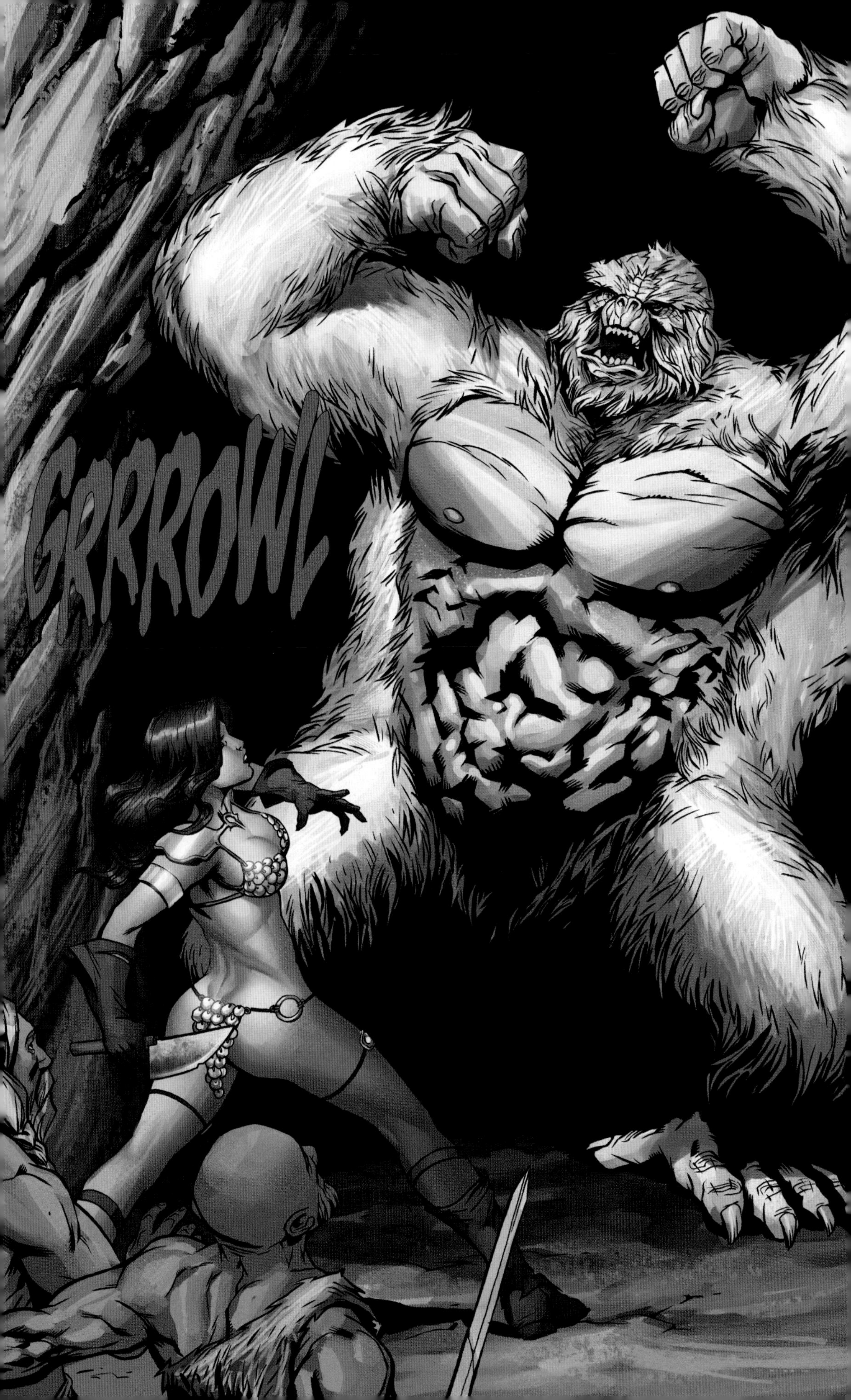
GRRROWL

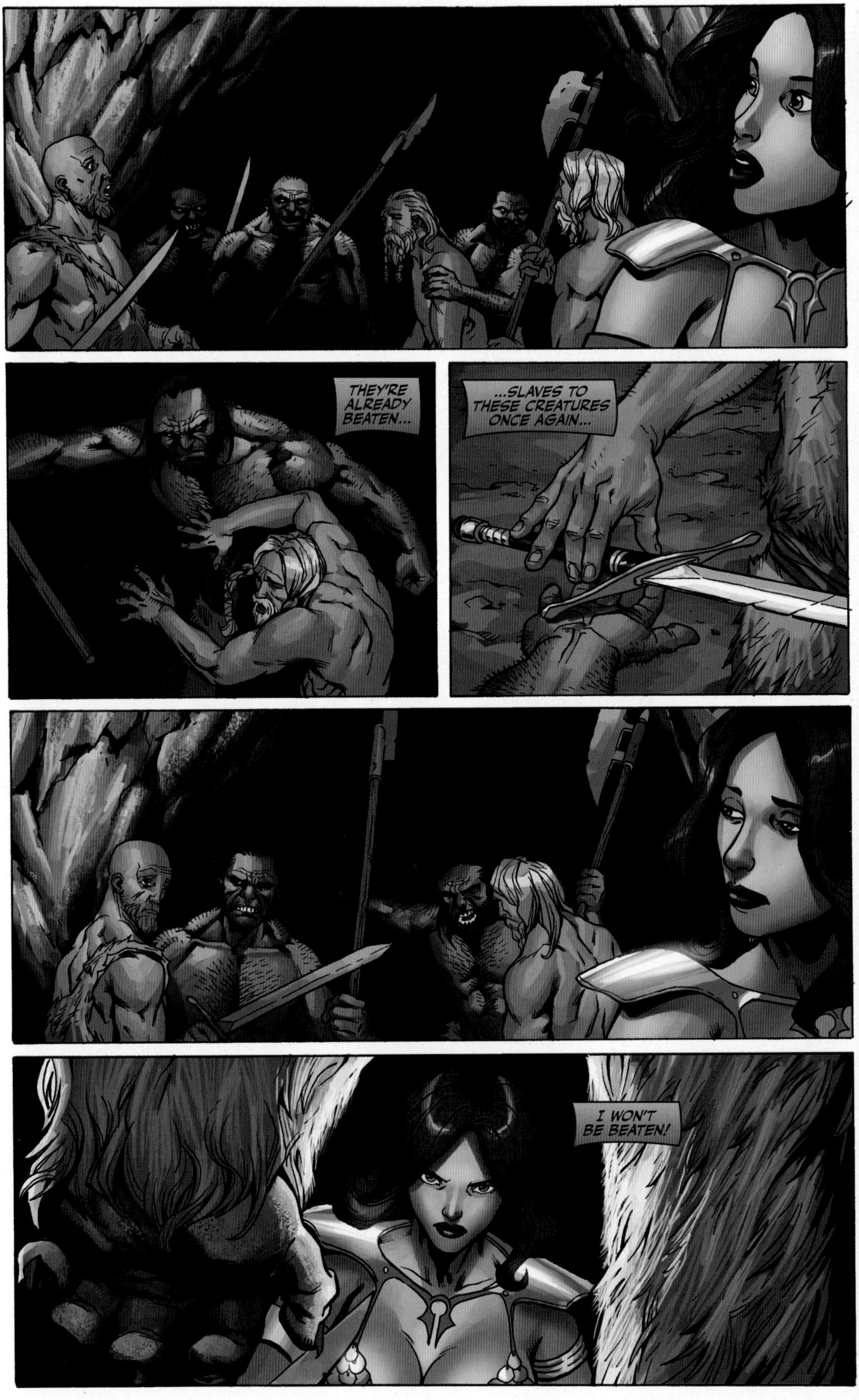
THEY'RE ALREADY BEATEN...
...SLAVES TO THESE CREATURES ONCE AGAIN...
I WON'T BE BEATEN!

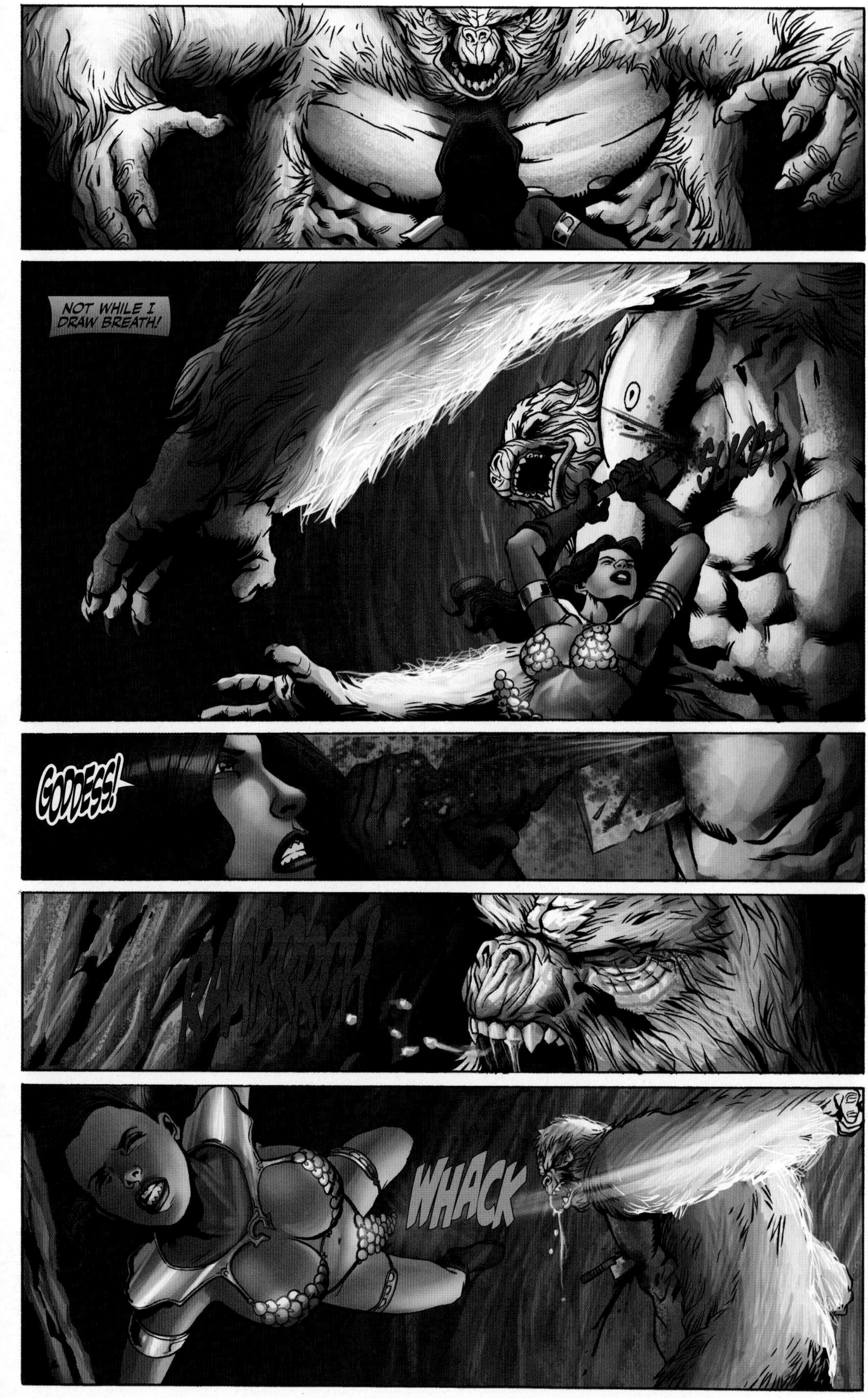
NOT WHILE I DRAW BREATH!
GODDESS!
WHACK

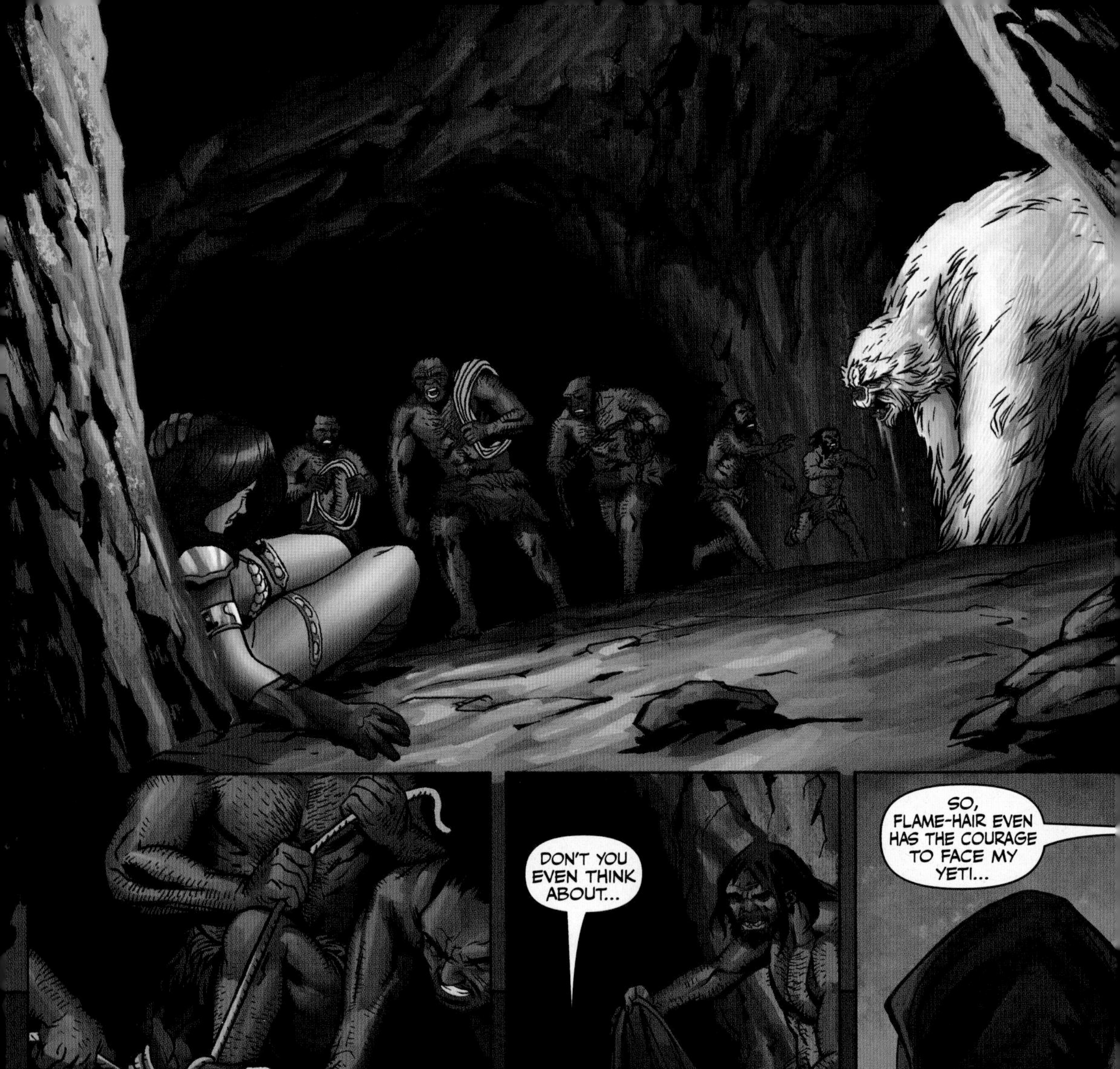
UNGH
DON'T YOU EVEN THINK ABOUT...
SO, FLAME-HAIR EVEN HAS THE COURAGE TO FACE MY YETI...

[redacted]

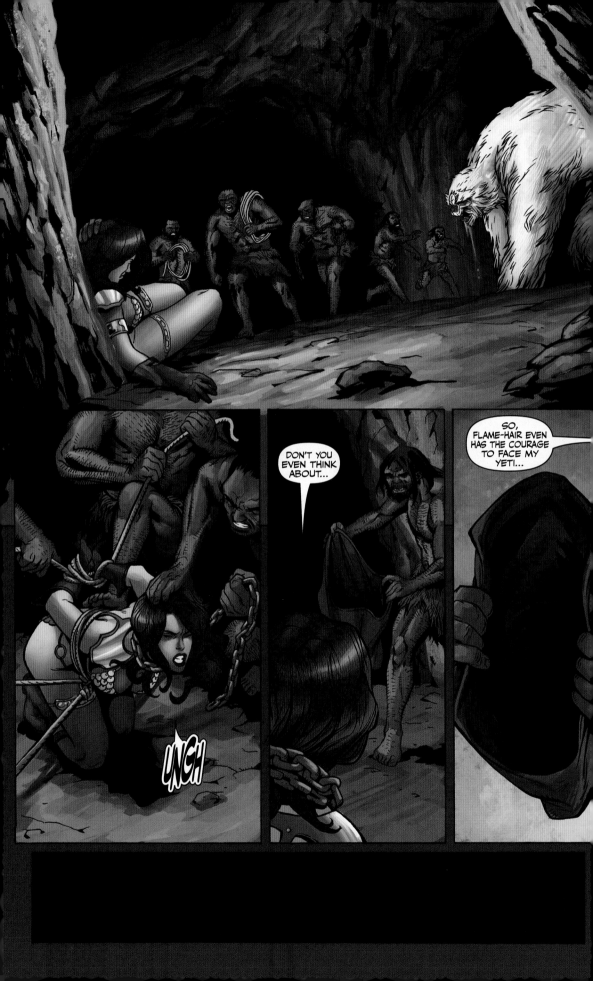

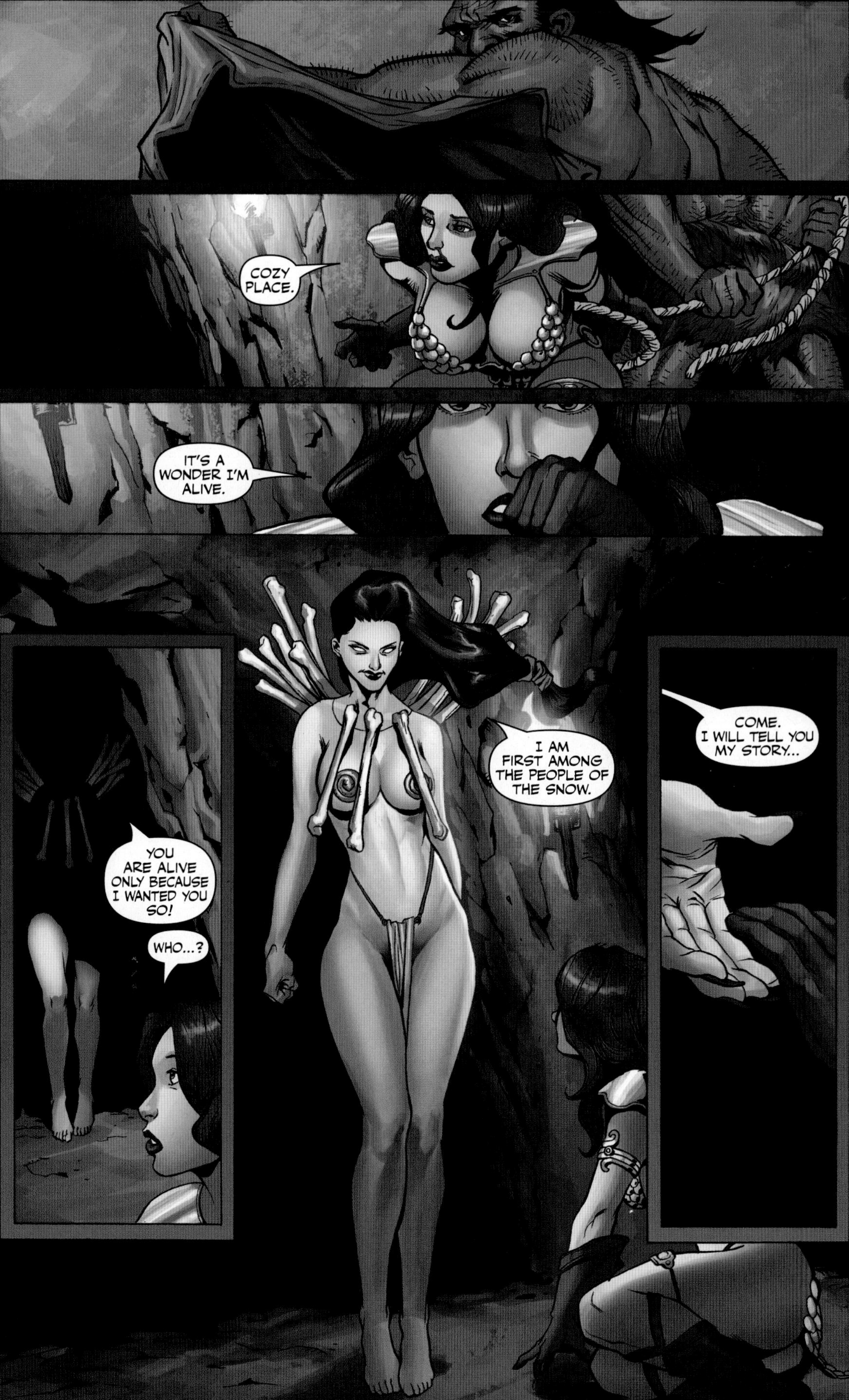
COZY PLACE.
IT'S A WONDER I'M ALIVE.
YOU ARE ALIVE ONLY BECAUSE I WANTED YOU SO!
WHO...?
I AM FIRST AMONG THE PEOPLE OF THE SNOW.
COME. I WILL TELL YOU MY STORY...

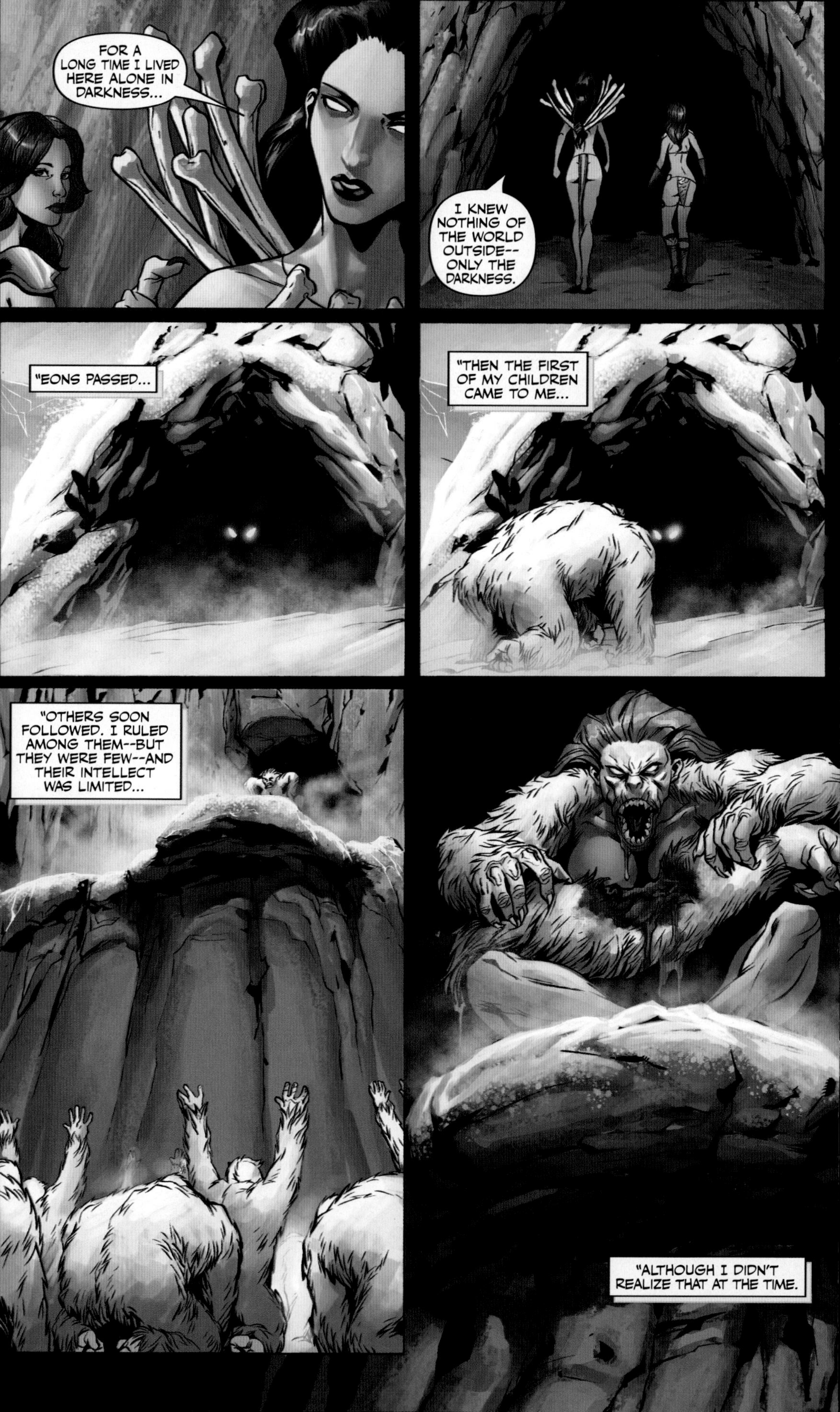
FOR A LONG TIME I LIVED HERE ALONE IN DARKNESS...
I KNEW NOTHING OF THE WORLD OUTSIDE--ONLY THE DARKNESS.
"EONS PASSED...
"THEN THE FIRST OF MY CHILDREN CAME TO ME...
"OTHERS SOON FOLLOWED. I RULED AMONG THEM--BUT THEY WERE FEW--AND THEIR INTELLECT WAS LIMITED...
"ALTHOUGH I DIDN'T REALIZE THAT AT THE TIME.

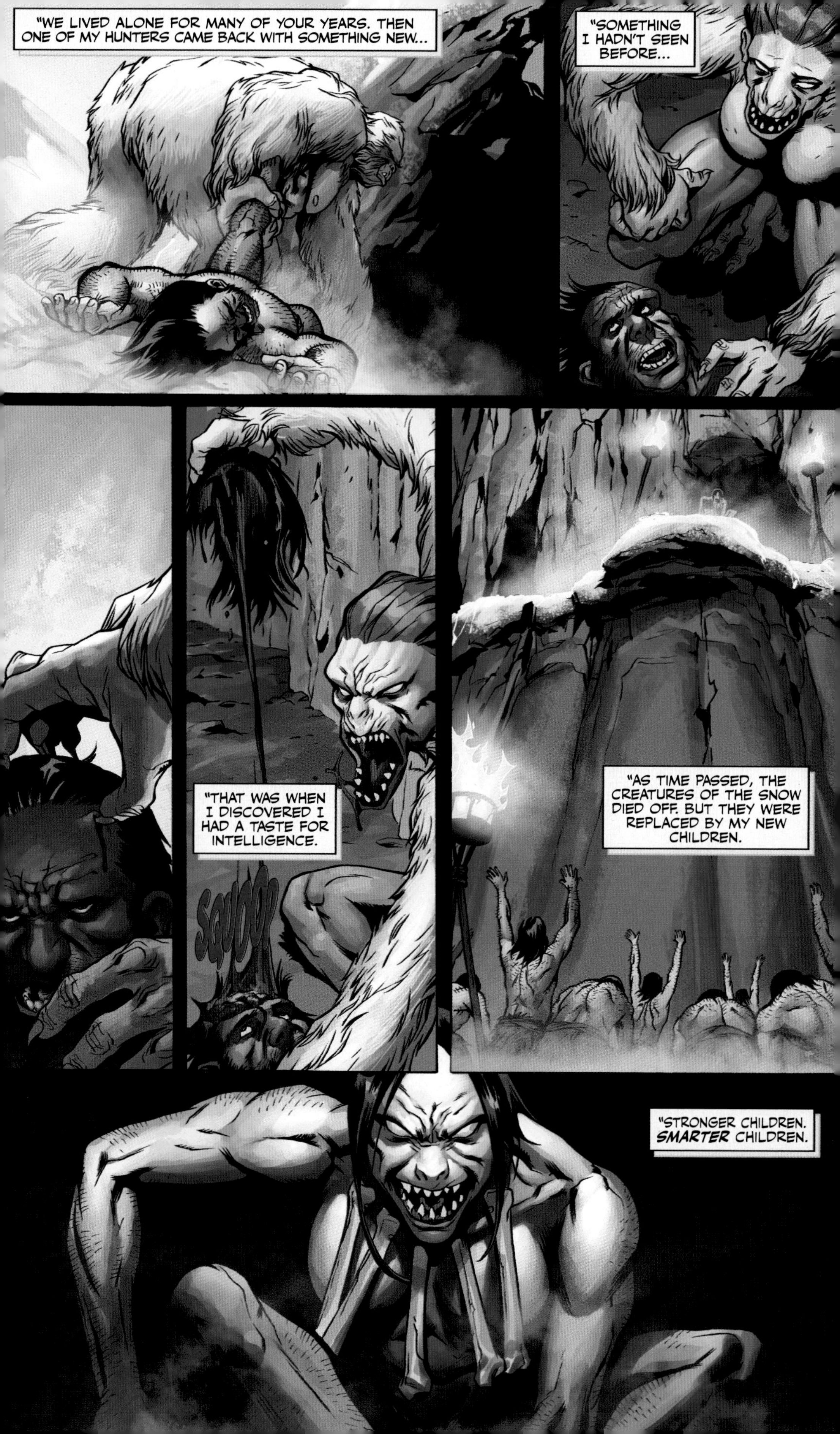
"WE LIVED ALONE FOR MANY OF YOUR YEARS. THEN ONE OF MY HUNTERS CAME BACK WITH SOMETHING NEW...
"SOMETHING I HADN'T SEEN BEFORE...
"THAT WAS WHEN I DISCOVERED I HAD A TASTE FOR INTELLIGENCE.
SQUOOP
"AS TIME PASSED, THE CREATURES OF THE SNOW DIED OFF. BUT THEY WERE REPLACED BY MY NEW CHILDREN.
"STRONGER CHILDREN. *SMARTER* CHILDREN.

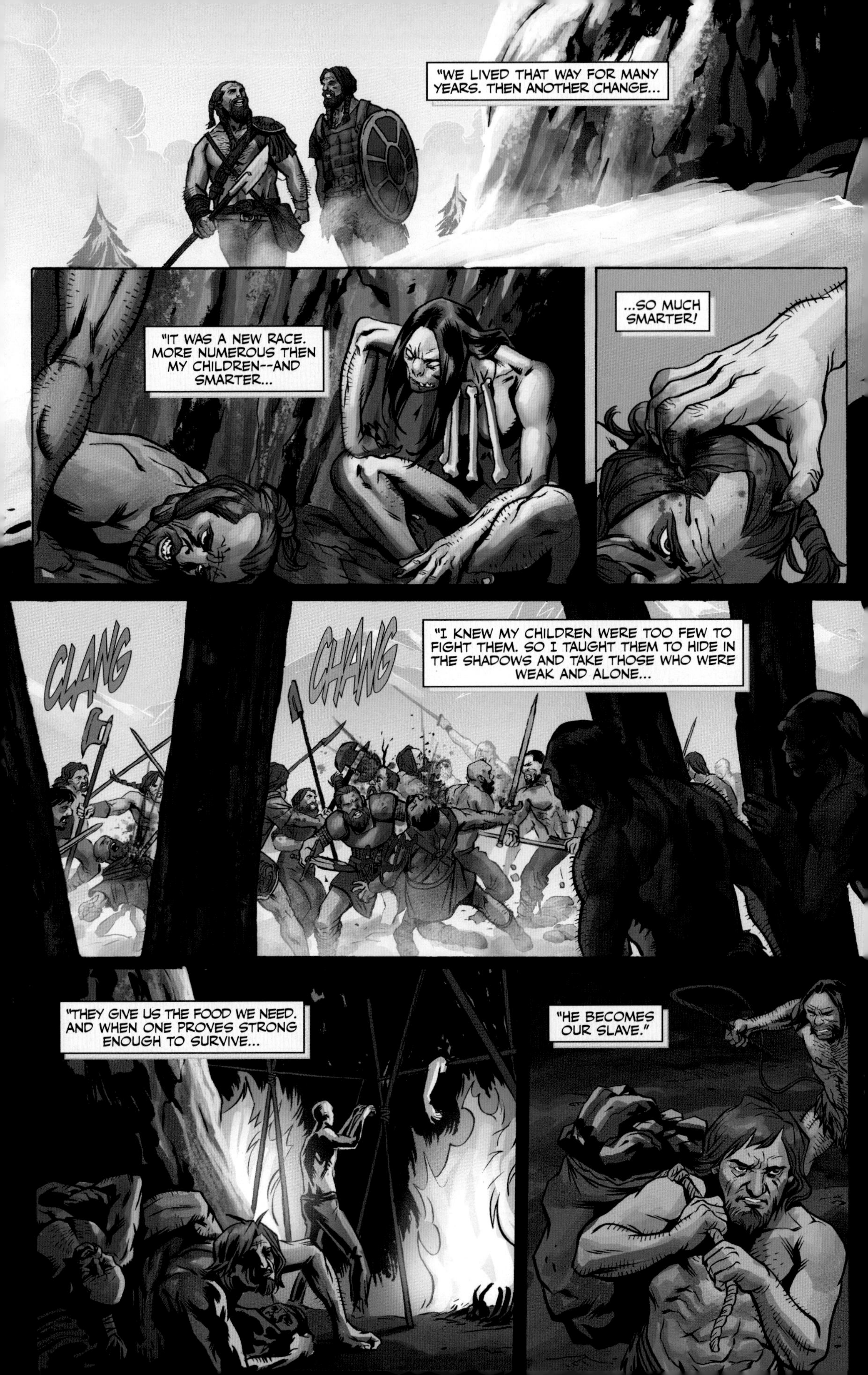
"WE LIVED THAT WAY FOR MANY YEARS. THEN ANOTHER CHANGE...
"IT WAS A NEW RACE. MORE NUMEROUS THEN MY CHILDREN--AND SMARTER...
...SO MUCH SMARTER!
CLANG
CHANG
"I KNEW MY CHILDREN WERE TOO FEW TO FIGHT THEM. SO I TAUGHT THEM TO HIDE IN THE SHADOWS AND TAKE THOSE WHO WERE WEAK AND ALONE...
"THEY GIVE US THE FOOD WE NEED. AND WHEN ONE PROVES STRONG ENOUGH TO SURVIVE...
"HE BECOMES OUR SLAVE."

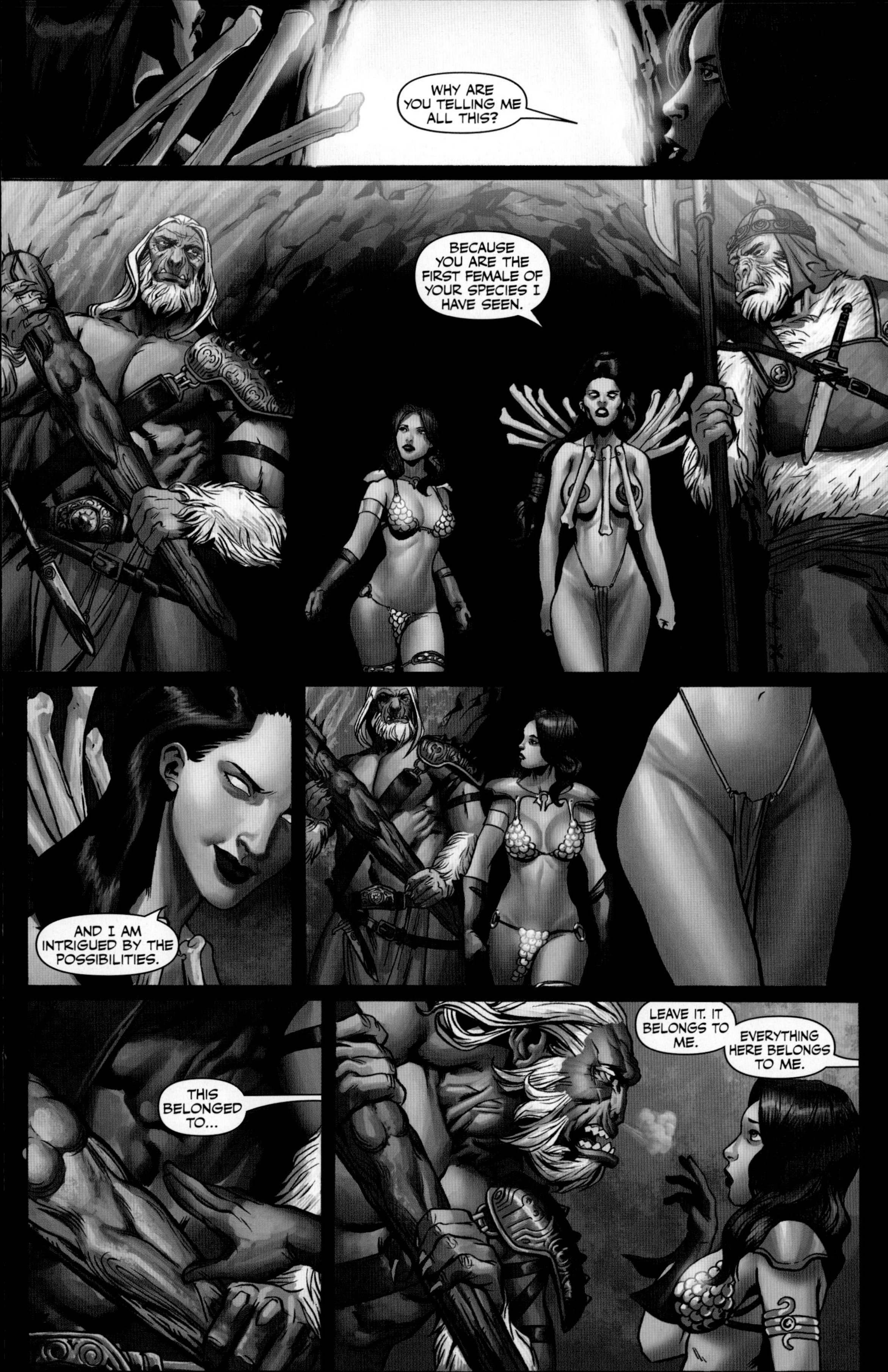
WHY ARE YOU TELLING ME ALL THIS?
BECAUSE YOU ARE THE FIRST FEMALE OF YOUR SPECIES I HAVE SEEN.
AND I AM INTRIGUED BY THE POSSIBILITIES.
THIS BELONGED TO...
LEAVE IT. IT BELONGS TO ME.
EVERYTHING HERE BELONGS TO ME.

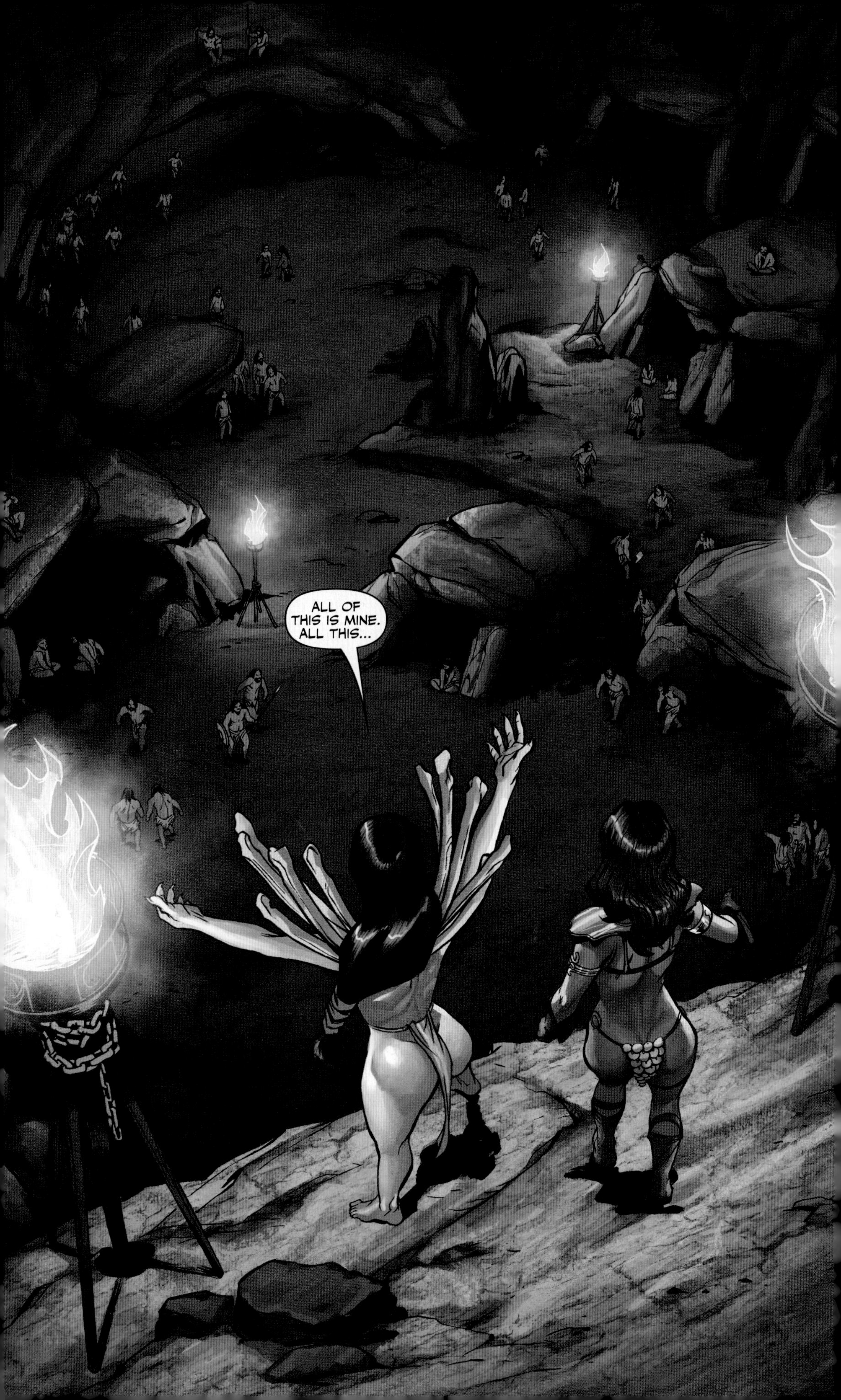
ALL OF THIS IS MINE. ALL THIS...

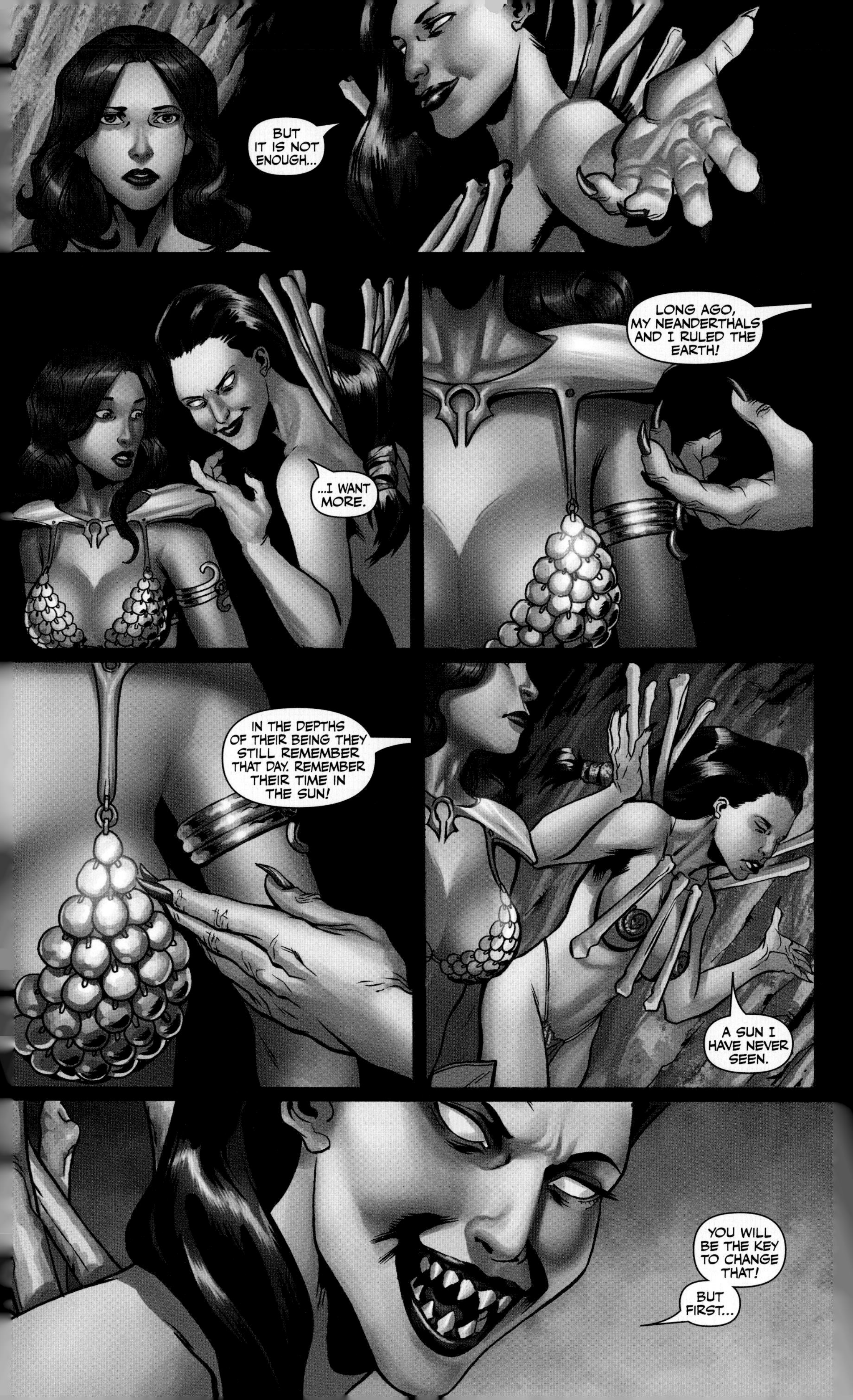
BUT IT IS NOT ENOUGH...
...I WANT MORE.
LONG AGO, MY NEANDERTHALS AND I RULED THE EARTH!
IN THE DEPTHS OF THEIR BEING THEY STILL REMEMBER THAT DAY. REMEMBER THEIR TIME IN THE SUN!
A SUN I HAVE NEVER SEEN.
YOU WILL BE THE KEY TO CHANGE THAT!
BUT FIRST...

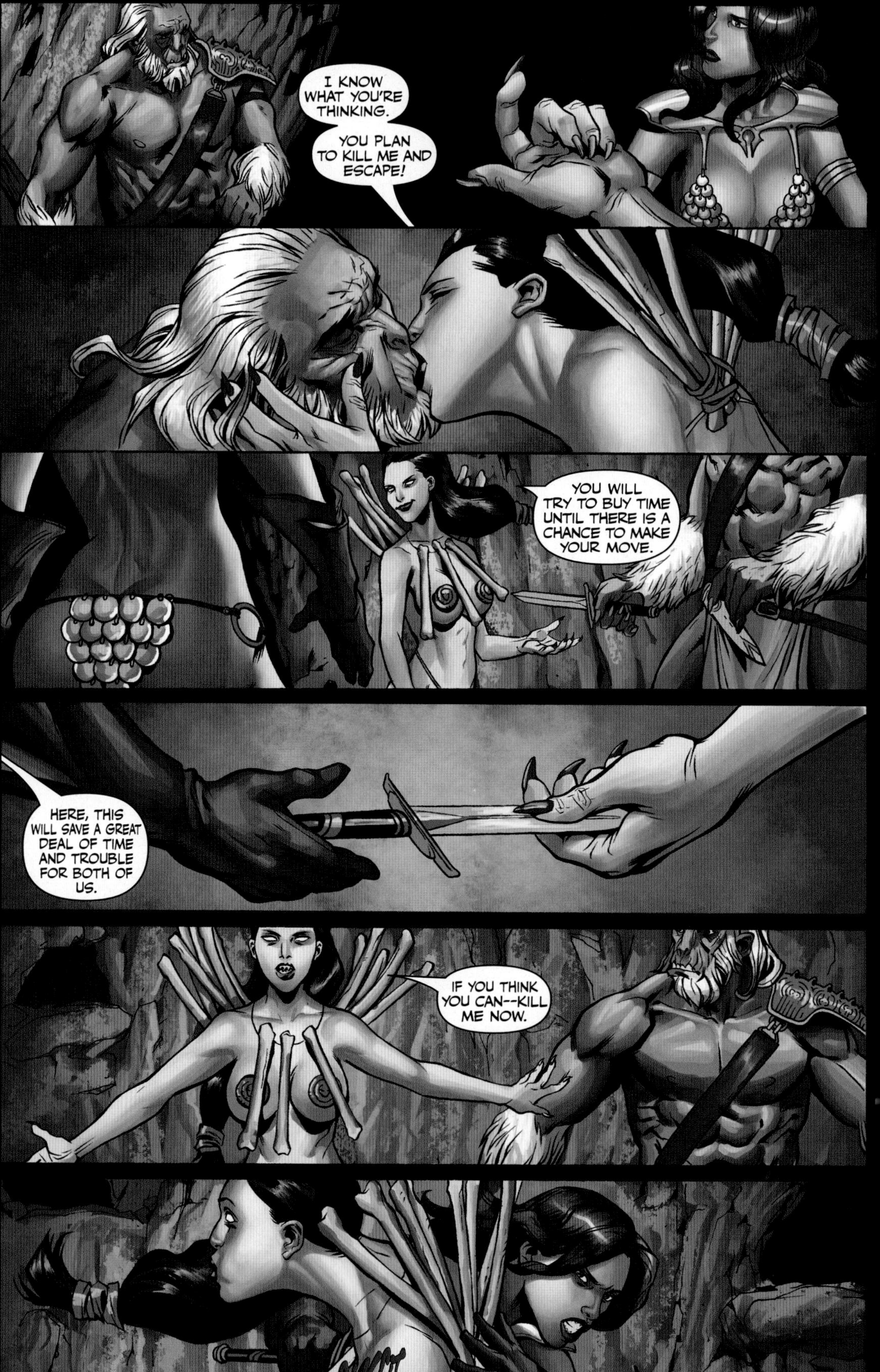
I KNOW WHAT YOU'RE THINKING.
YOU PLAN TO KILL ME AND ESCAPE!
YOU WILL TRY TO BUY TIME UNTIL THERE IS A CHANCE TO MAKE YOUR MOVE.
HERE, THIS WILL SAVE A GREAT DEAL OF TIME AND TROUBLE FOR BOTH OF US.
IF YOU THINK YOU CAN--KILL ME NOW.

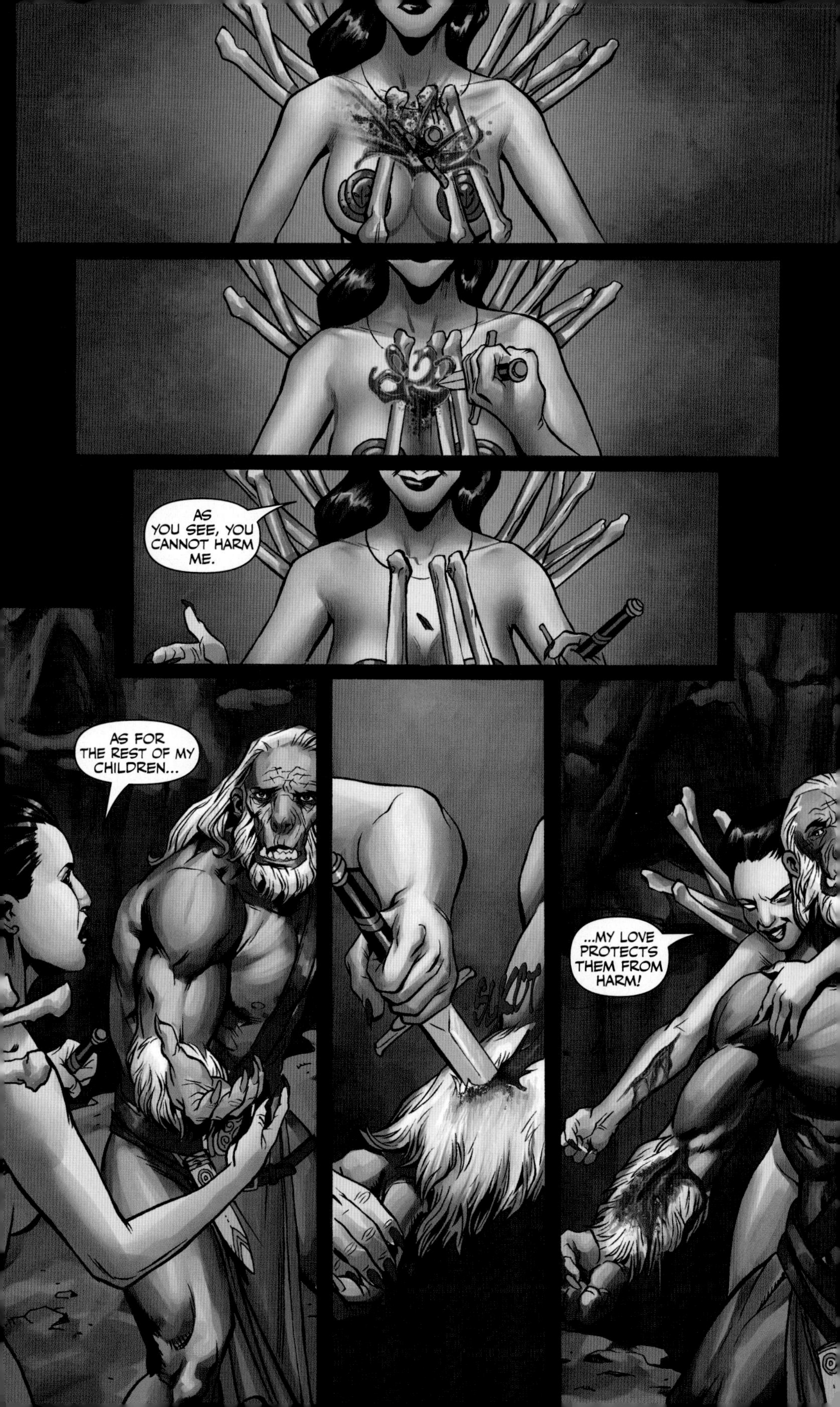
AS YOU SEE, YOU CANNOT HARM ME.
AS FOR THE REST OF MY CHILDREN...
...MY LOVE PROTECTS THEM FROM HARM!

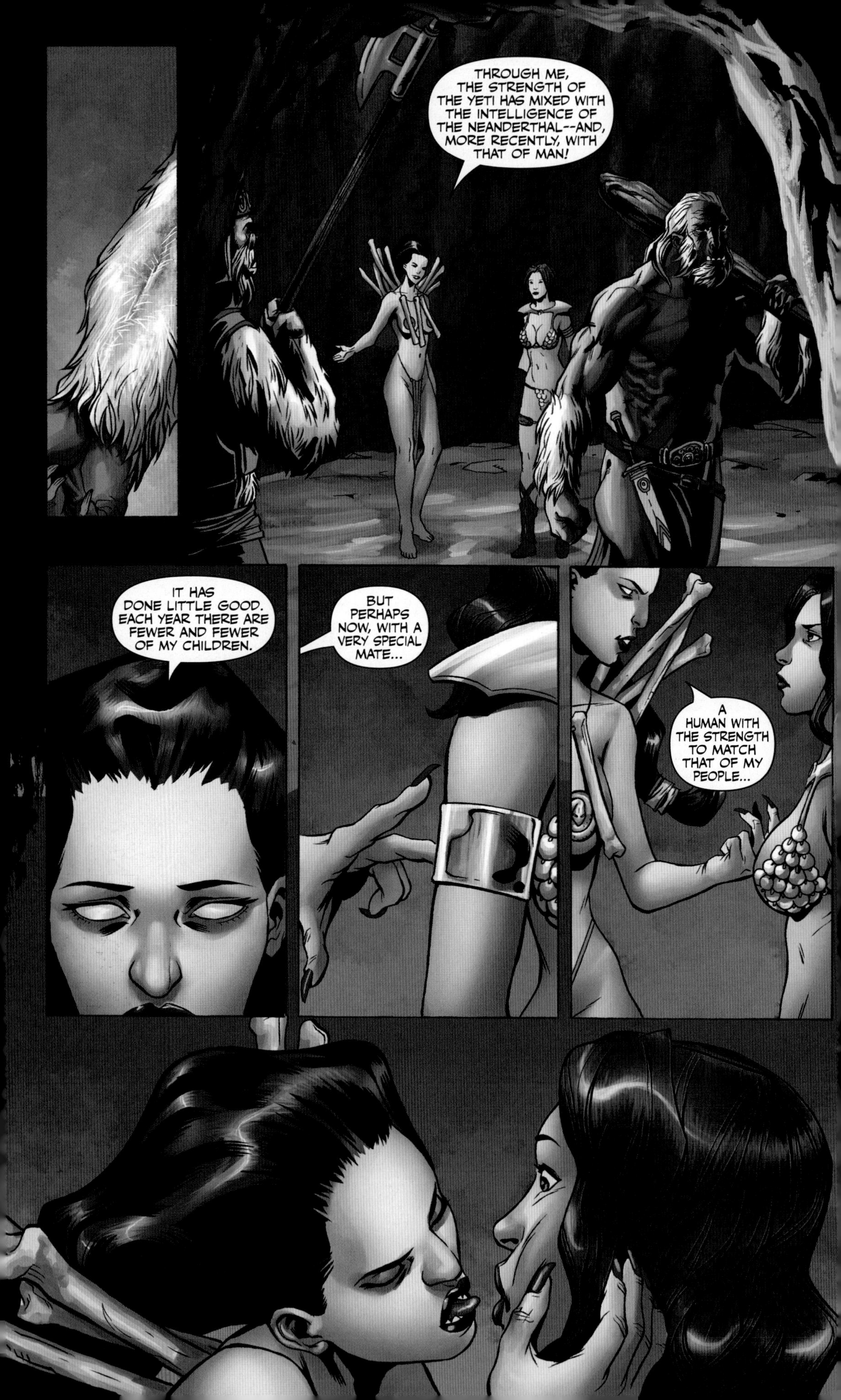
THROUGH ME, THE STRENGTH OF THE YETI HAS MIXED WITH THE INTELLIGENCE OF THE NEANDERTHAL--AND, MORE RECENTLY, WITH THAT OF MAN!
IT HAS DONE LITTLE GOOD. EACH YEAR THERE ARE FEWER AND FEWER OF MY CHILDREN.
BUT PERHAPS NOW, WITH A VERY SPECIAL MATE...
A HUMAN WITH THE STRENGTH TO MATCH THAT OF MY PEOPLE...

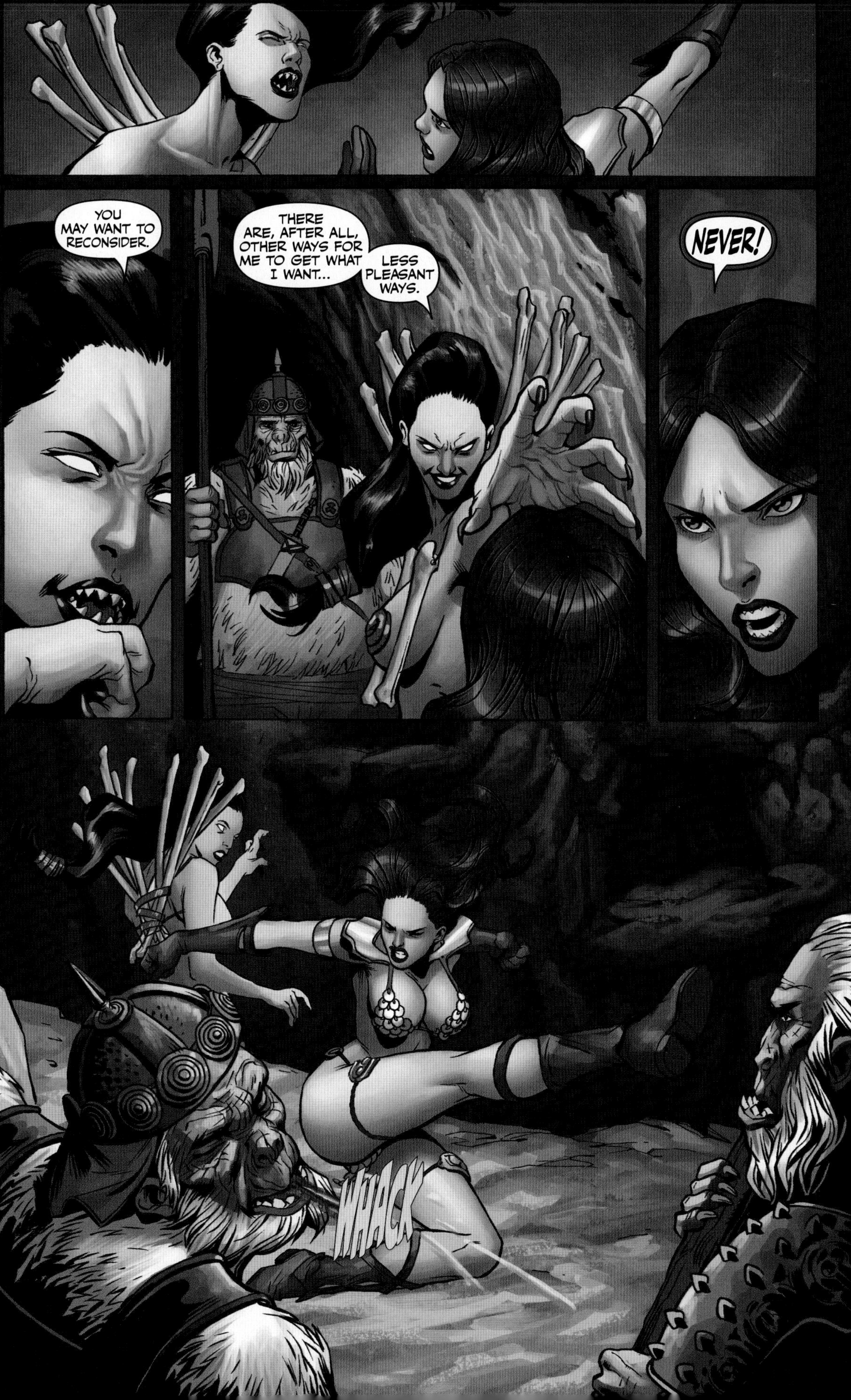
YOU MAY WANT TO RECONSIDER.
THERE ARE, AFTER ALL, OTHER WAYS FOR ME TO GET WHAT I WANT...
LESS PLEASANT WAYS.
NEVER!
WHACK

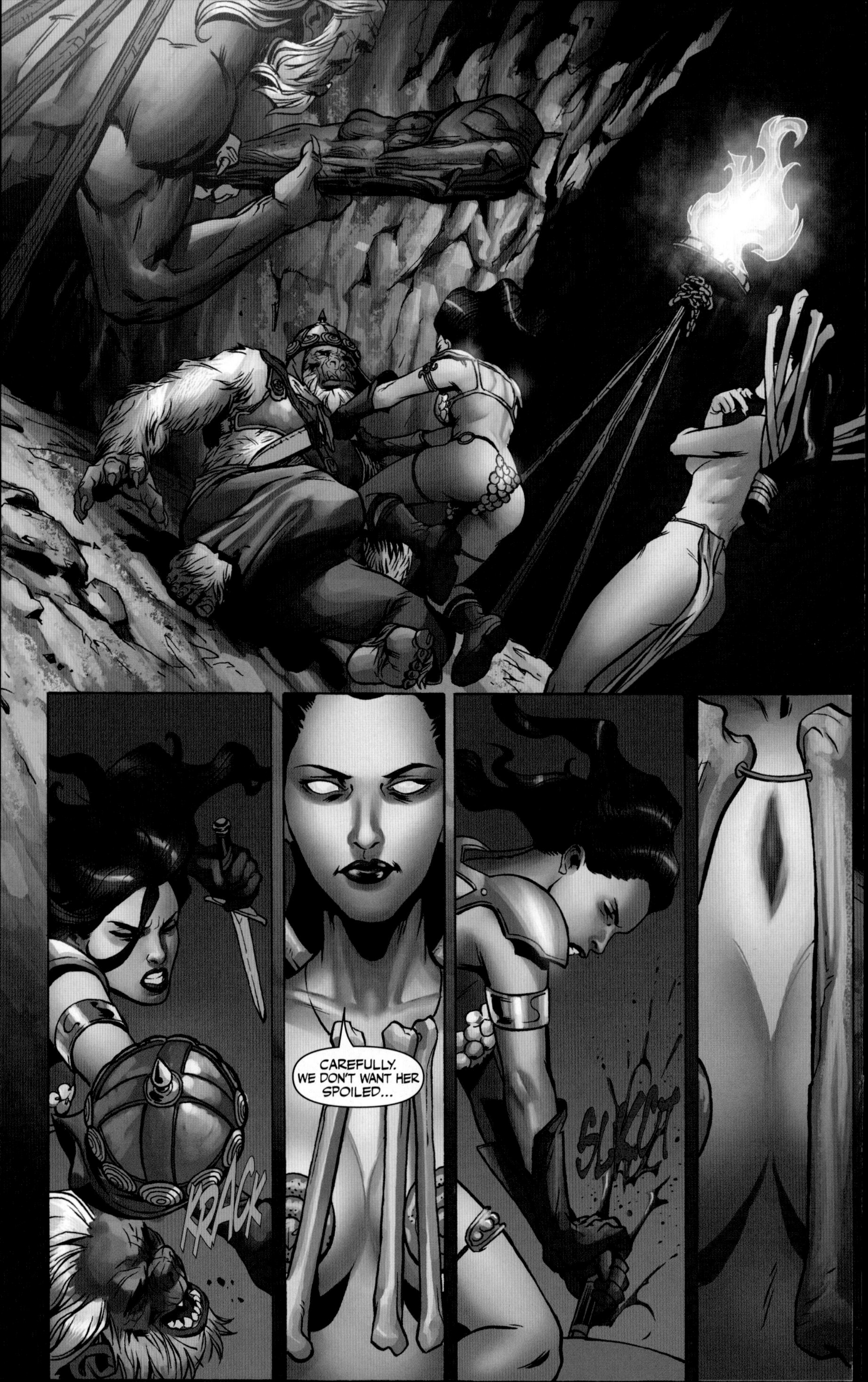
KRACK
CAREFULLY. WE DON'T WANT HER SPOILED...
SLKCH

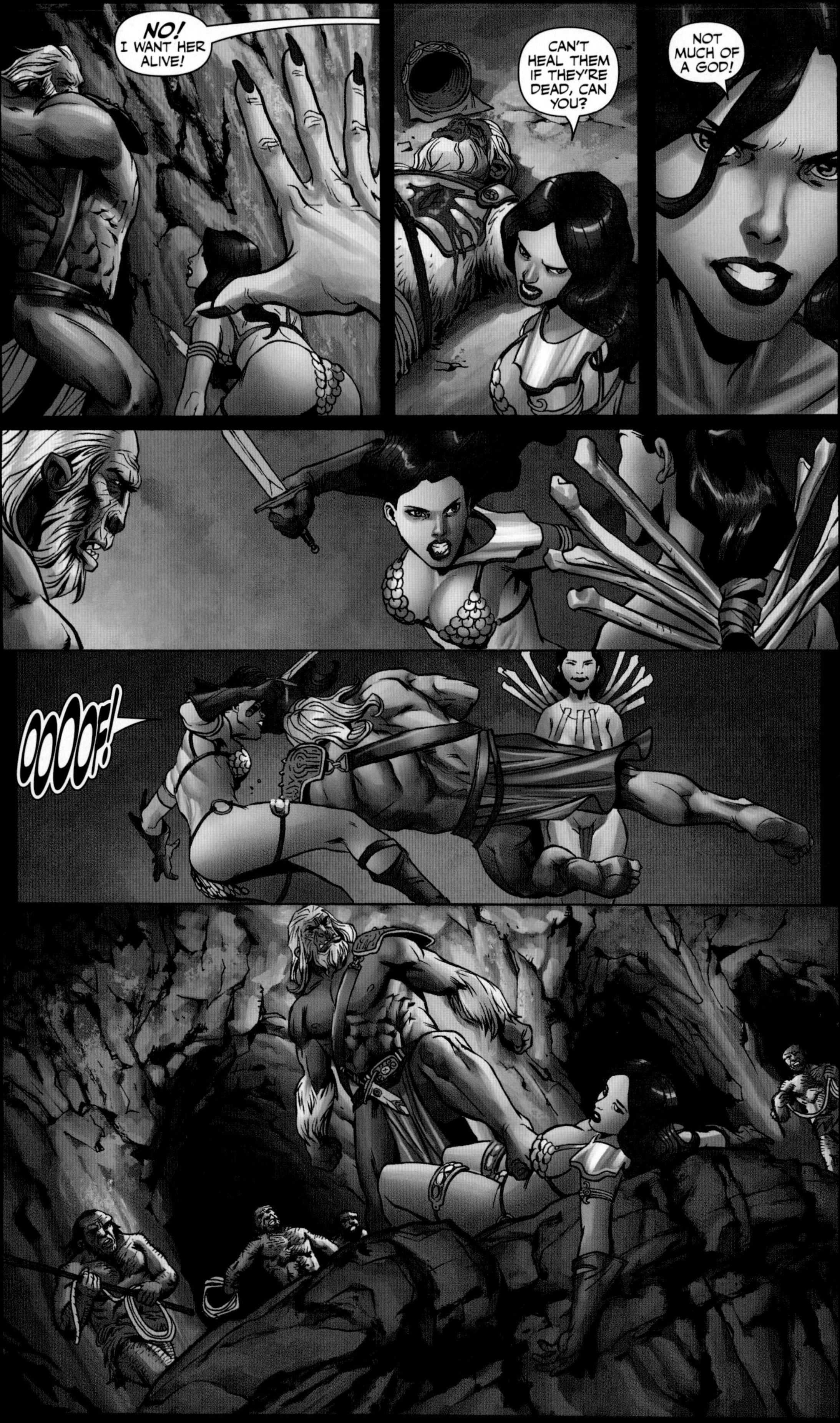
NO! I WANT HER ALIVE!
CAN'T HEAL THEM IF THEY'RE DEAD, CAN YOU?
NOT MUCH OF A GOD!
OOOOF!

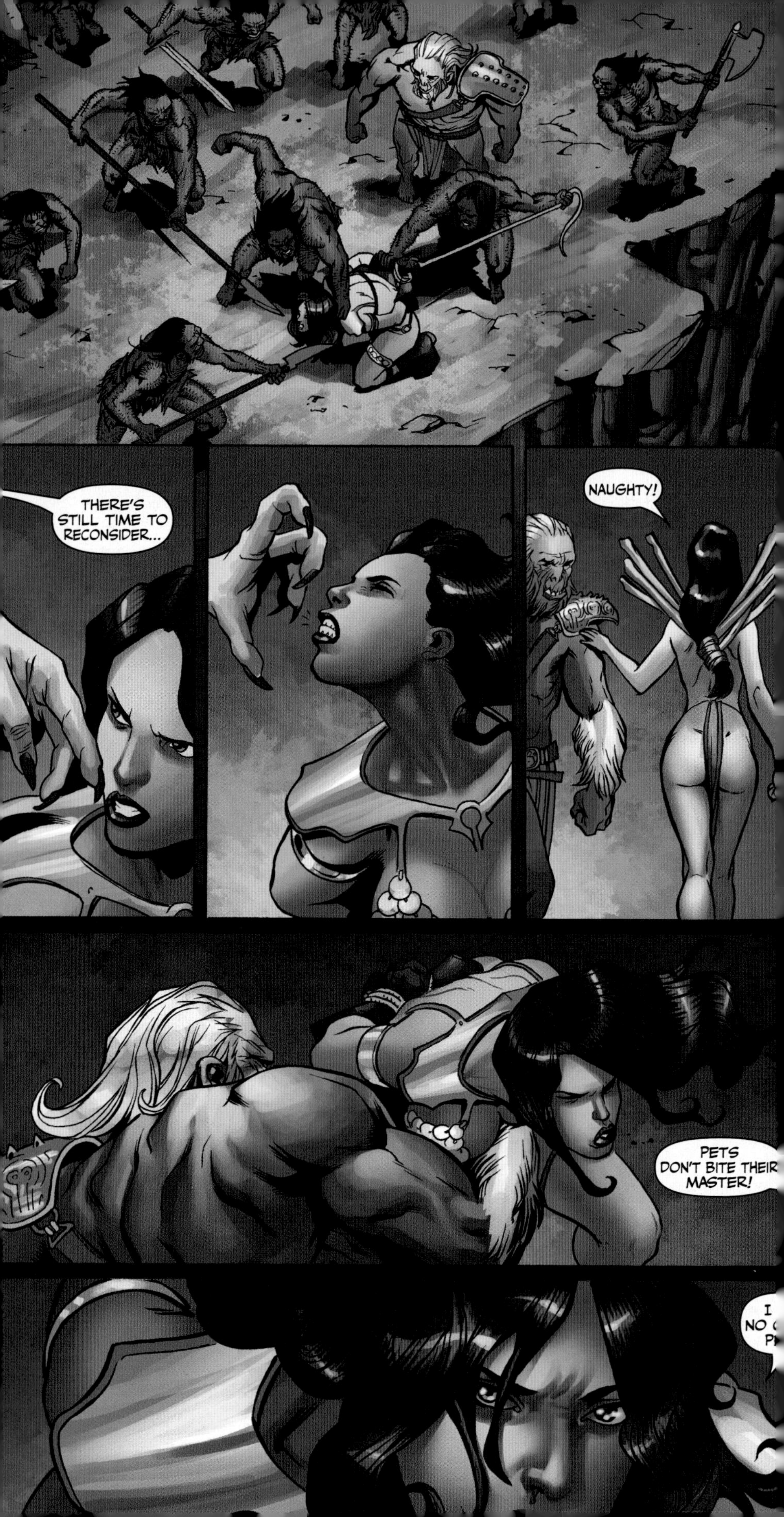
THERE'S STILL TIME TO RECONSIDER...
NAUGHTY!
PETS DON'T BITE THEIR MASTER!

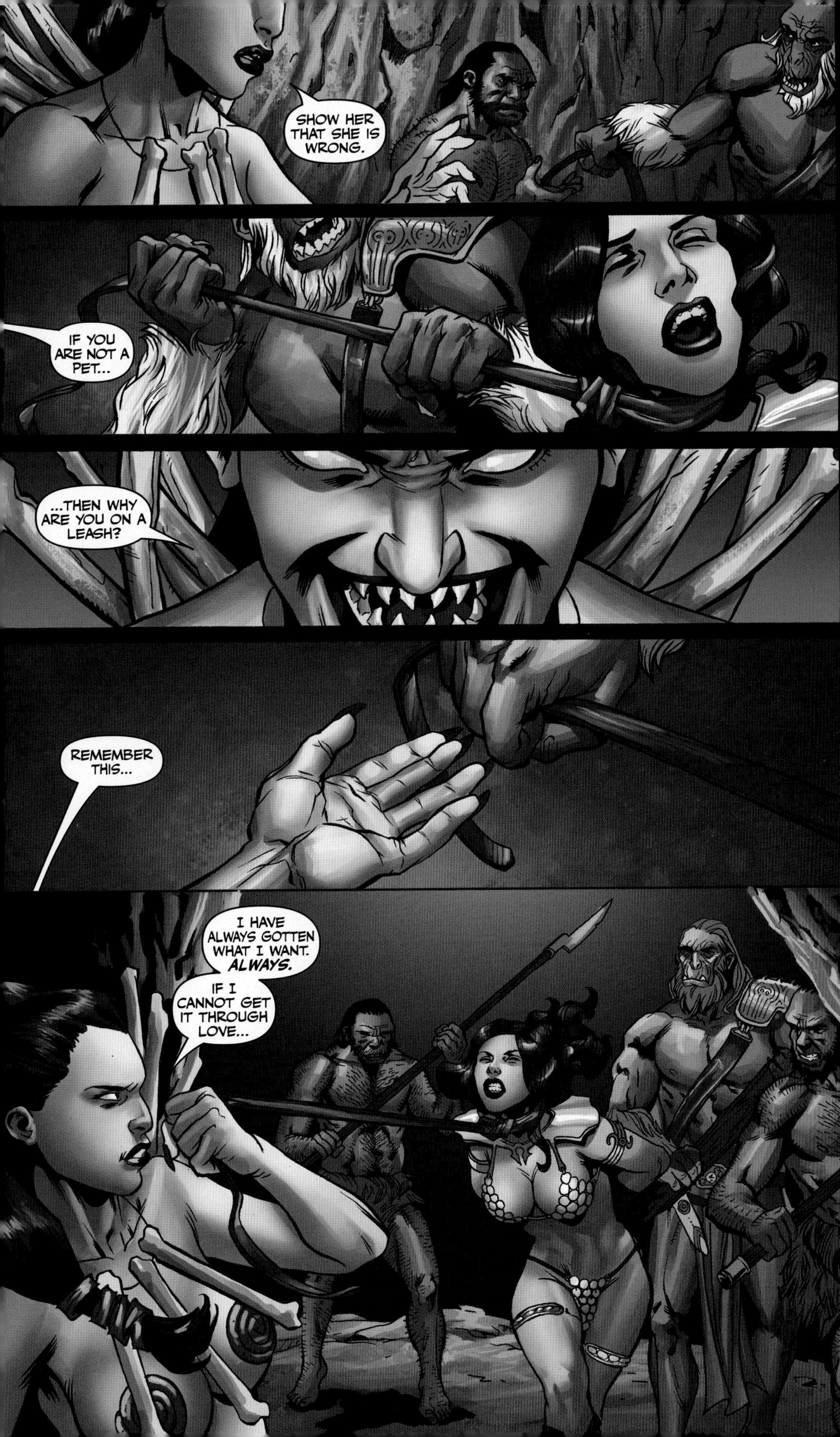
SHOW HER THAT SHE IS WRONG.
IF YOU ARE NOT A PET...
...THEN WHY ARE YOU ON A LEASH?
REMEMBER THIS...
I HAVE ALWAYS GOTTEN WHAT I WANT. ***ALWAYS.***
IF I CANNOT GET IT THROUGH LOVE...

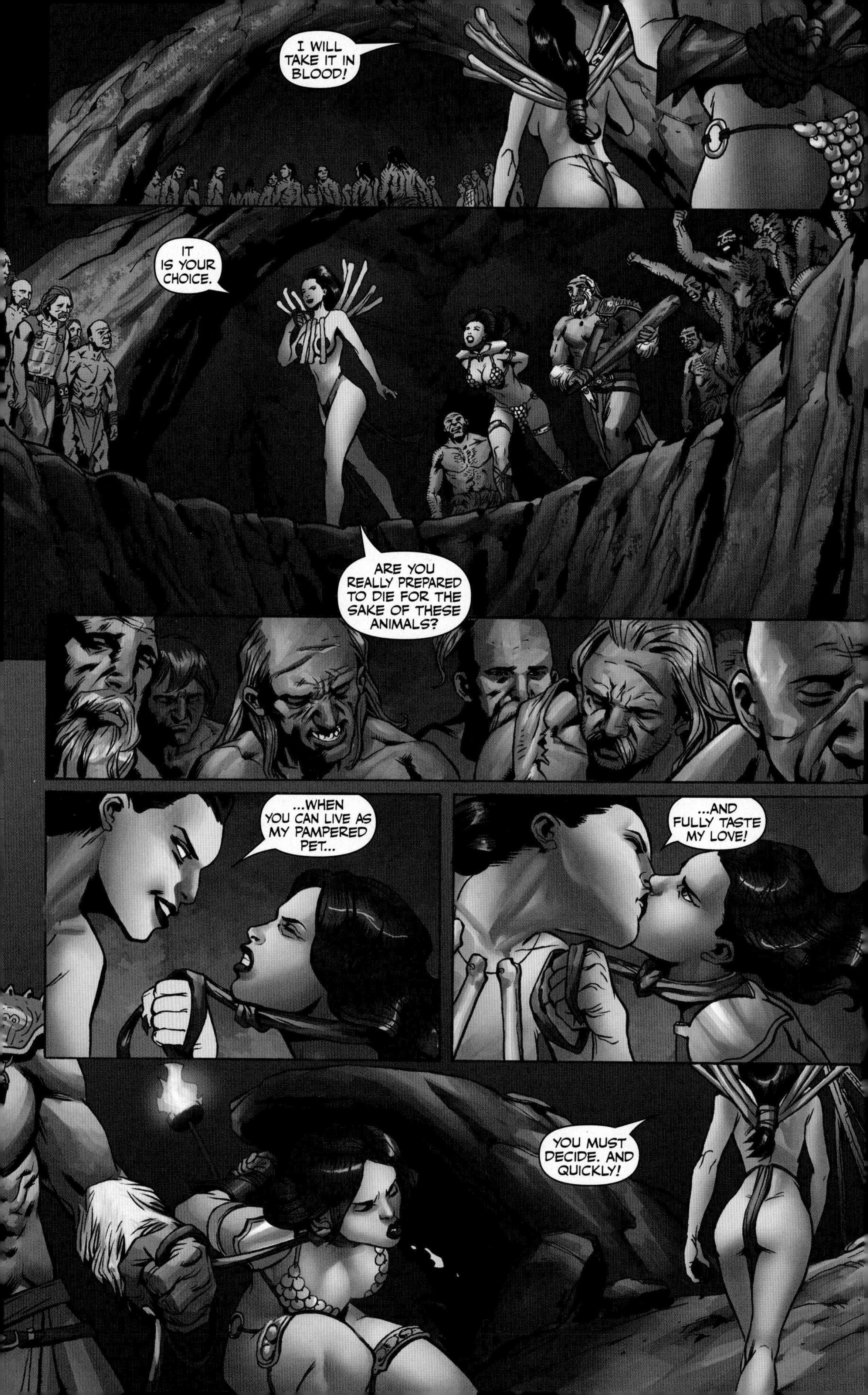
I WILL TAKE IT IN BLOOD!
IT IS YOUR CHOICE.
ARE YOU REALLY PREPARED TO DIE FOR THE SAKE OF THESE ANIMALS?
...WHEN YOU CAN LIVE AS MY PAMPERED PET...
...AND FULLY TASTE MY LOVE!
YOU MUST DECIDE. AND QUICKLY!

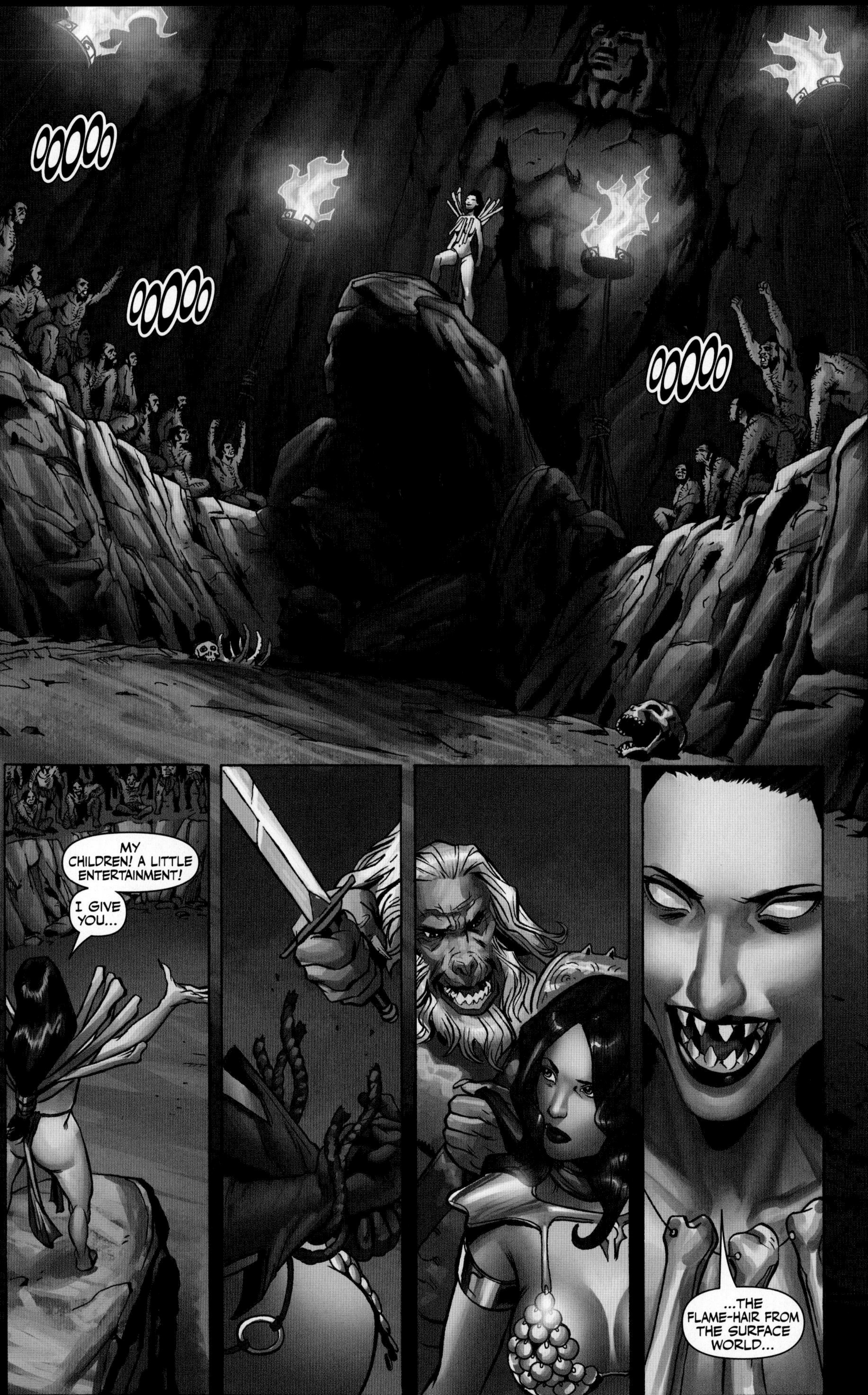
OOOOO
OOOOO
OOOOO
MY CHILDREN! A LITTLE ENTERTAINMENT!
I GIVE YOU...
...THE FLAME-HAIR FROM THE SURFACE WORLD...

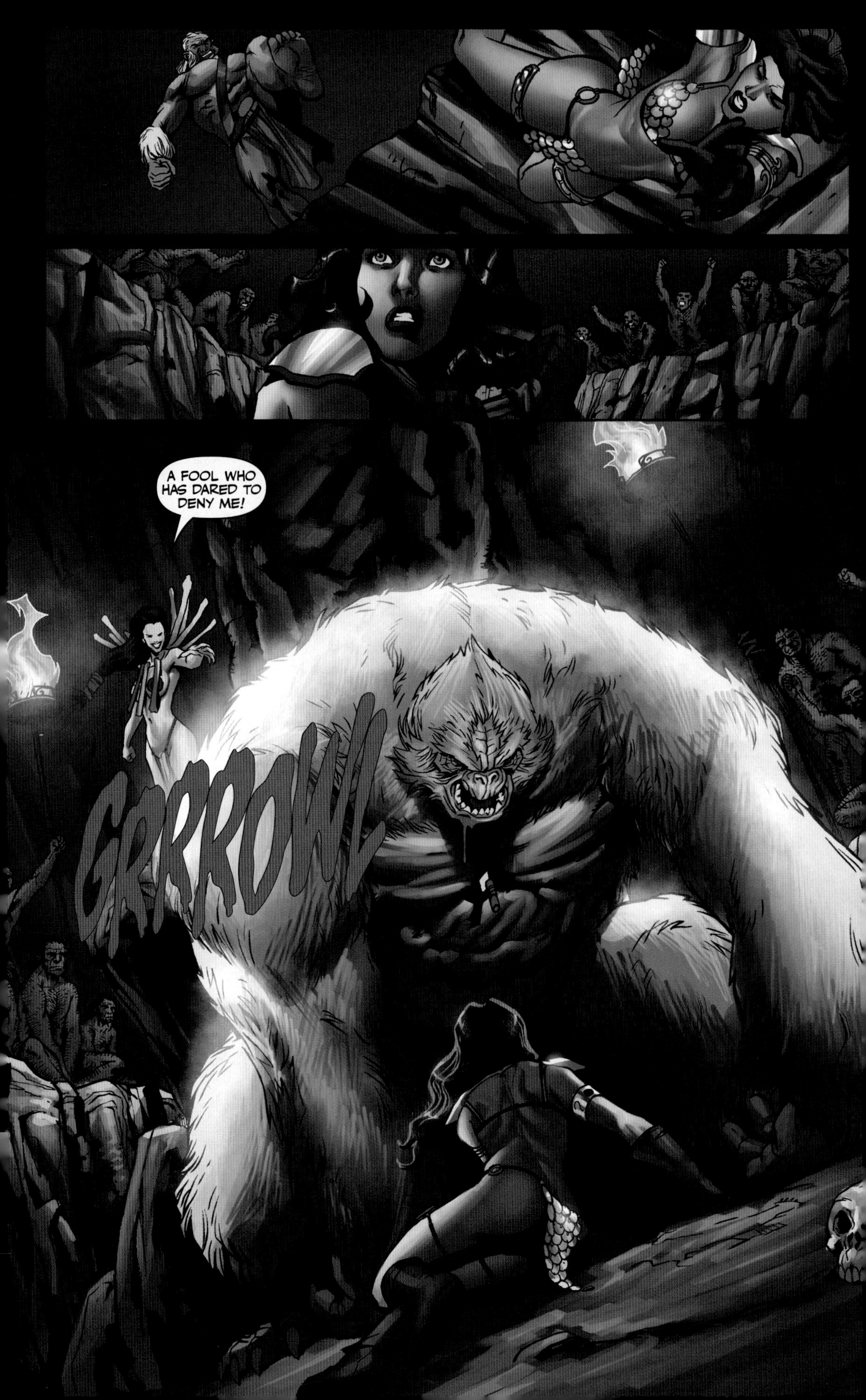
A FOOL WHO HAS DARED TO DENY ME!
GRRROWL

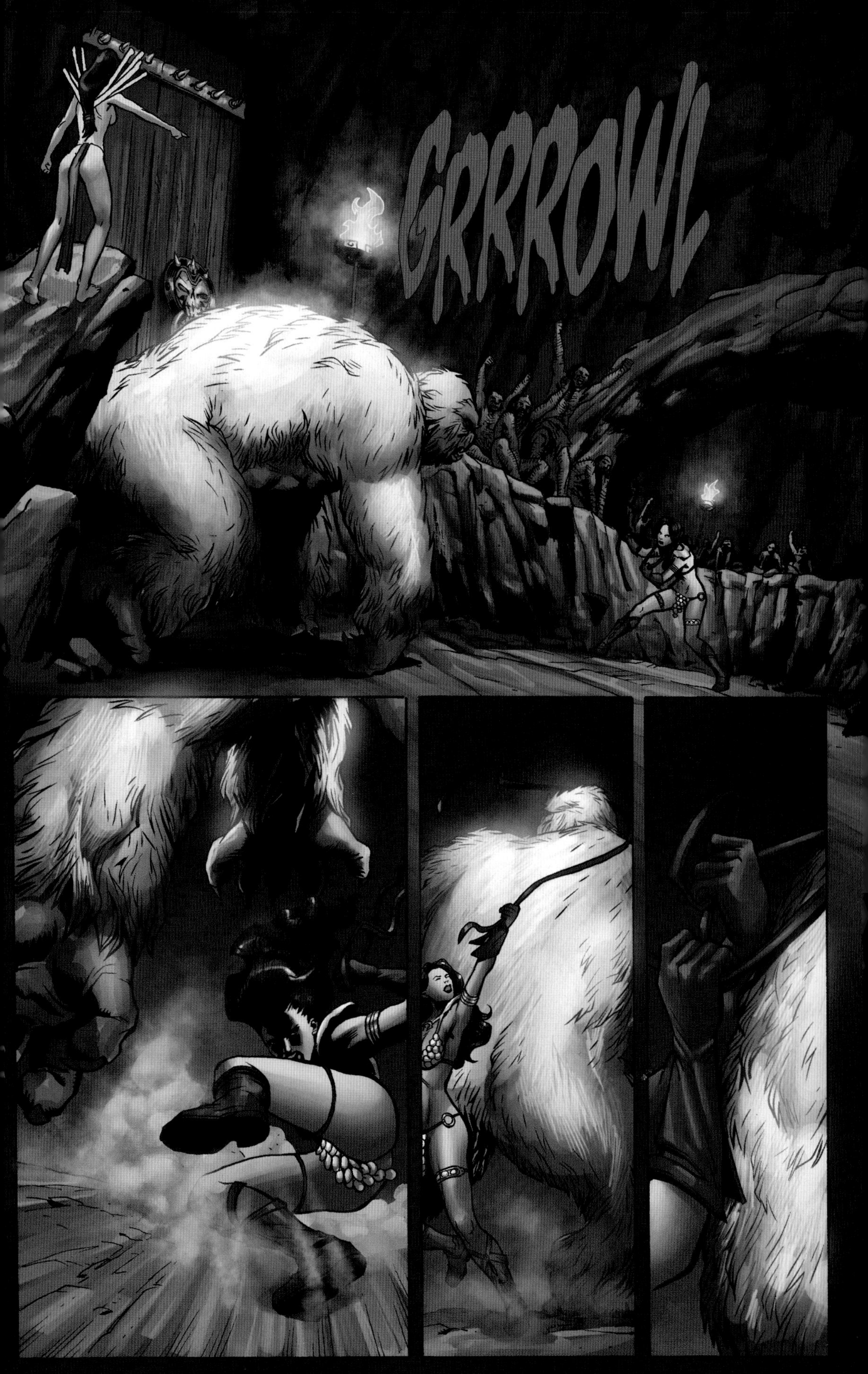
GRRROWL

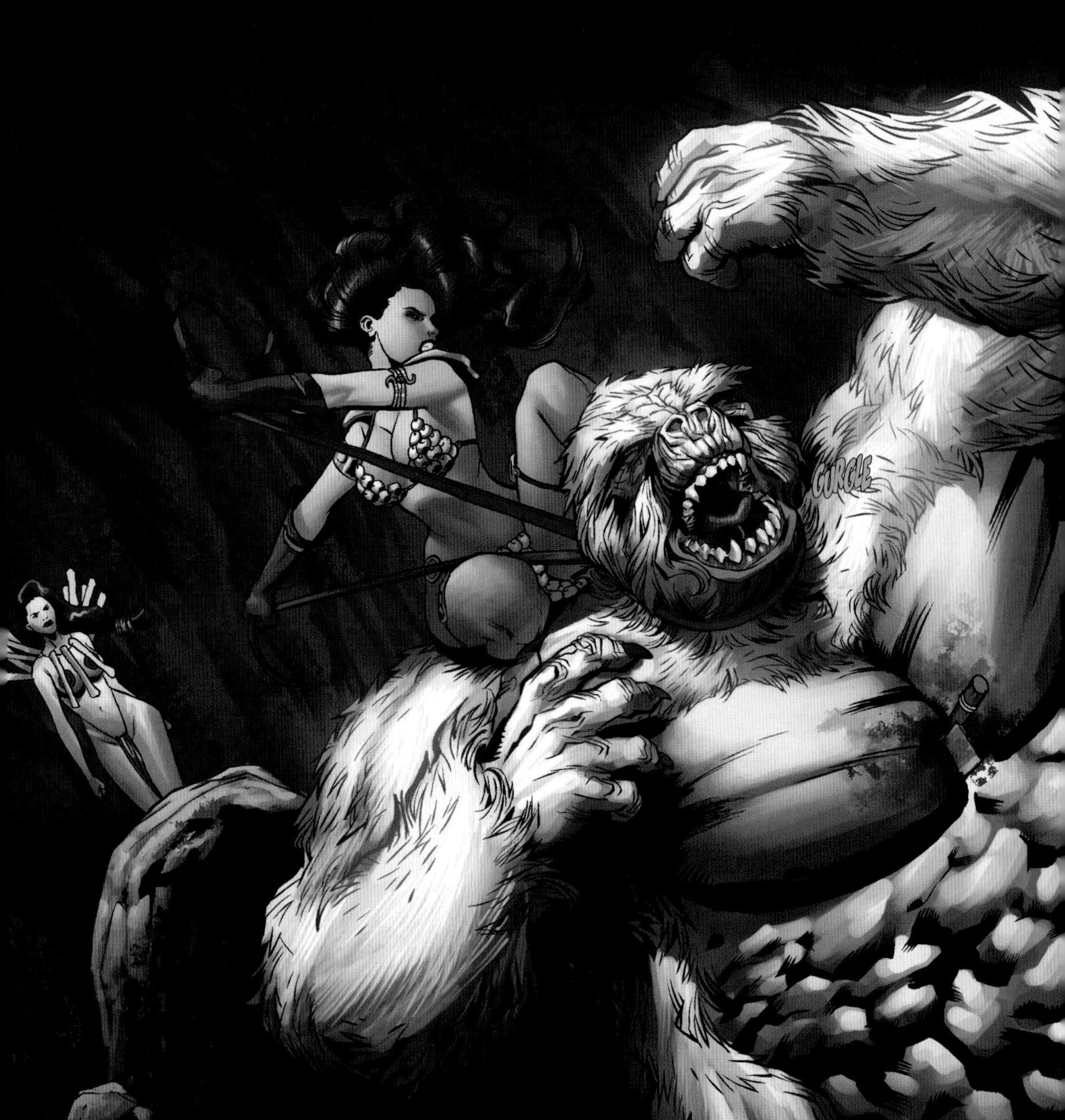
GURGLE
ALL AROUND ME, WHILE I FIGHT, I SEE...SHOCK, SURPRISE...AND SOMETHING ELSE...

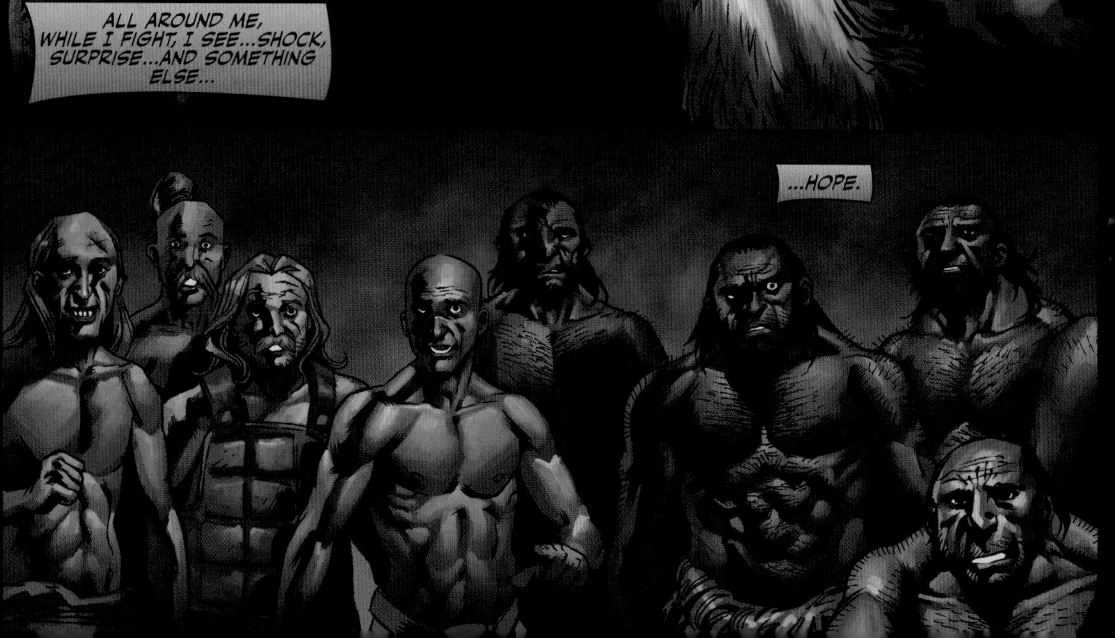
...HOPE.

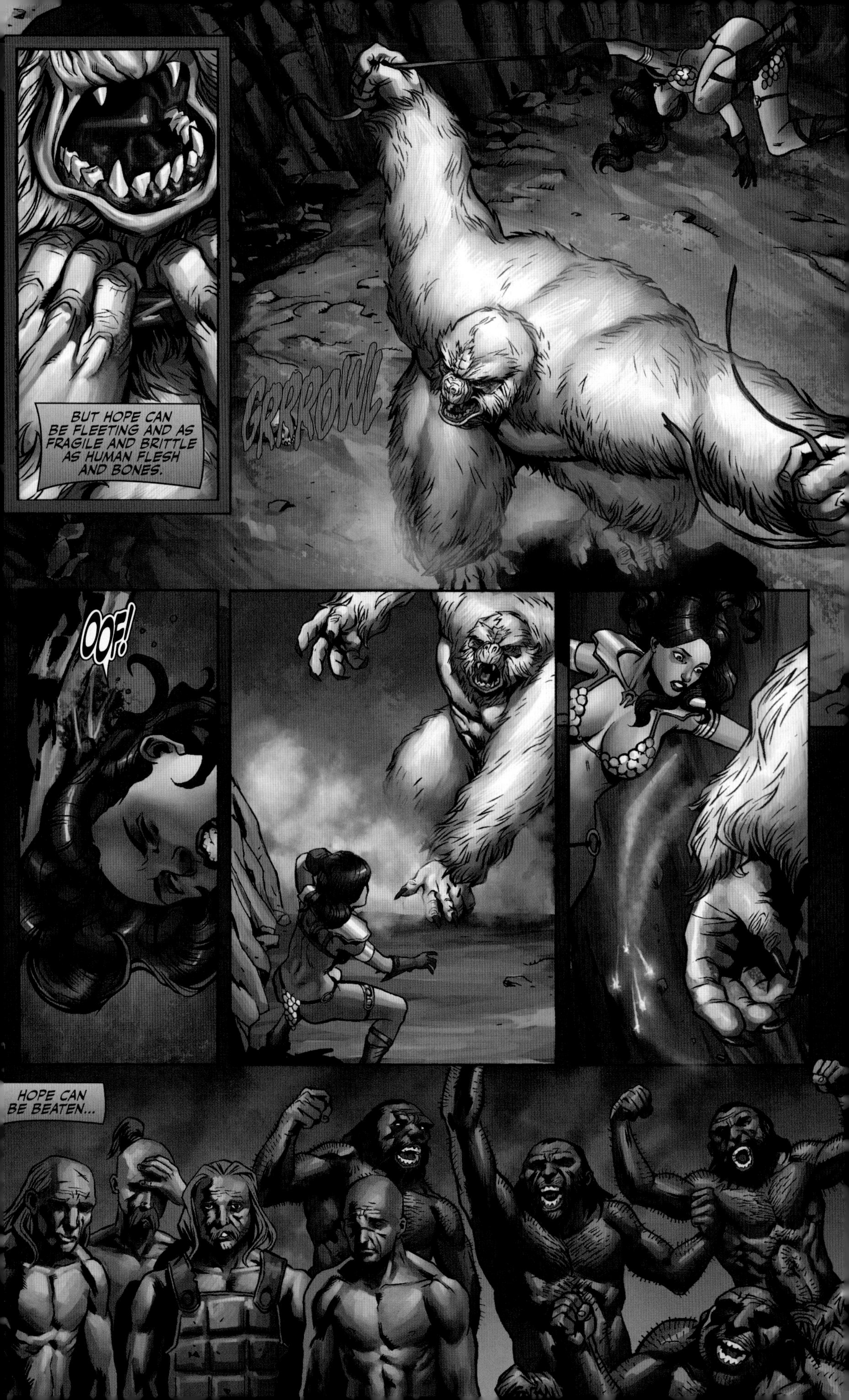
BUT HOPE CAN BE FLEETING AND AS FRAGILE AND BRITTLE AS HUMAN FLESH AND BONES.
GRRROWL
OOF!
HOPE CAN BE BEATEN...

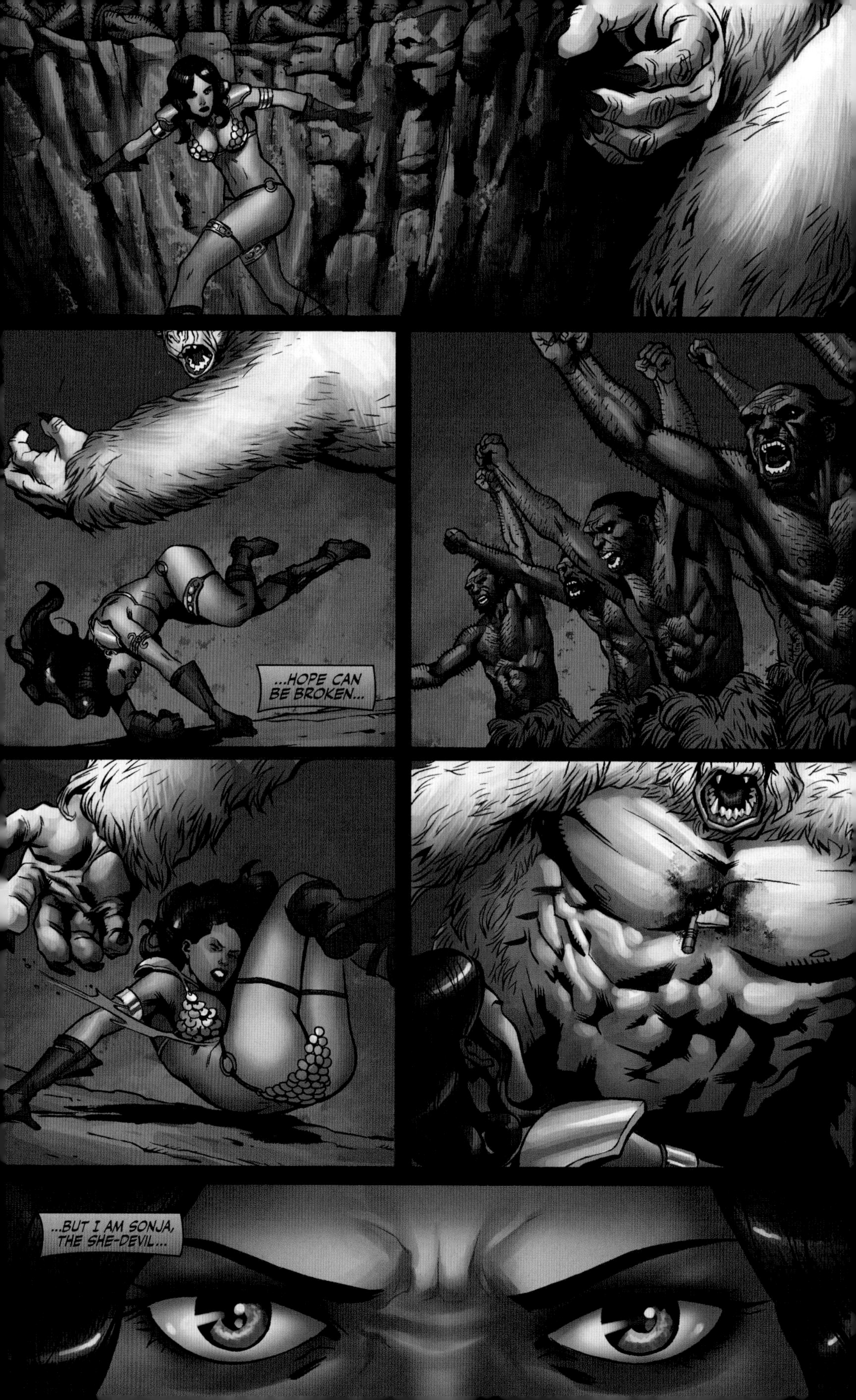
...HOPE CAN BE BROKEN...
...BUT I AM SONJA, THE SHE-DEVIL...

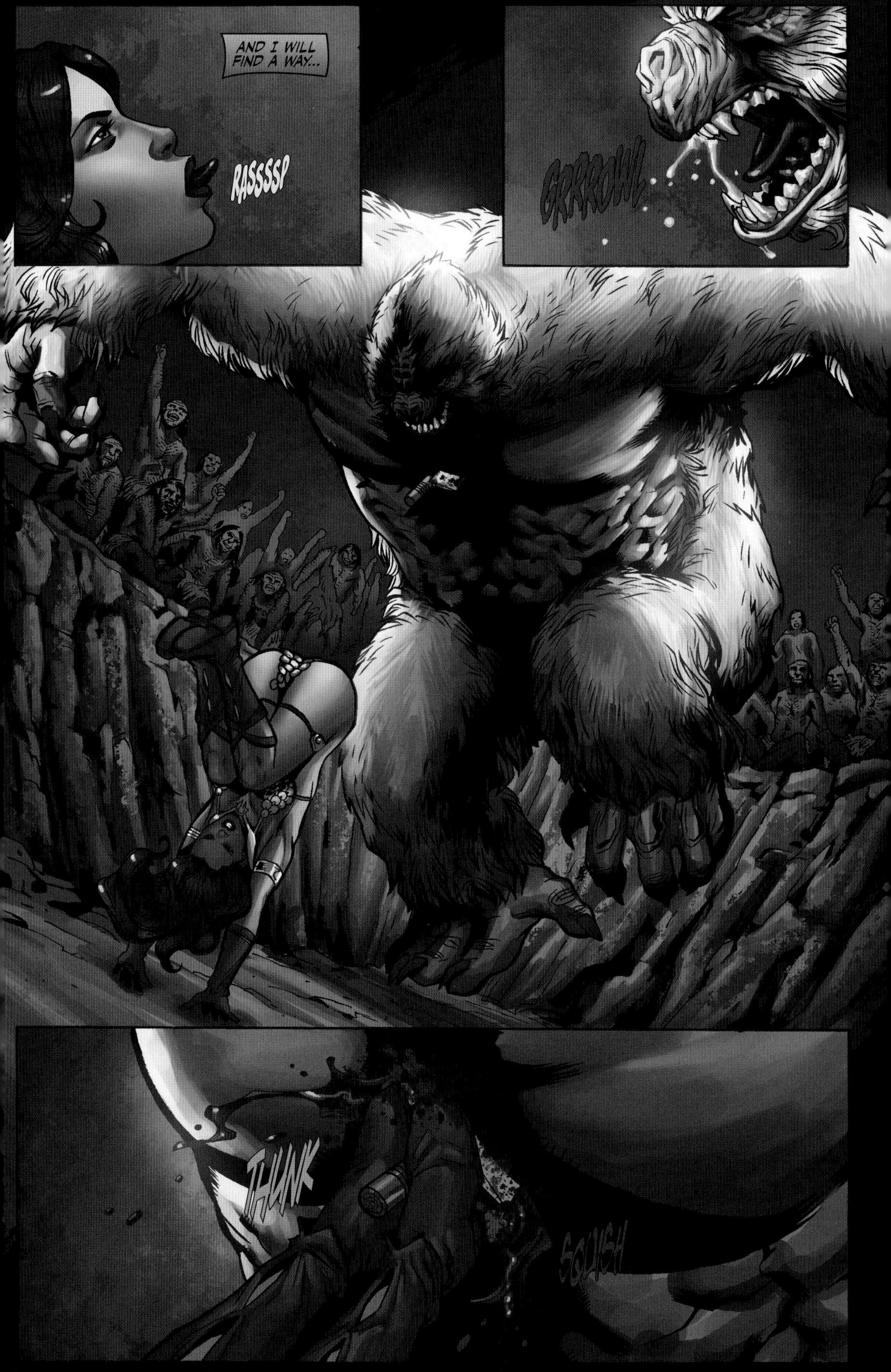
AND I WILL FIND A WAY...
RASSSSP
GRRROWL
THUNK
SQUISH

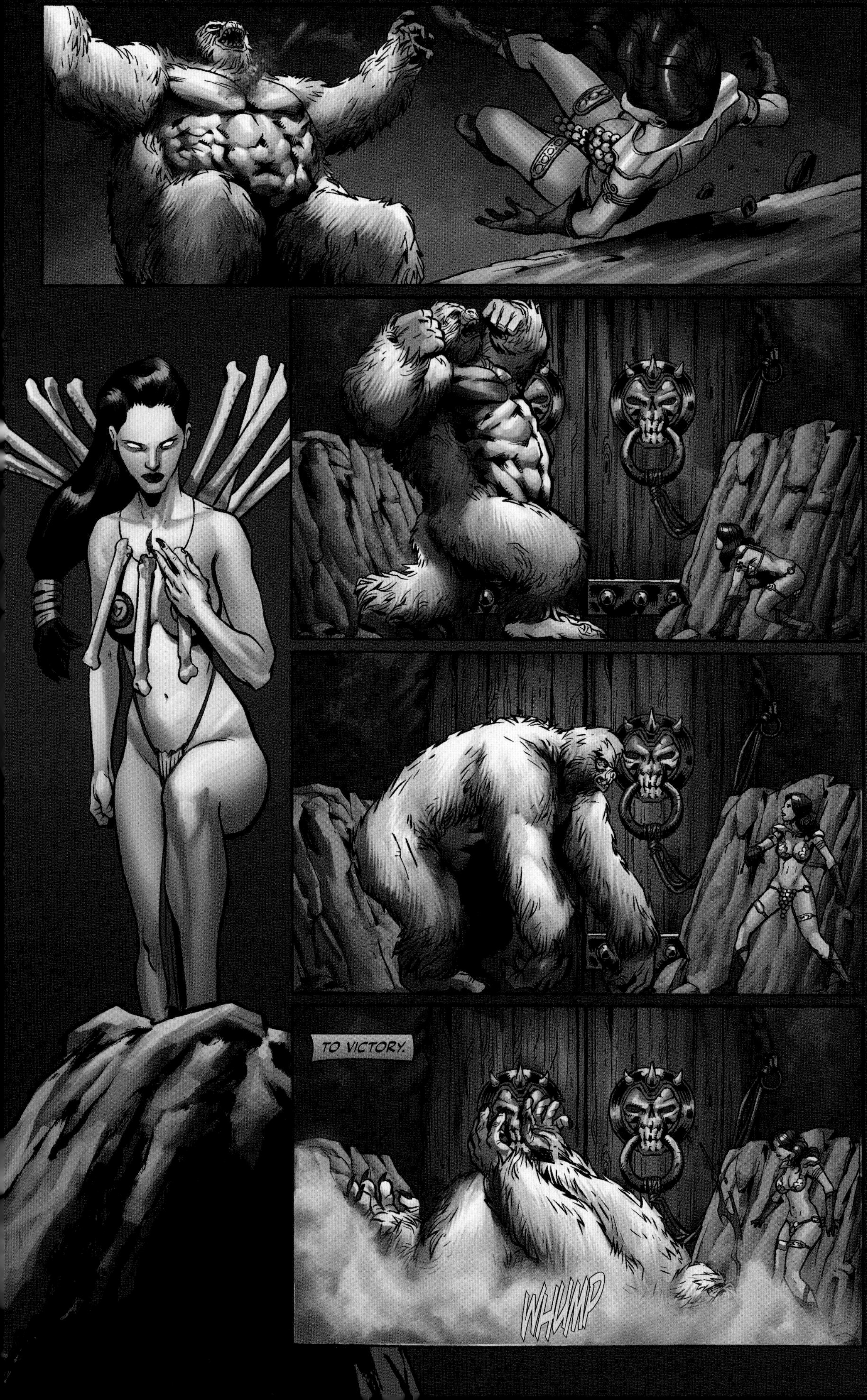
TO VICTORY.
WHUMP

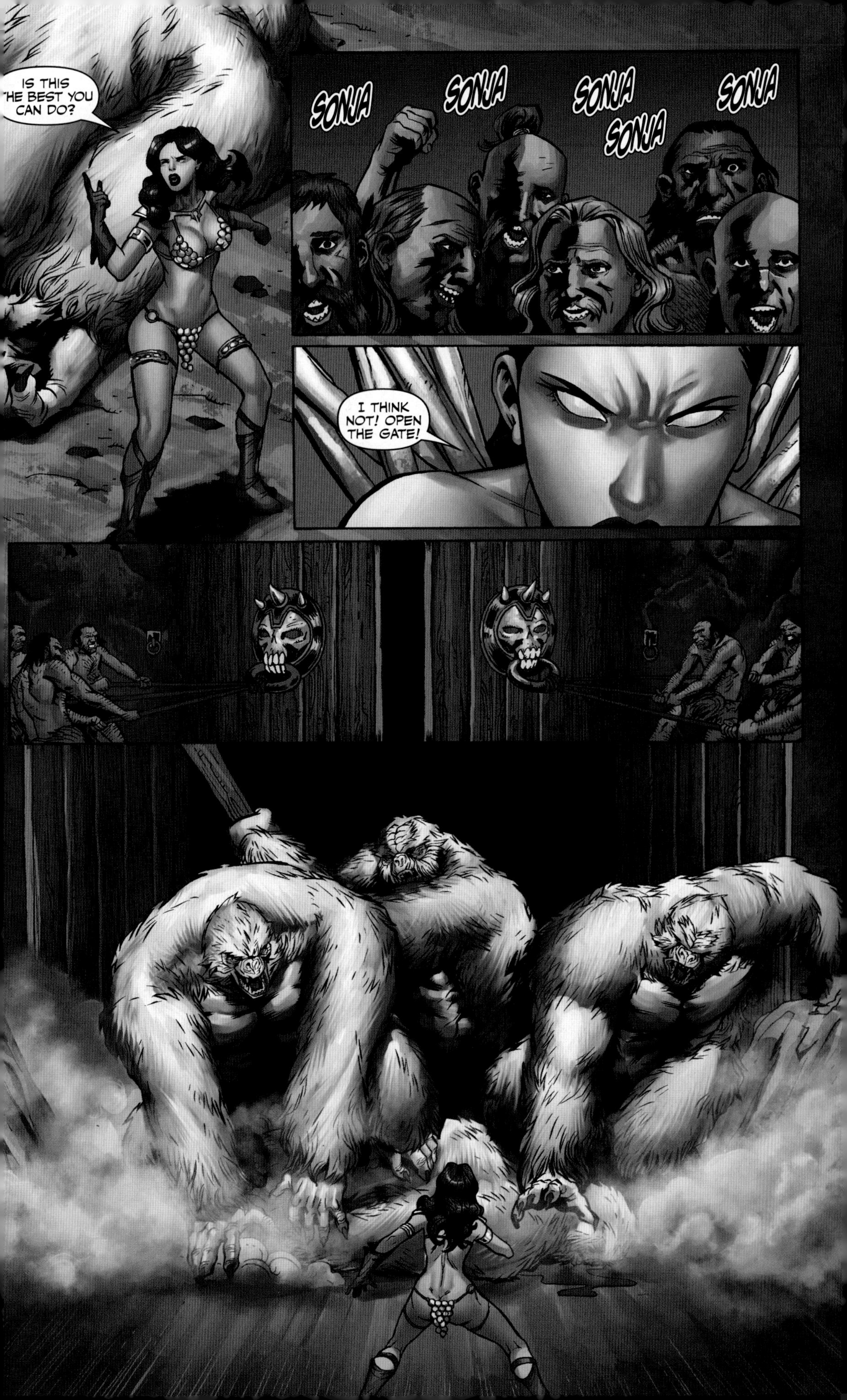
IS THIS THE BEST YOU CAN DO?
SONJA
SONJA
SONJA
SONJA
SONJA
I THINK NOT! OPEN THE GATE!

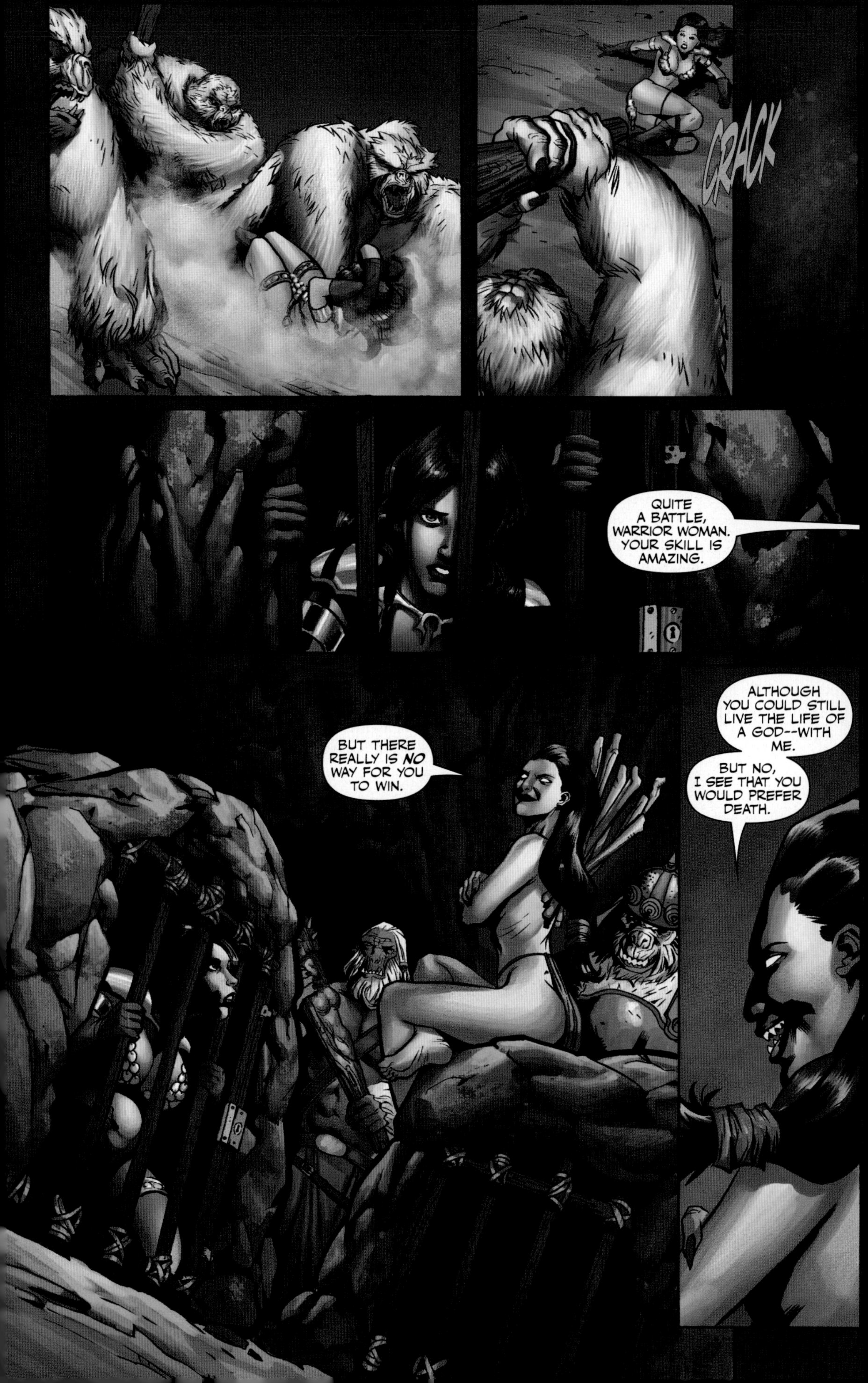
CRACK
QUITE A BATTLE, WARRIOR WOMAN. YOUR SKILL IS AMAZING.
BUT THERE REALLY IS **NO** WAY FOR YOU TO WIN.
ALTHOUGH YOU COULD STILL LIVE THE LIFE OF A GOD--WITH ME.
BUT NO, I SEE THAT YOU WOULD PREFER DEATH.

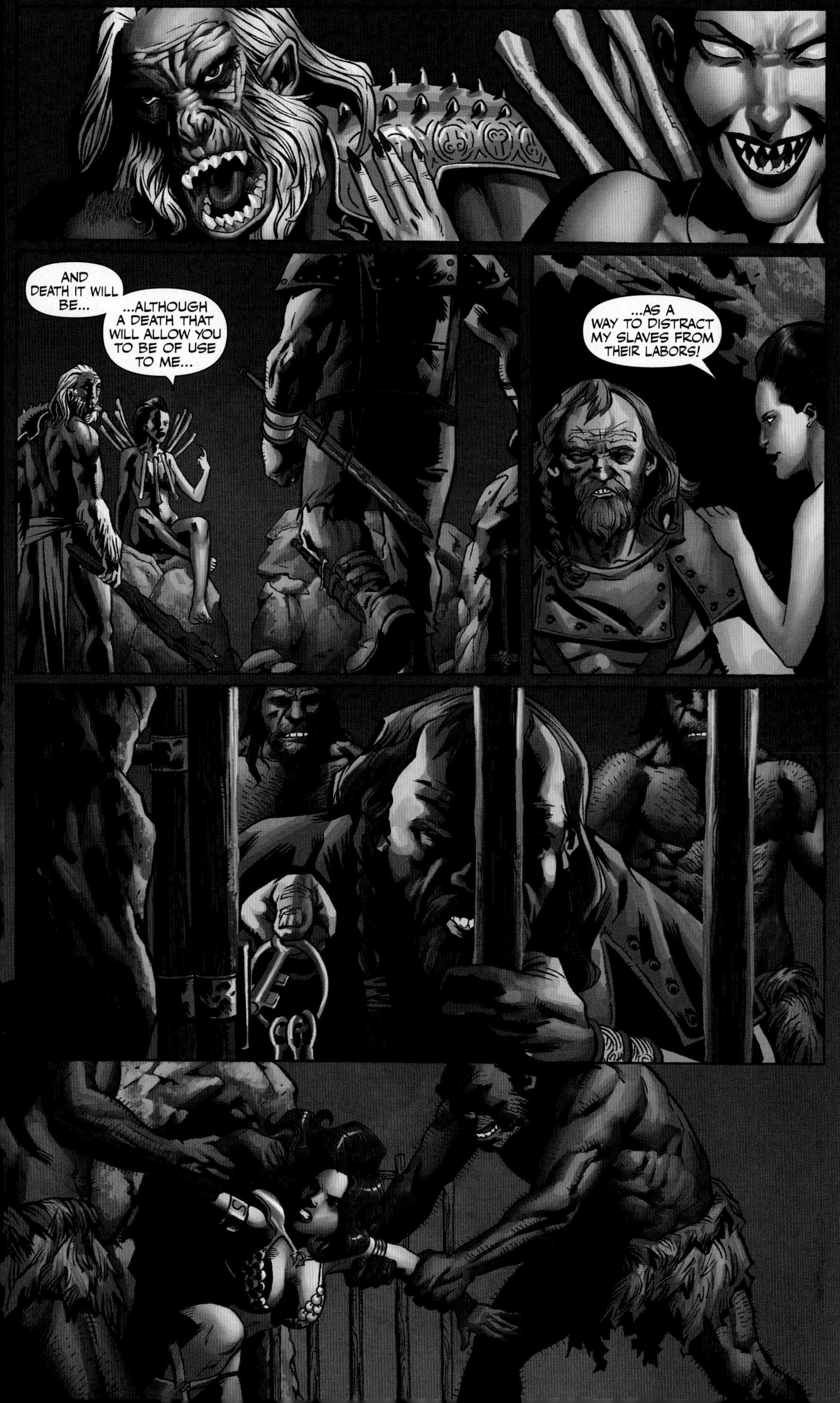

AND DEATH IT WILL BE...
...ALTHOUGH A DEATH THAT WILL ALLOW YOU TO BE OF USE TO ME...
...AS A WAY TO DISTRACT MY SLAVES FROM THEIR LABORS!

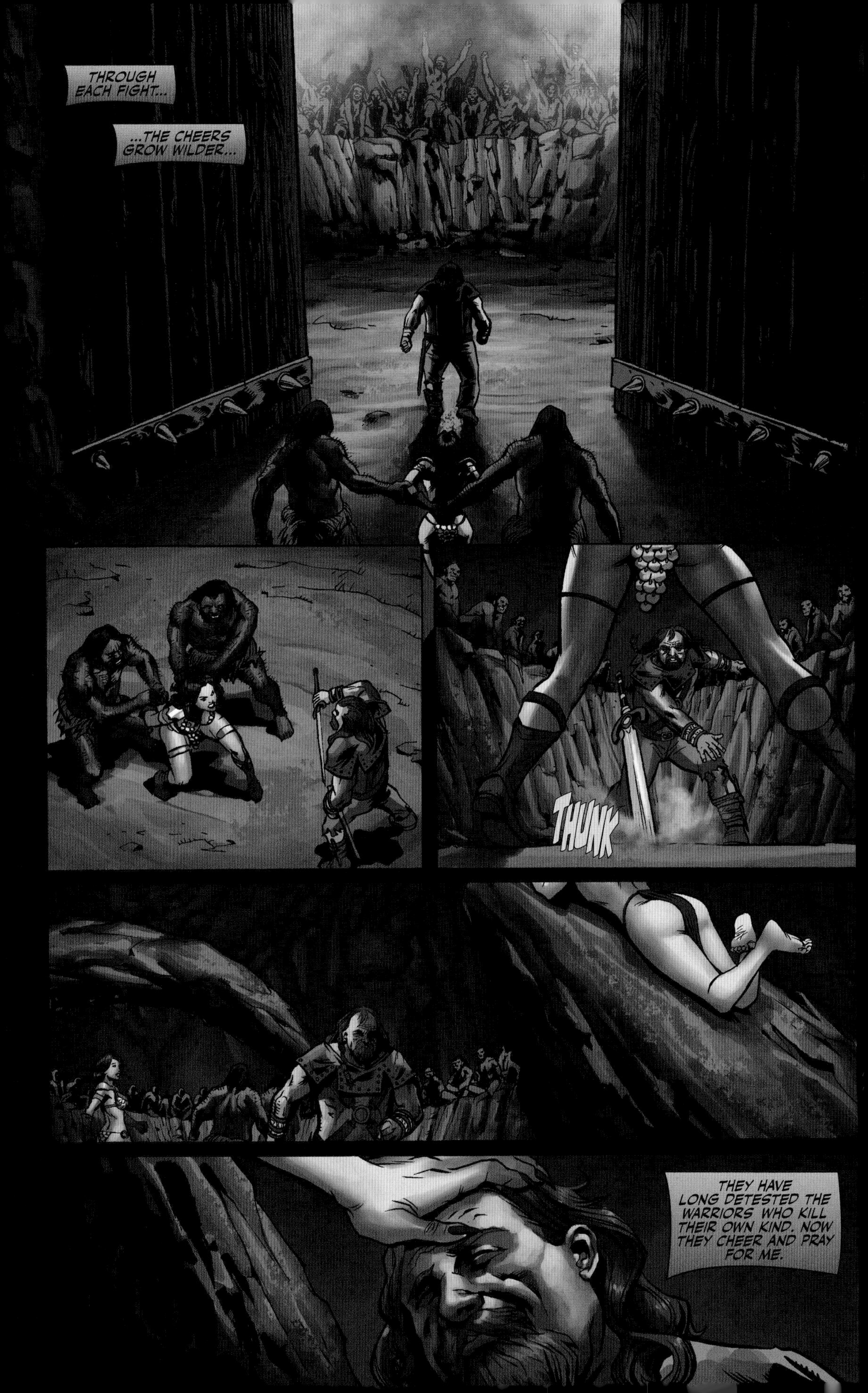
THROUGH EACH FIGHT...
...THE CHEERS GROW WILDER...
THUNK
THEY HAVE LONG DETESTED THE WARRIORS WHO KILL THEIR OWN KIND. NOW THEY CHEER AND PRAY FOR ME.

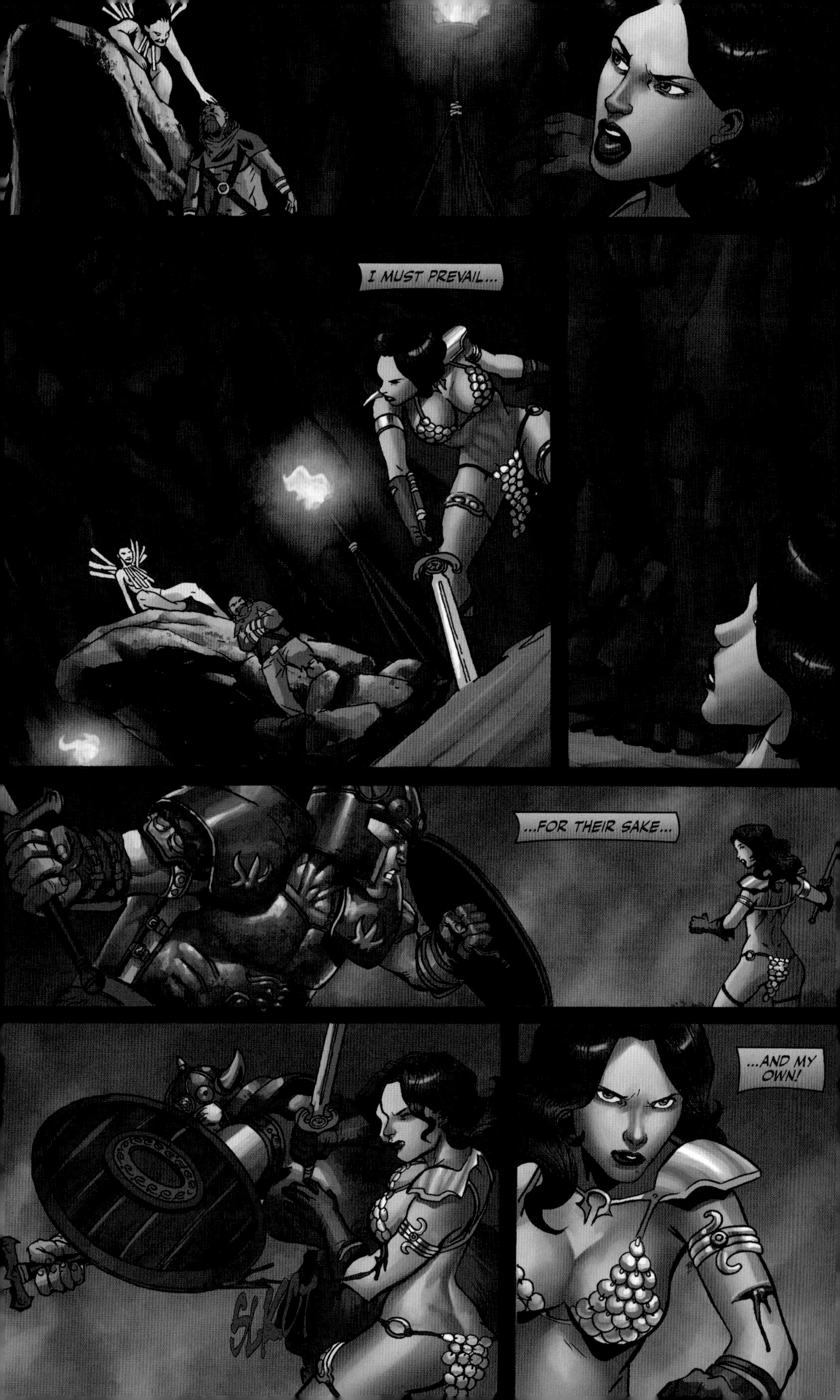
I MUST PREVAIL...
...FOR THEIR SAKE...
...AND MY OWN!

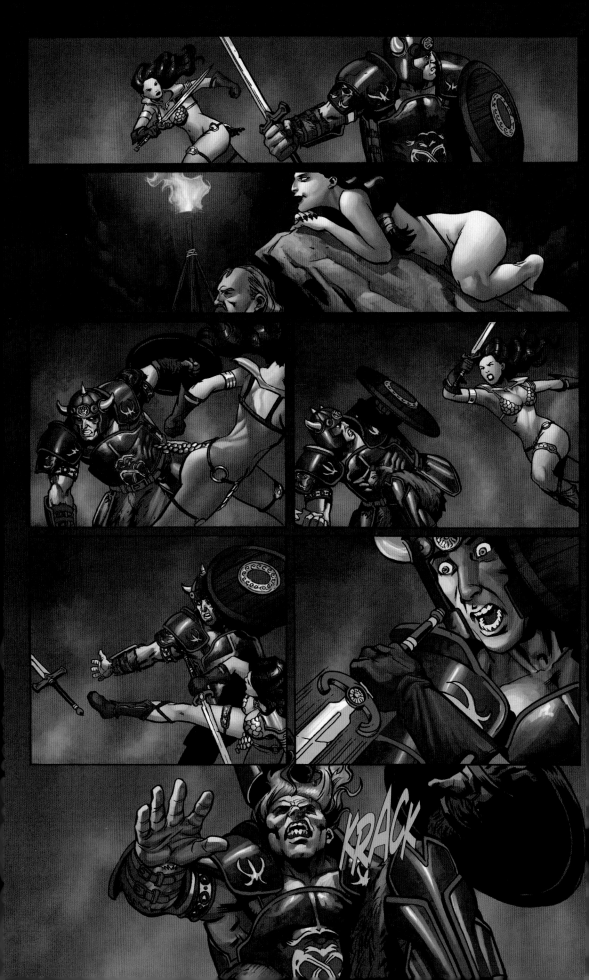

KRACK

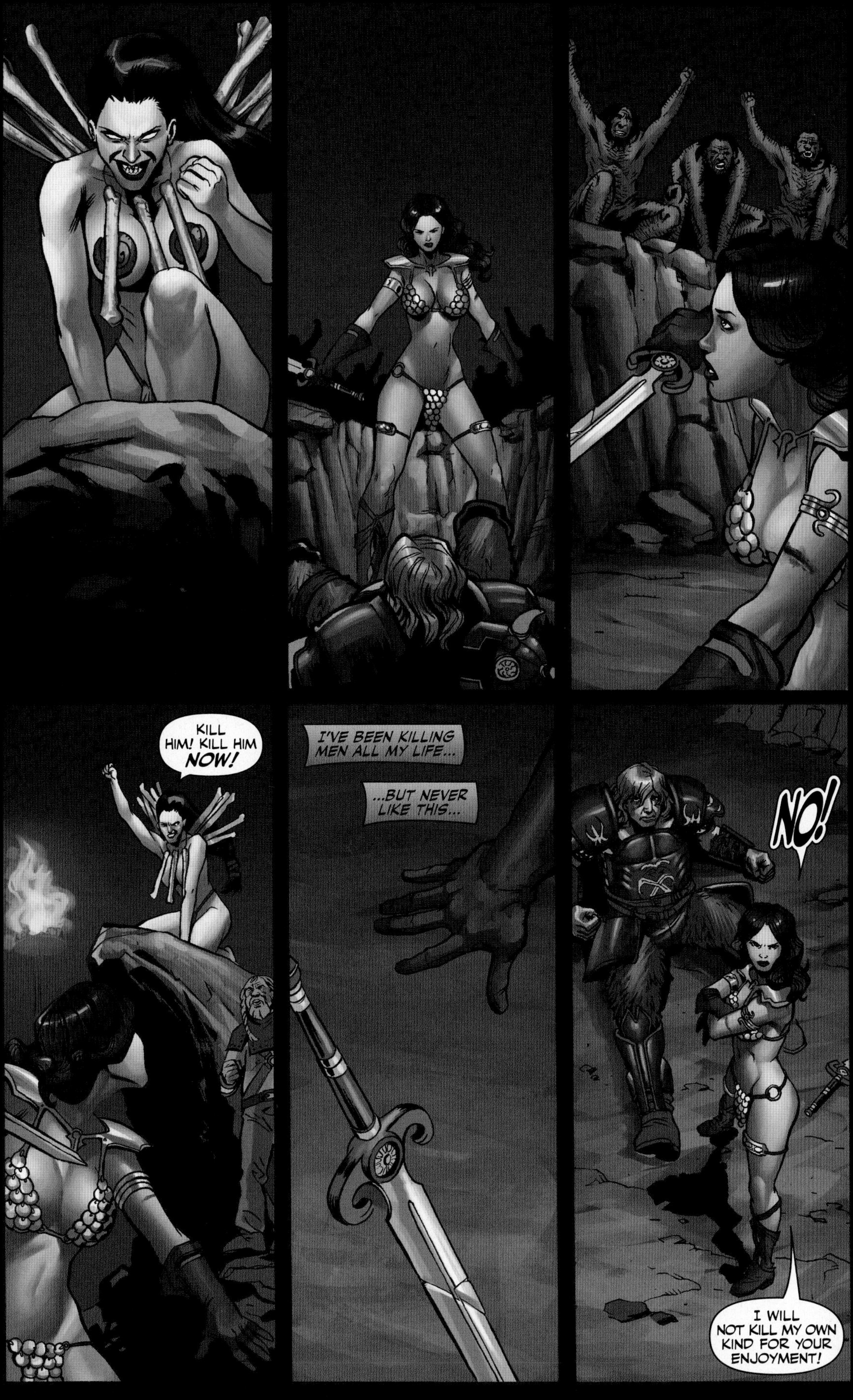
KILL HIM! KILL HIM NOW!
I'VE BEEN KILLING MEN ALL MY LIFE...
...BUT NEVER LIKE THIS...
NO!
I WILL NOT KILL MY OWN KIND FOR YOUR ENJOYMENT!

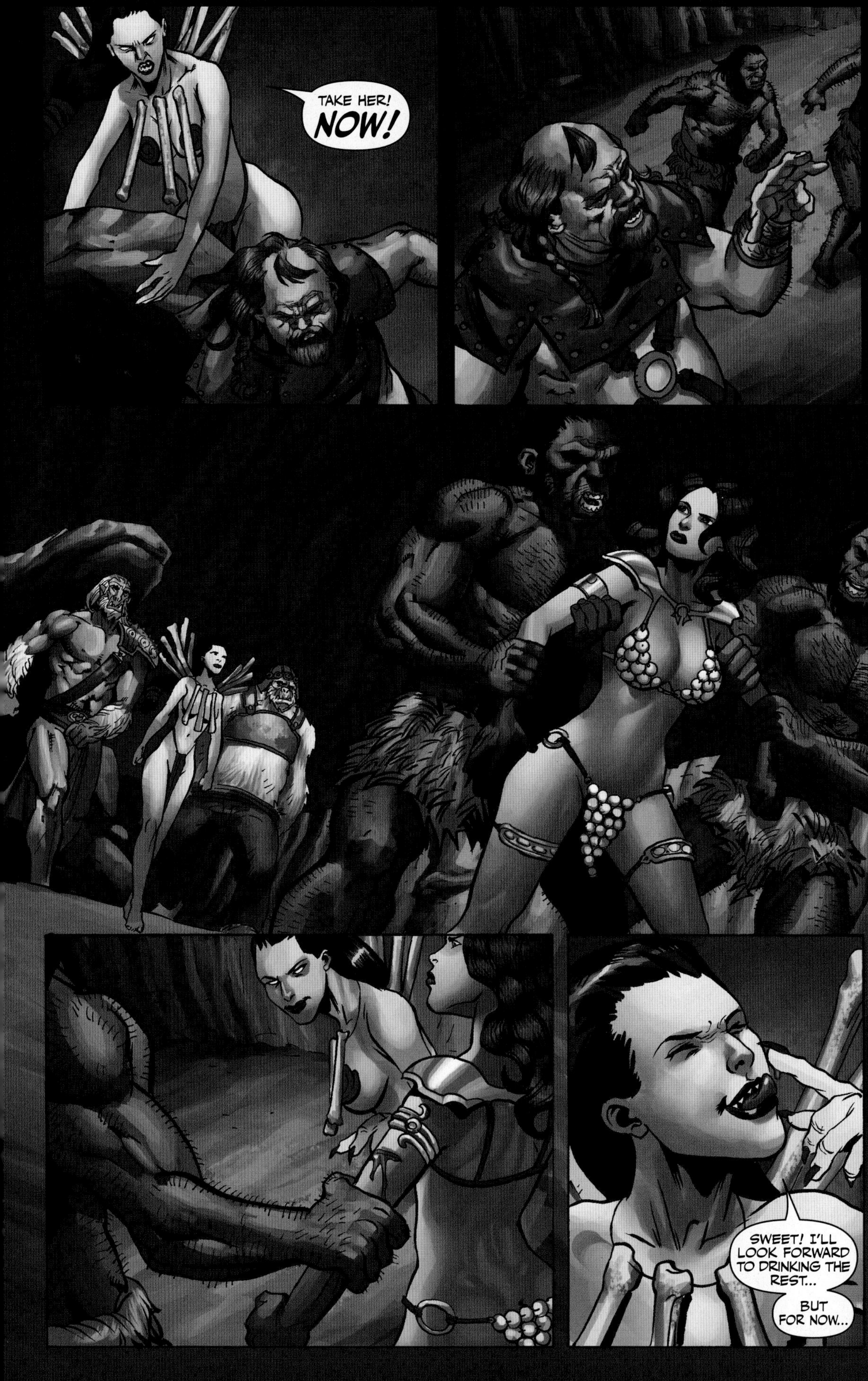
TAKE HER! NOW!
SWEET! I'LL LOOK FORWARD TO DRINKING THE REST...
BUT FOR NOW...

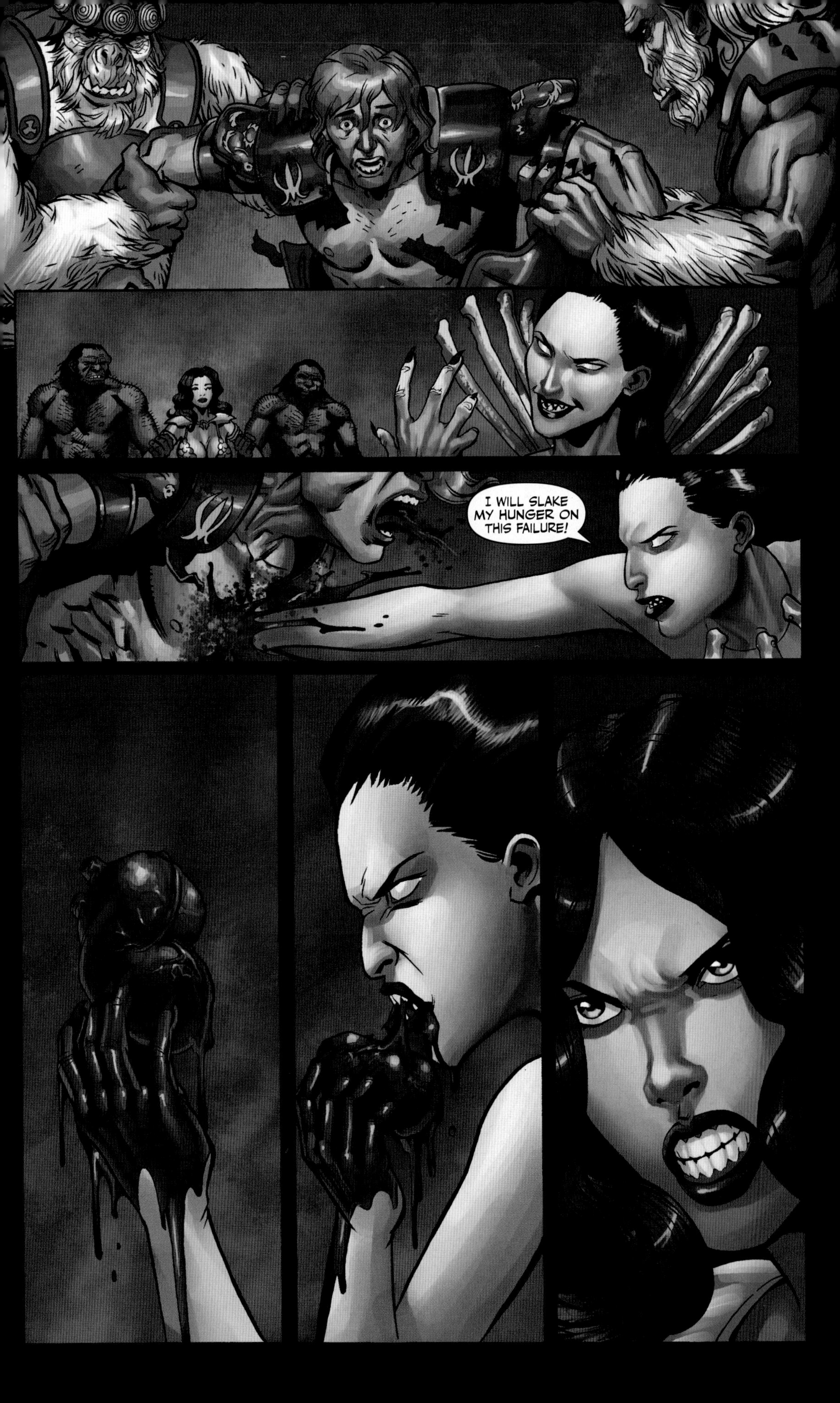
I WILL SLAKE MY HUNGER ON THIS FAILURE!

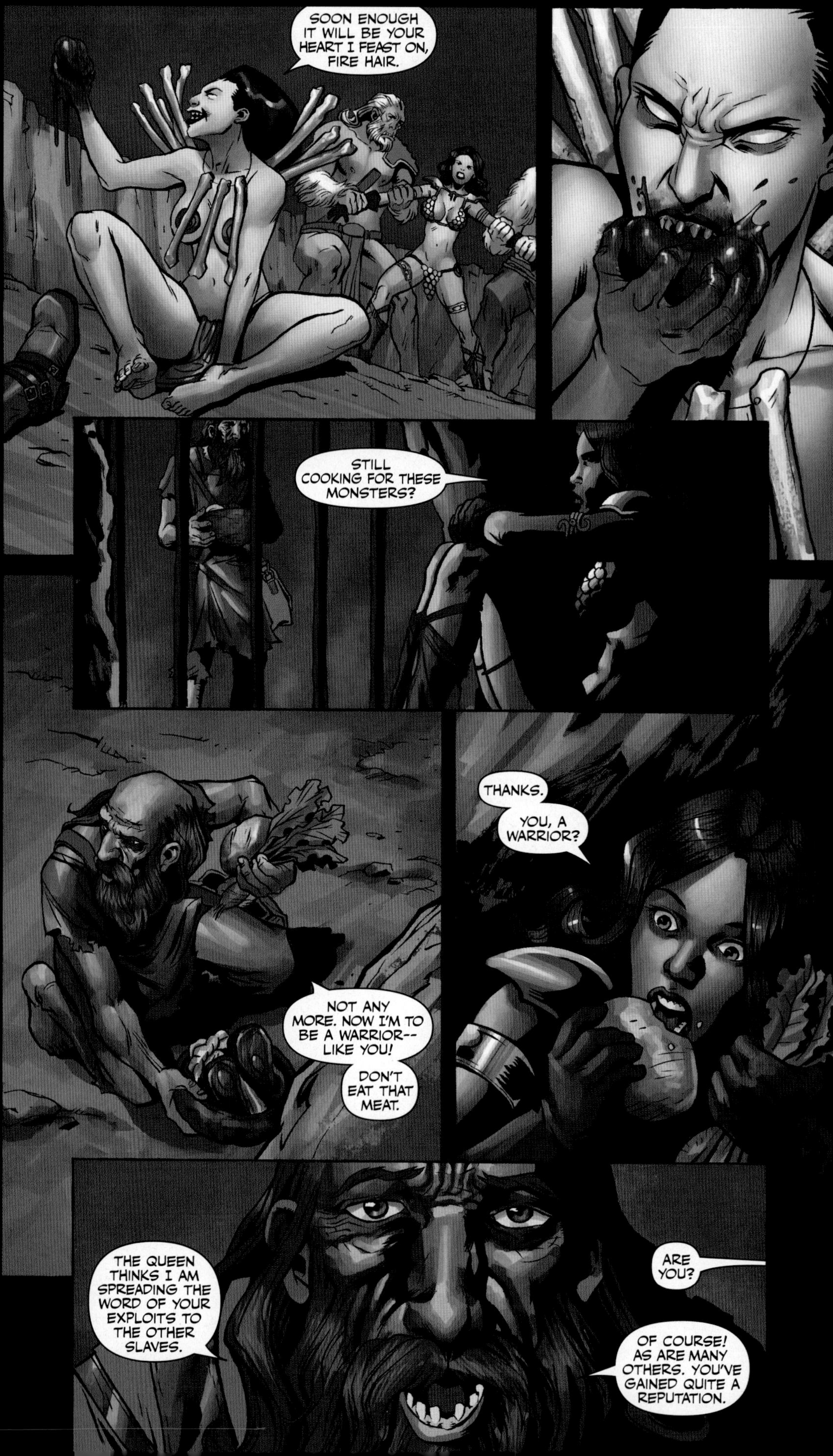
SOON ENOUGH IT WILL BE YOUR HEART I FEAST ON, FIRE HAIR.
STILL COOKING FOR THESE MONSTERS?
NOT ANY MORE. NOW I'M TO BE A WARRIOR-- LIKE YOU!
DON'T EAT THAT MEAT.
THANKS.
YOU, A WARRIOR?
THE QUEEN THINKS I AM SPREADING THE WORD OF YOUR EXPLOITS TO THE OTHER SLAVES.
ARE YOU?
OF COURSE! AS ARE MANY OTHERS. YOU'VE GAINED QUITE A REPUTATION.

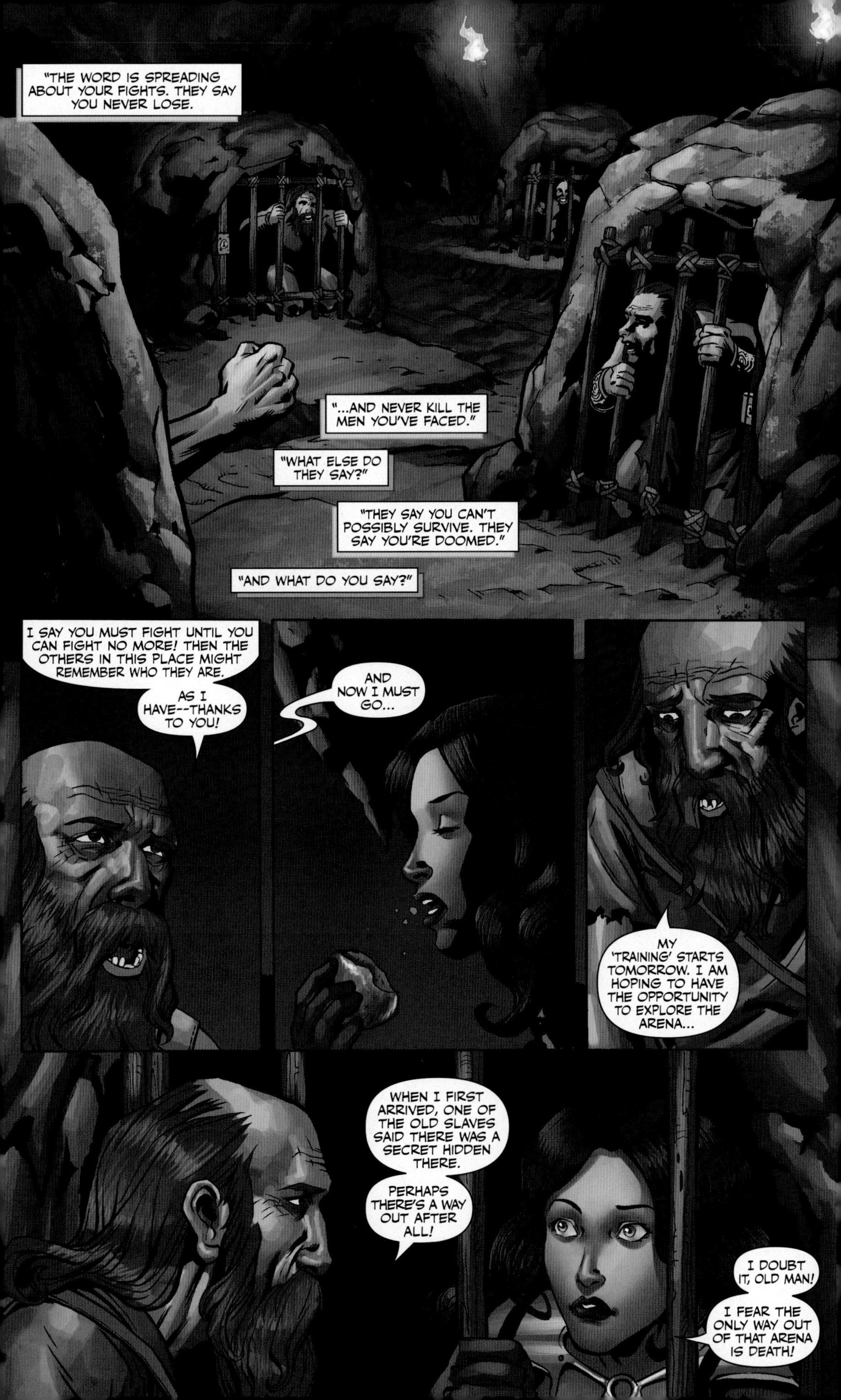
"THE WORD IS SPREADING ABOUT YOUR FIGHTS. THEY SAY YOU NEVER LOSE.
"...AND NEVER KILL THE MEN YOU'VE FACED."
"WHAT ELSE DO THEY SAY?"
"THEY SAY YOU CAN'T POSSIBLY SURVIVE. THEY SAY YOU'RE DOOMED."
"AND WHAT DO YOU SAY?"
I SAY YOU MUST FIGHT UNTIL YOU CAN FIGHT NO MORE! THEN THE OTHERS IN THIS PLACE MIGHT REMEMBER WHO THEY ARE.
AS I HAVE--THANKS TO YOU!
AND NOW I MUST GO...
MY 'TRAINING' STARTS TOMORROW. I AM HOPING TO HAVE THE OPPORTUNITY TO EXPLORE THE ARENA...
WHEN I FIRST ARRIVED, ONE OF THE OLD SLAVES SAID THERE WAS A SECRET HIDDEN THERE.
PERHAPS THERE'S A WAY OUT AFTER ALL!
I DOUBT IT, OLD MAN!
I FEAR THE ONLY WAY OUT OF THAT ARENA IS DEATH!

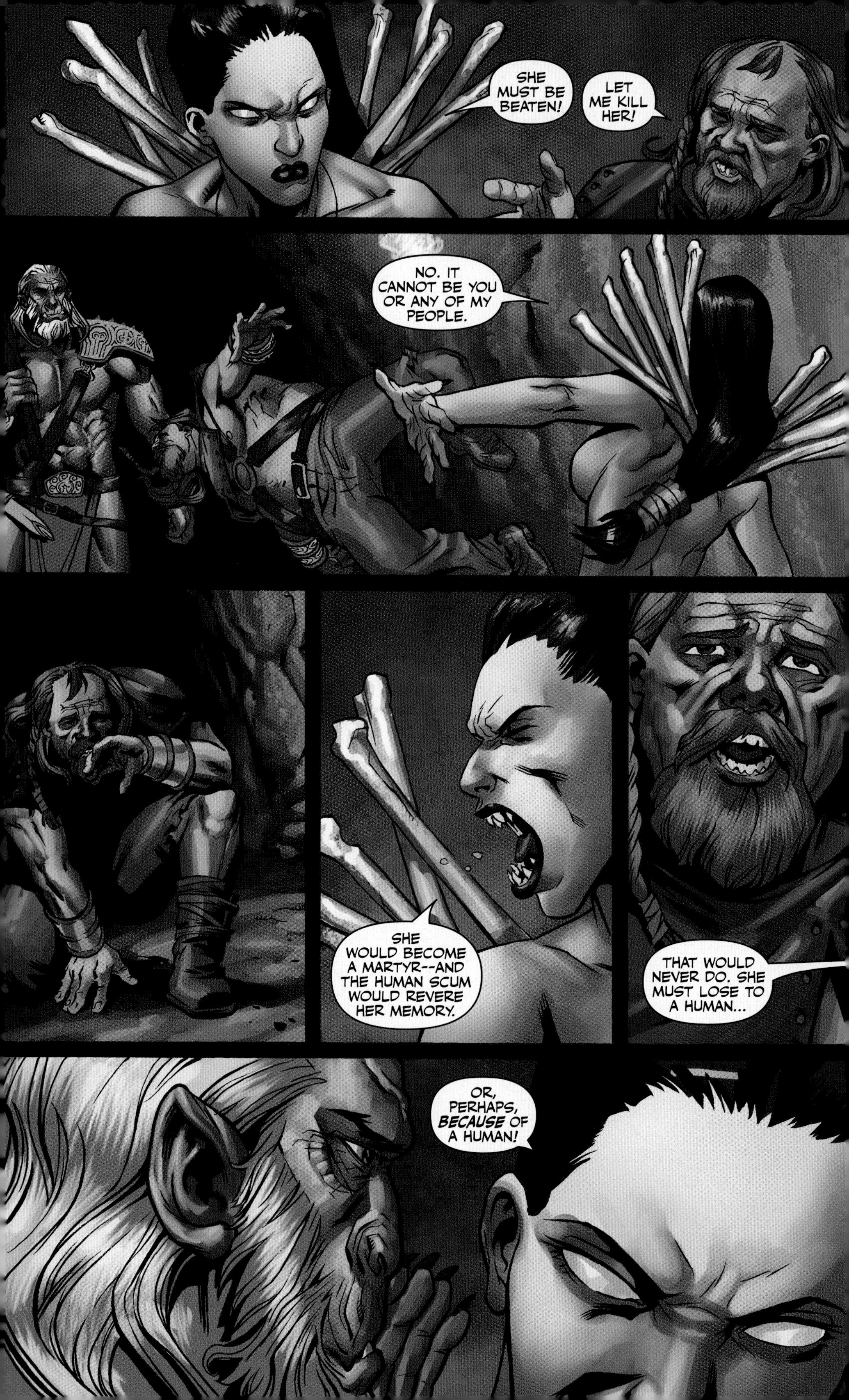
SHE MUST BE BEATEN!
LET ME KILL HER!
NO. IT CANNOT BE YOU OR ANY OF MY PEOPLE.
SHE WOULD BECOME A MARTYR--AND THE HUMAN SCUM WOULD REVERE HER MEMORY.
THAT WOULD NEVER DO. SHE MUST LOSE TO A HUMAN...
OR, PERHAPS, *BECAUSE* OF A HUMAN!

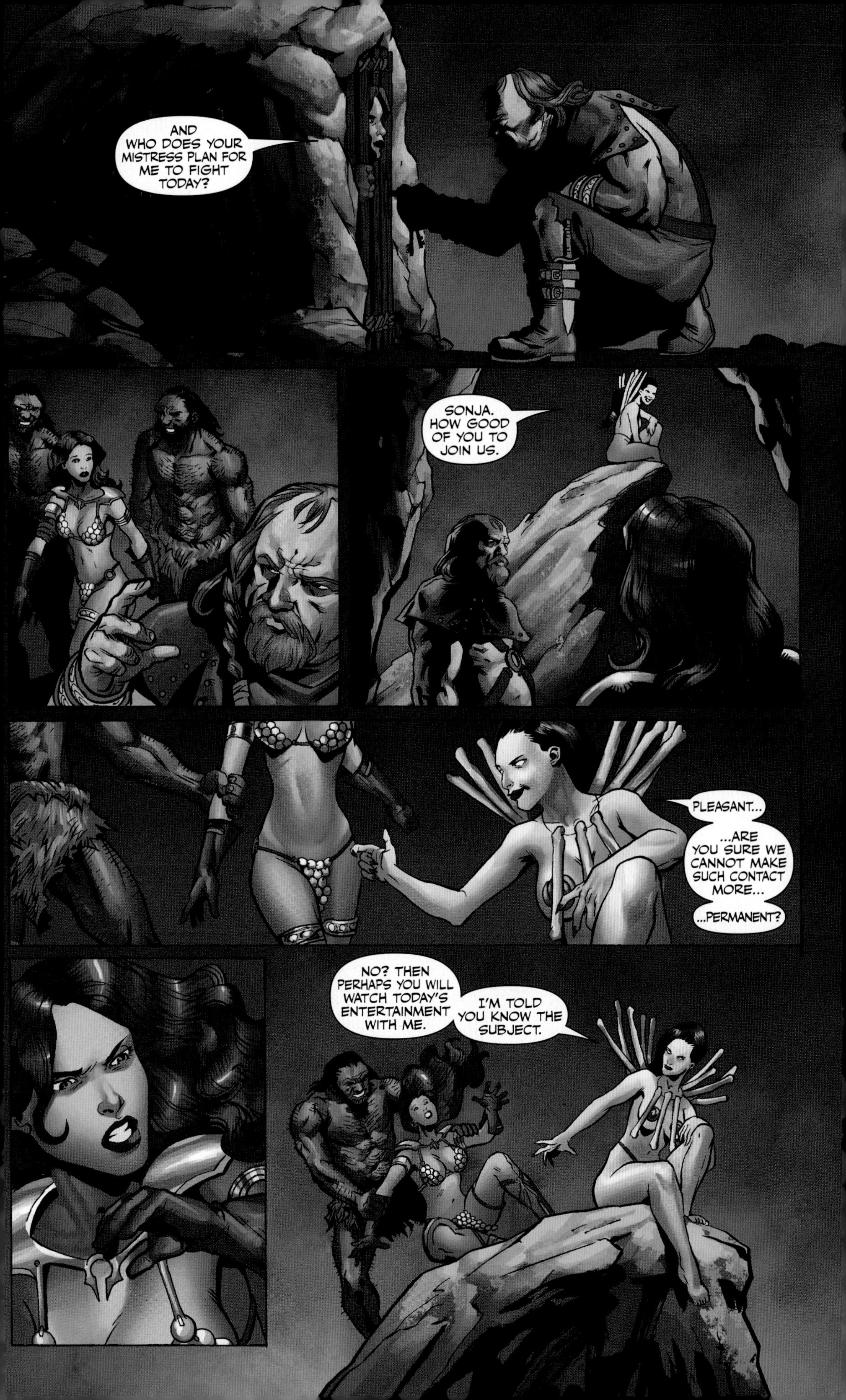
AND WHO DOES YOUR MISTRESS PLAN FOR ME TO FIGHT TODAY?
SONJA. HOW GOOD OF YOU TO JOIN US.
PLEASANT...
...ARE YOU SURE WE CANNOT MAKE SUCH CONTACT MORE...
...PERMANENT?
NO? THEN PERHAPS YOU WILL WATCH TODAY'S ENTERTAINMENT WITH ME.
I'M TOLD YOU KNOW THE SUBJECT.

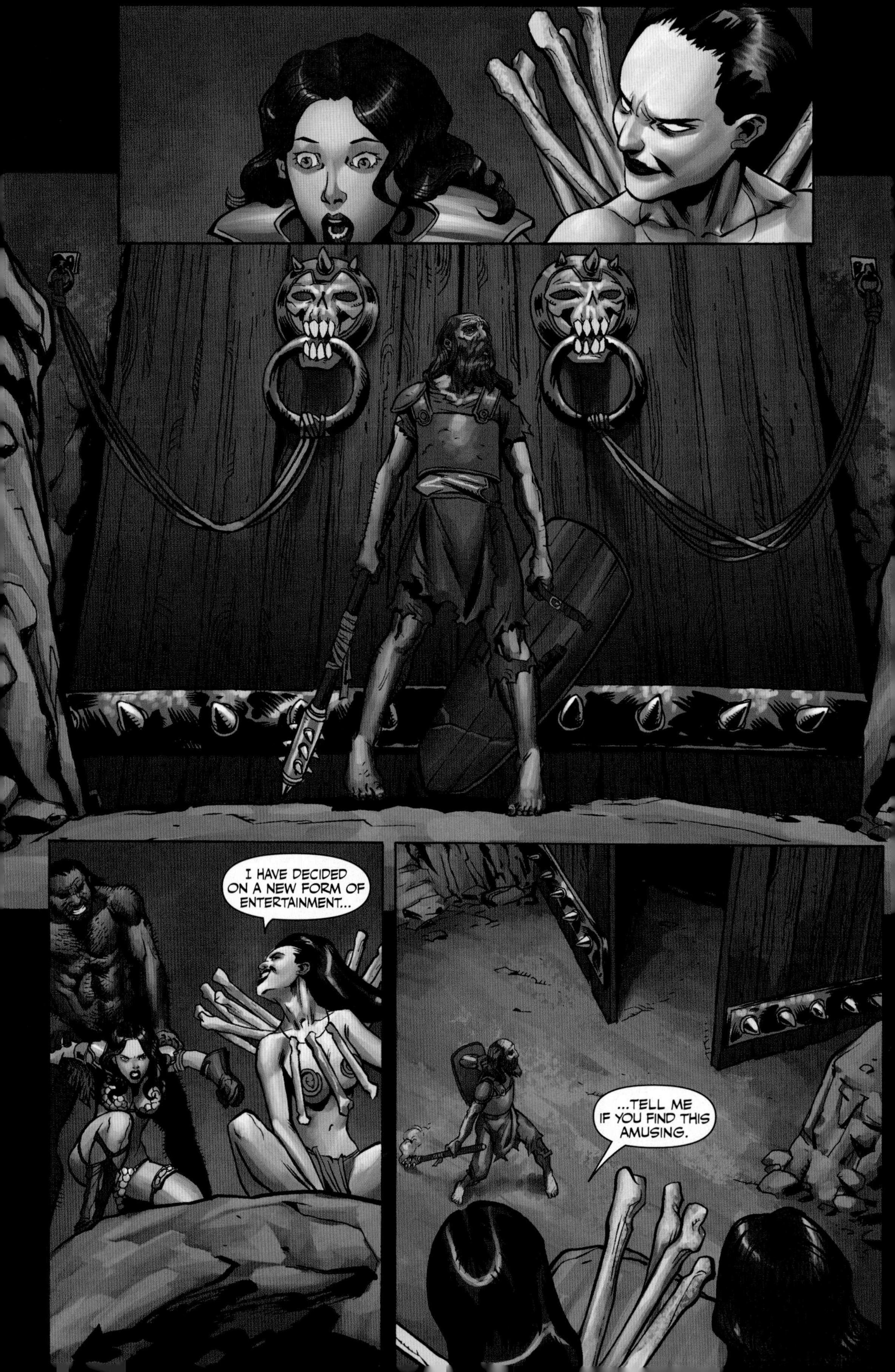
I HAVE DECIDED ON A NEW FORM OF ENTERTAINMENT...
...TELL ME IF YOU FIND THIS AMUSING.

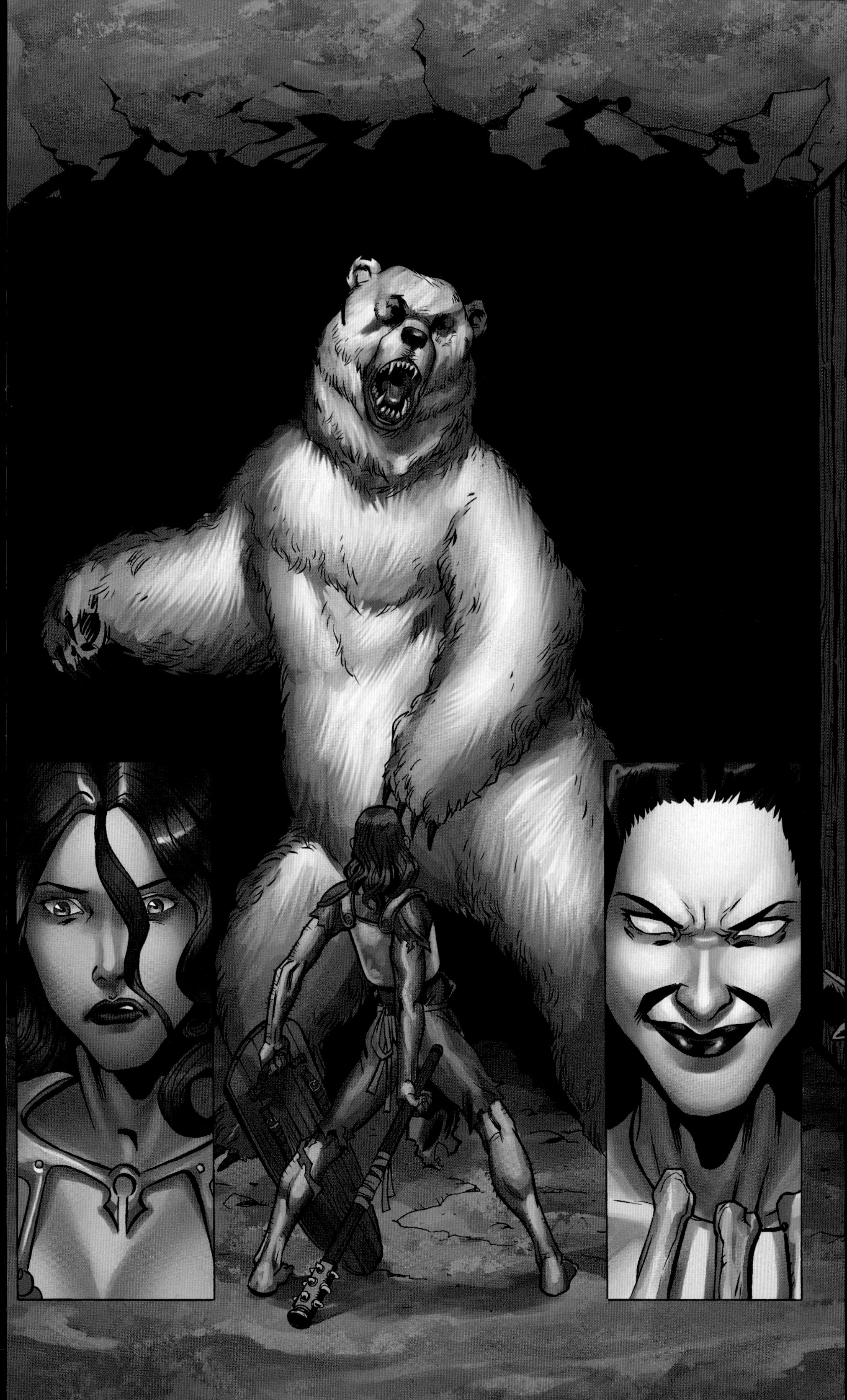

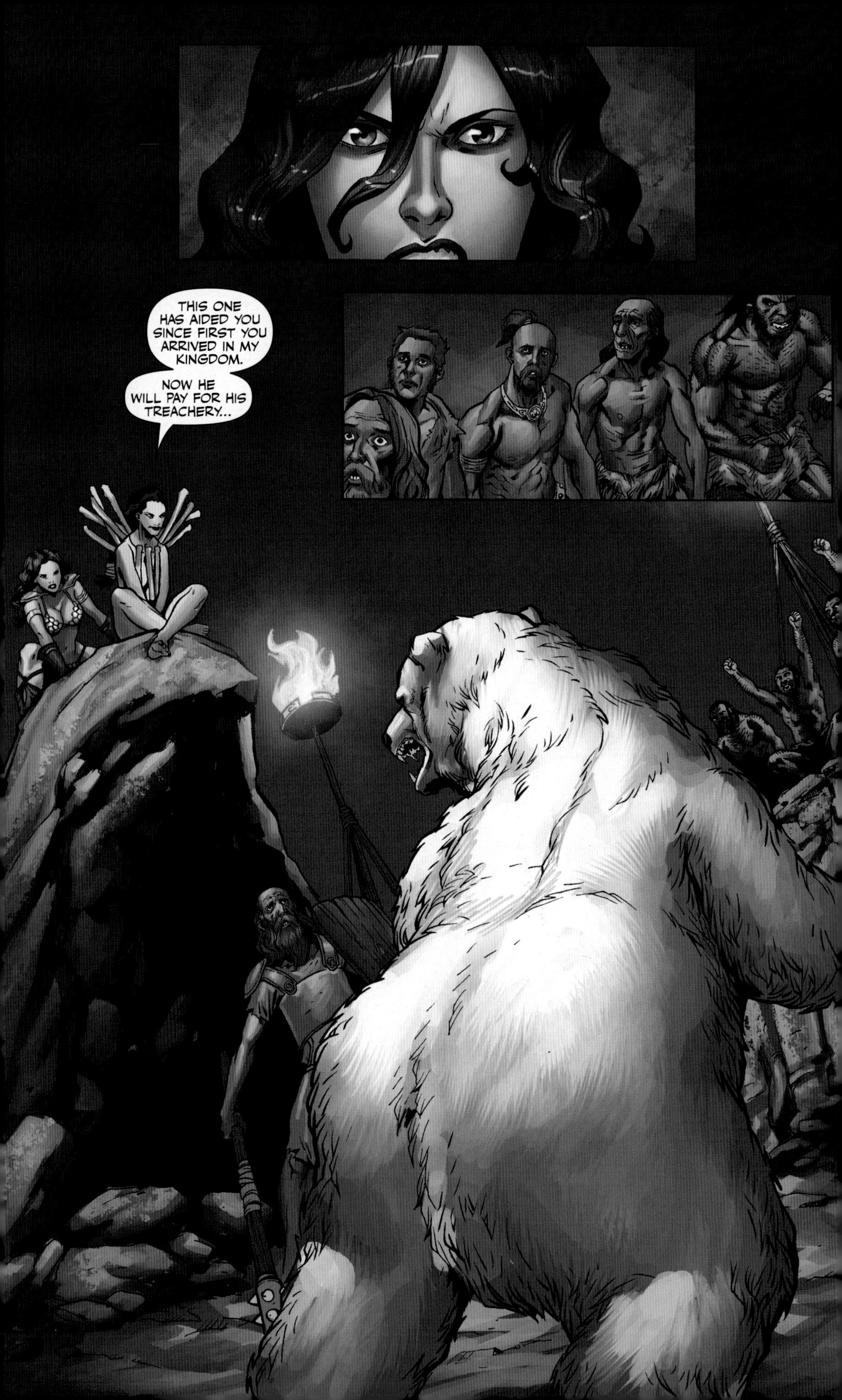
THIS ONE HAS AIDED YOU SINCE FIRST YOU ARRIVED IN MY KINGDOM.
NOW HE WILL PAY FOR HIS TREACHERY...

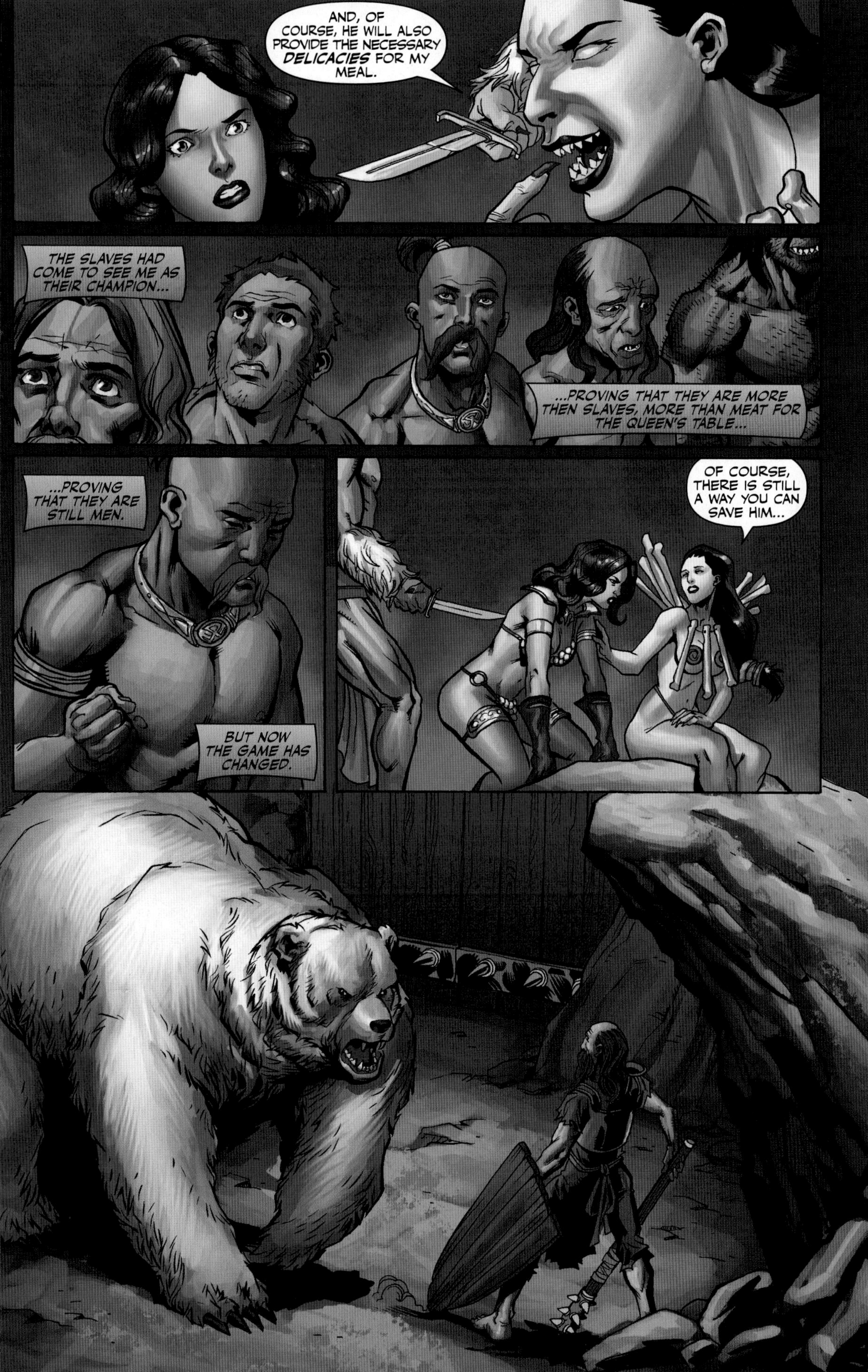
AND, OF COURSE, HE WILL ALSO PROVIDE THE NECESSARY DELICACIES FOR MY MEAL.
THE SLAVES HAD COME TO SEE ME AS THEIR CHAMPION...
...PROVING THAT THEY ARE MORE THEN SLAVES, MORE THAN MEAT FOR THE QUEEN'S TABLE...
...PROVING THAT THEY ARE STILL MEN.
BUT NOW THE GAME HAS CHANGED.
OF COURSE, THERE IS STILL A WAY YOU CAN SAVE HIM...

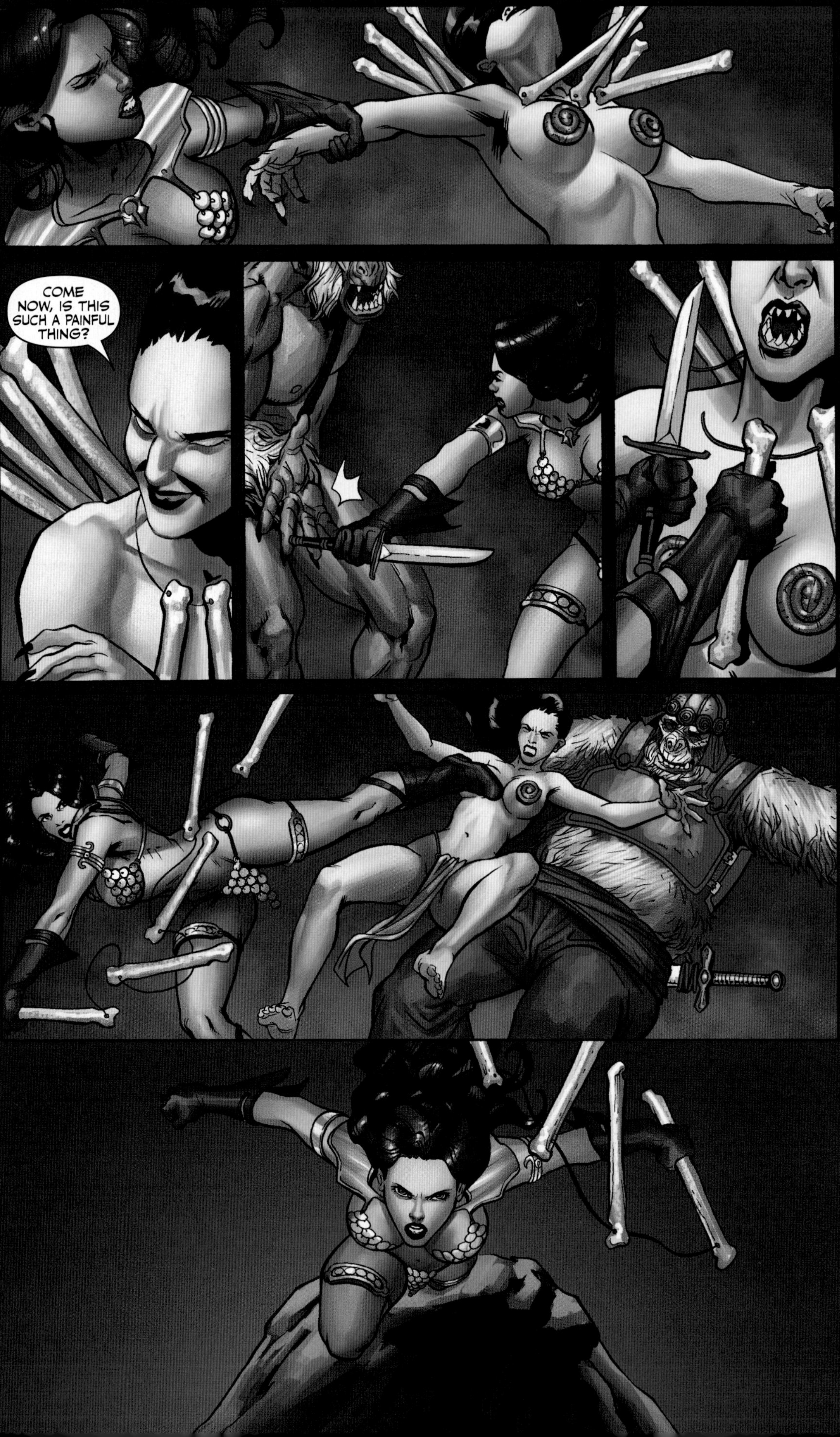
COME NOW, IS THIS SUCH A PAINFUL THING?

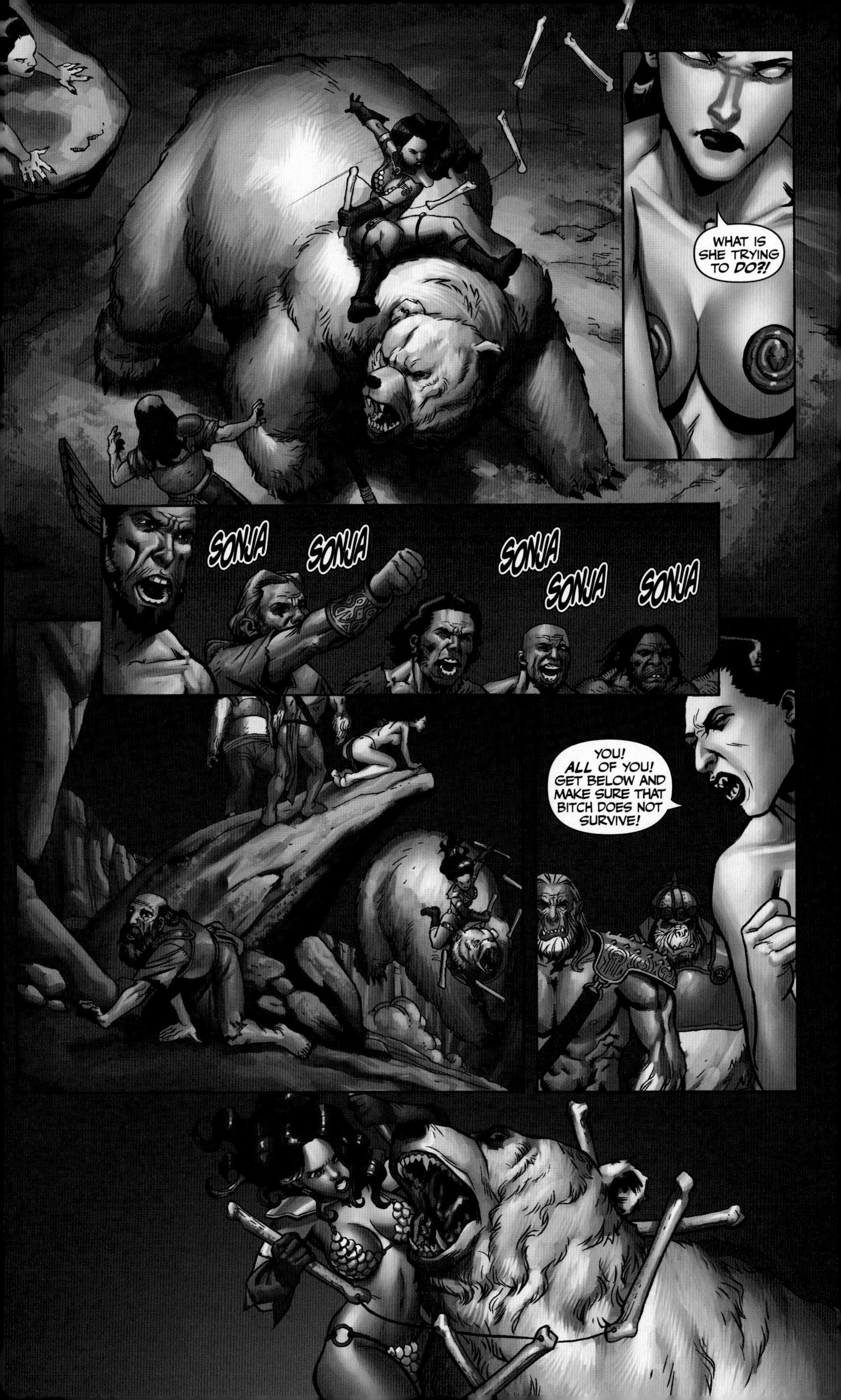
WHAT IS SHE TRYING TO DO?!
SONJA
SONJA
SONJA
SONJA
SONJA
YOU! ALL OF YOU! GET BELOW AND MAKE SURE THAT BITCH DOES NOT SURVIVE!

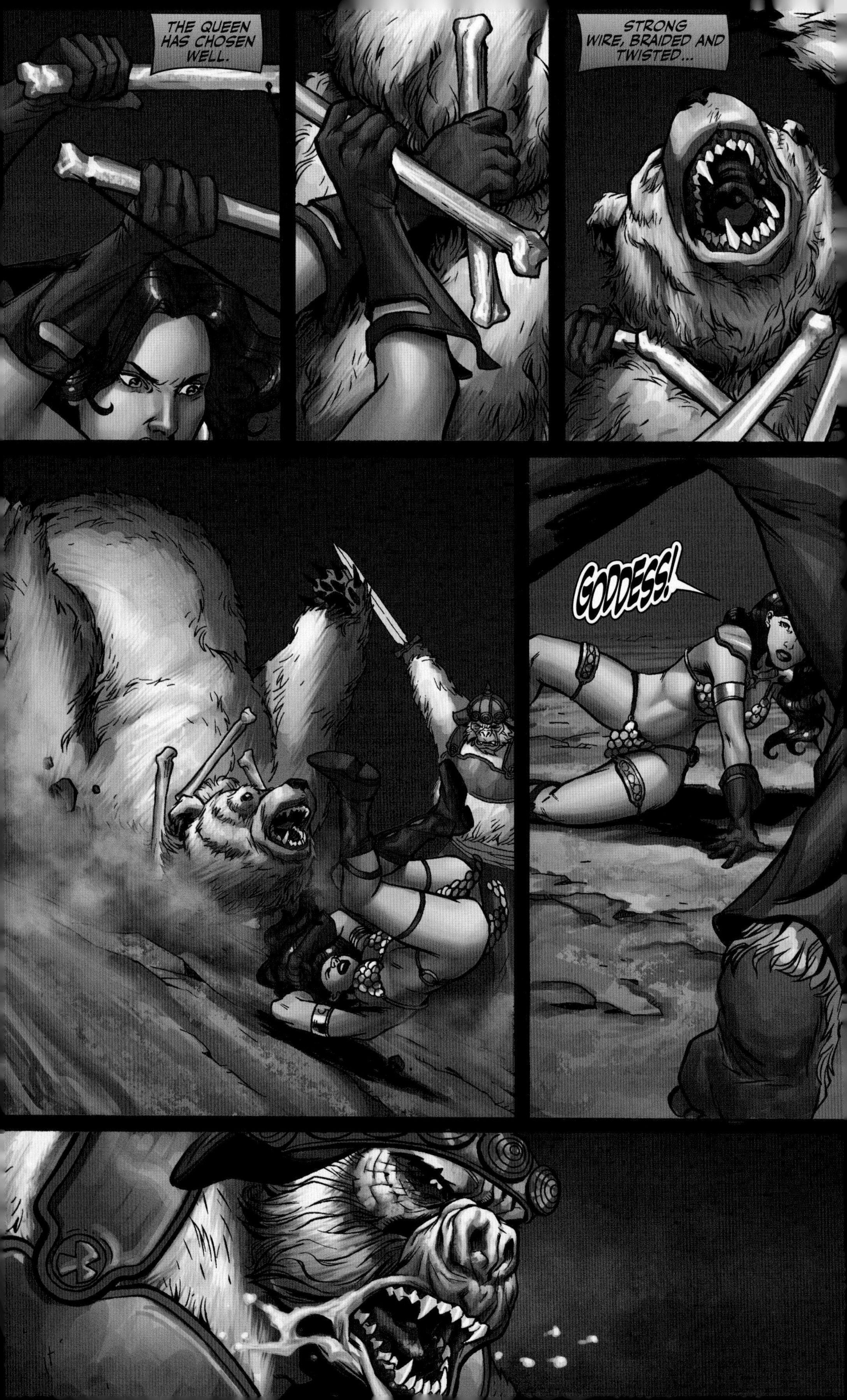
THE QUEEN HAS CHOSEN WELL.
STRONG WIRE, BRAIDED AND TWISTED...
GODDESS!

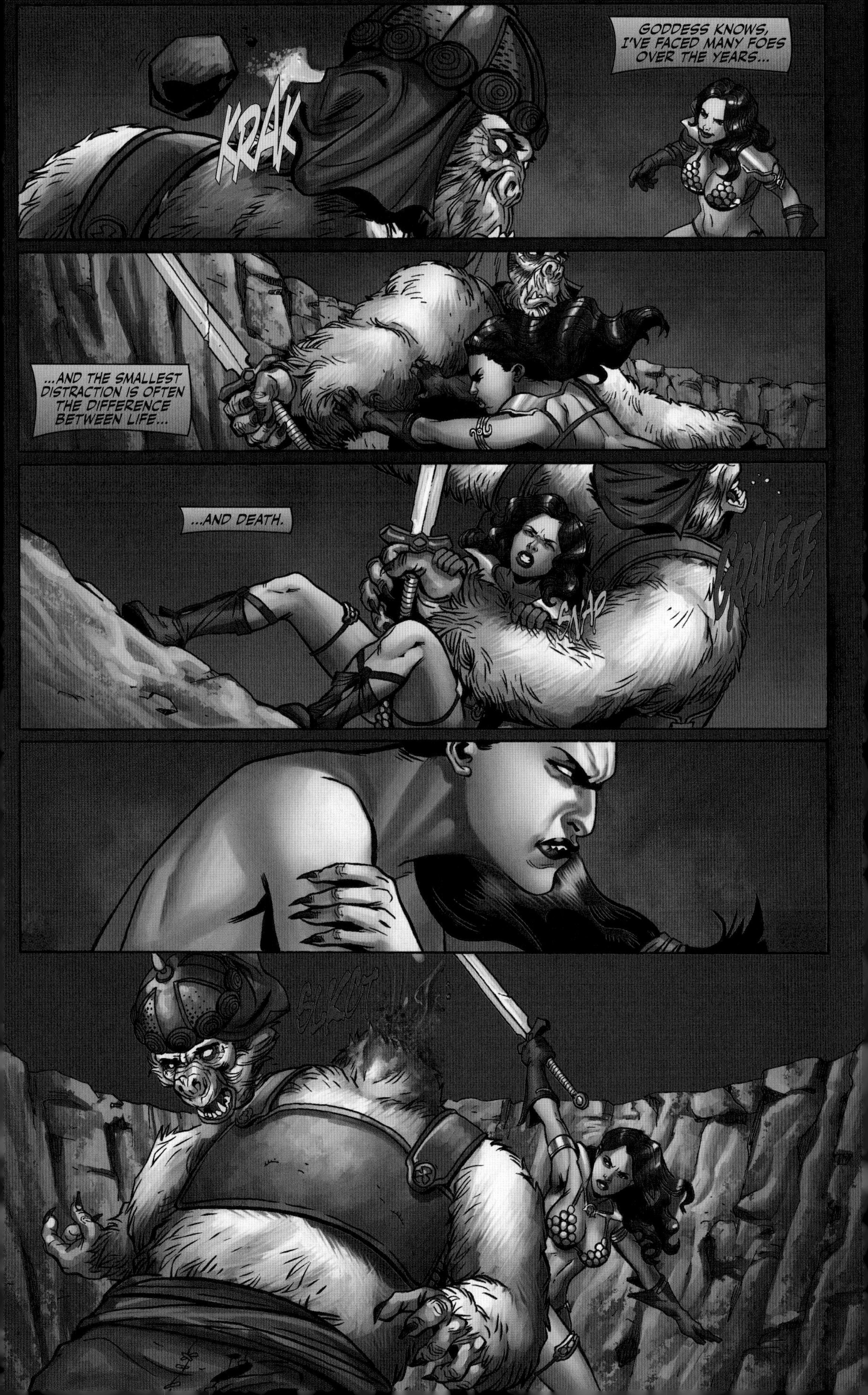
GODDESS KNOWS, I'VE FACED MANY FOES OVER THE YEARS...
KRAK
...AND THE SMALLEST DISTRACTION IS OFTEN THE DIFFERENCE BETWEEN LIFE...
...AND DEATH.
SNAP
GRAIEEE

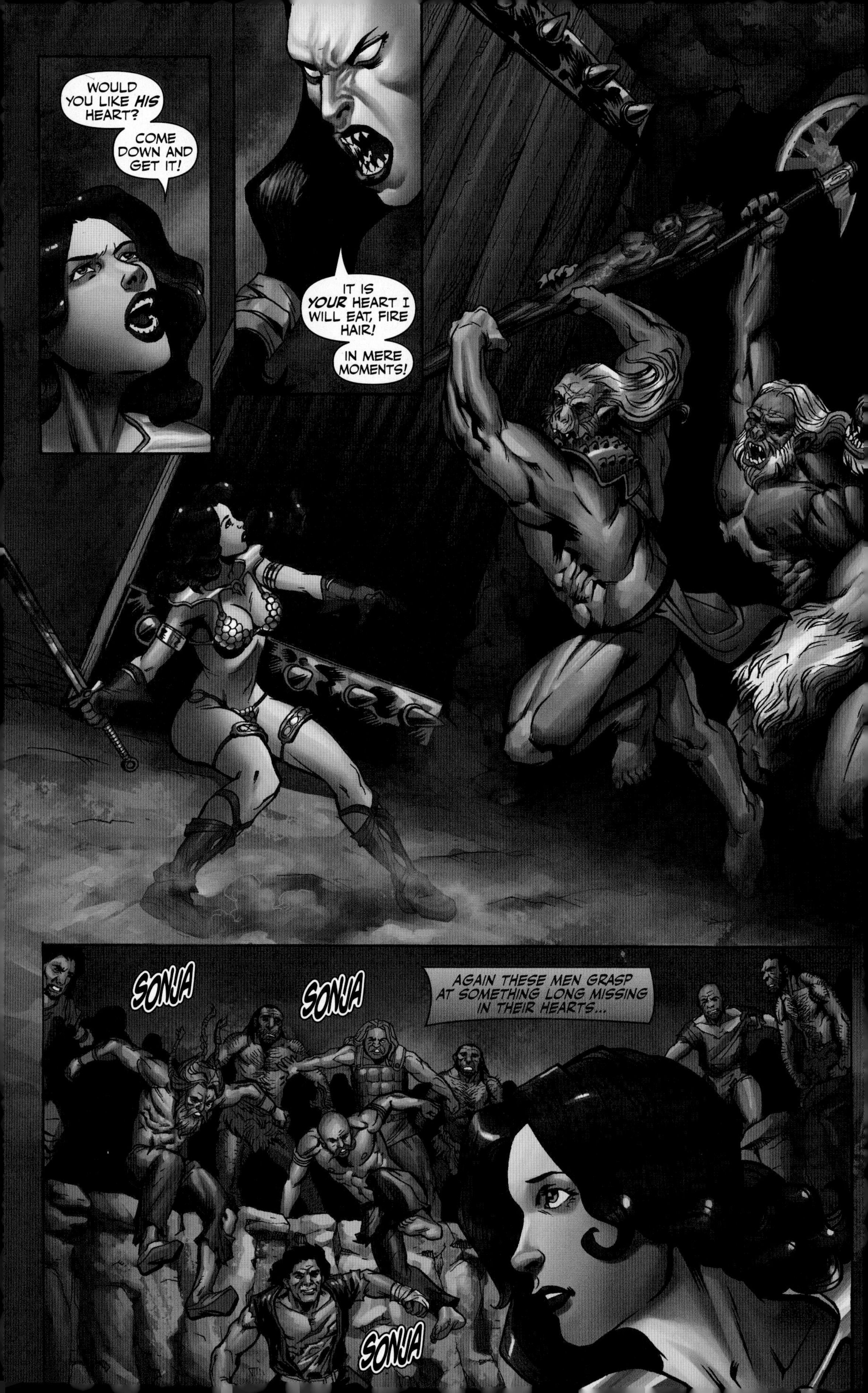
WOULD YOU LIKE *HIS* HEART?
COME DOWN AND GET IT!
IT IS *YOUR* HEART I WILL EAT, FIRE HAIR!
IN MERE MOMENTS!
SONJA
SONJA
AGAIN THESE MEN GRASP AT SOMETHING LONG MISSING IN THEIR HEARTS...
SONJA

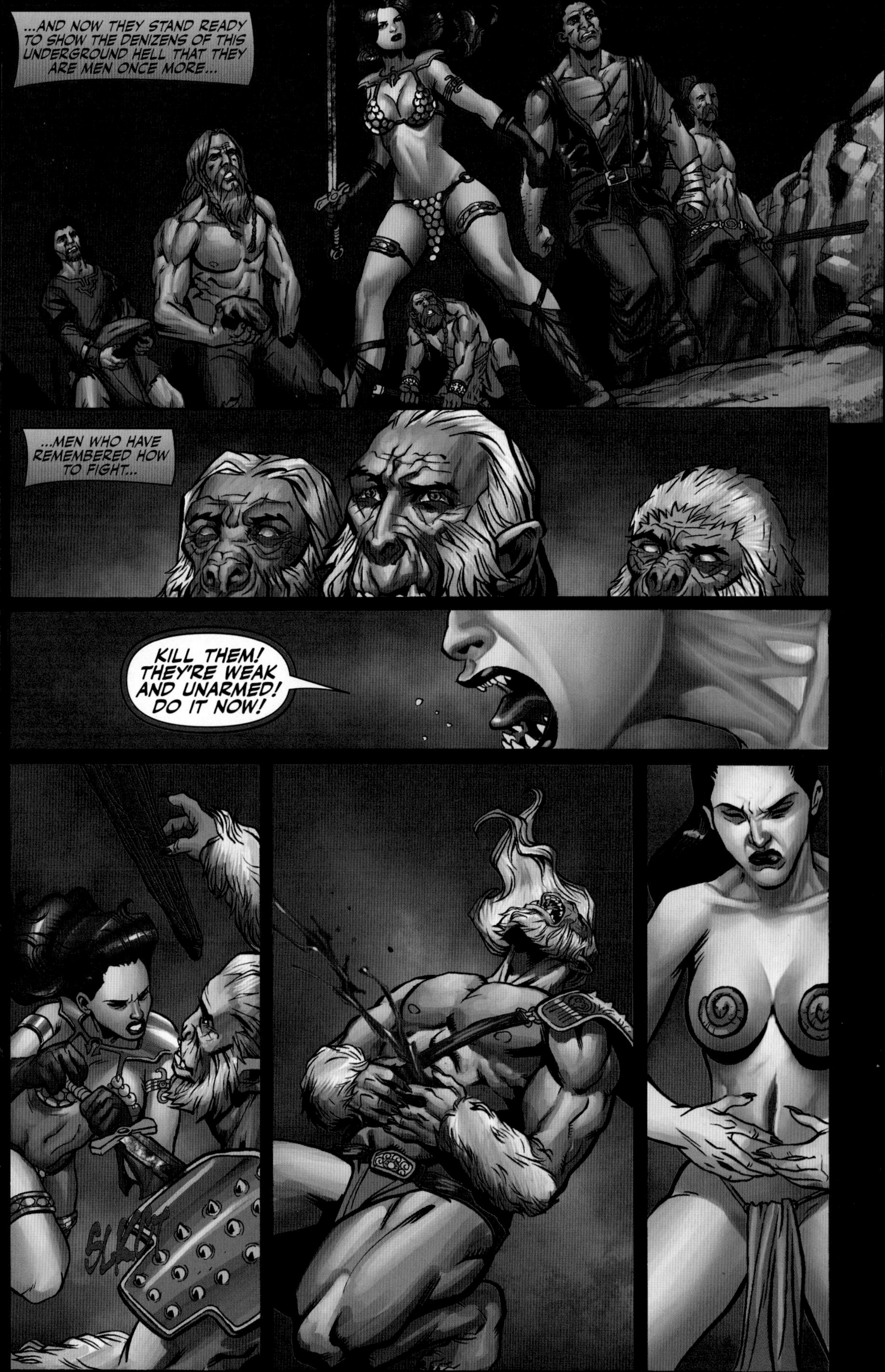
...AND NOW THEY STAND READY TO SHOW THE DENIZENS OF THIS UNDERGROUND HELL THAT THEY ARE MEN ONCE MORE...
...MEN WHO HAVE REMEMBERED HOW TO FIGHT...
KILL THEM! THEY'RE WEAK AND UNARMED! DO IT NOW!
SLKT

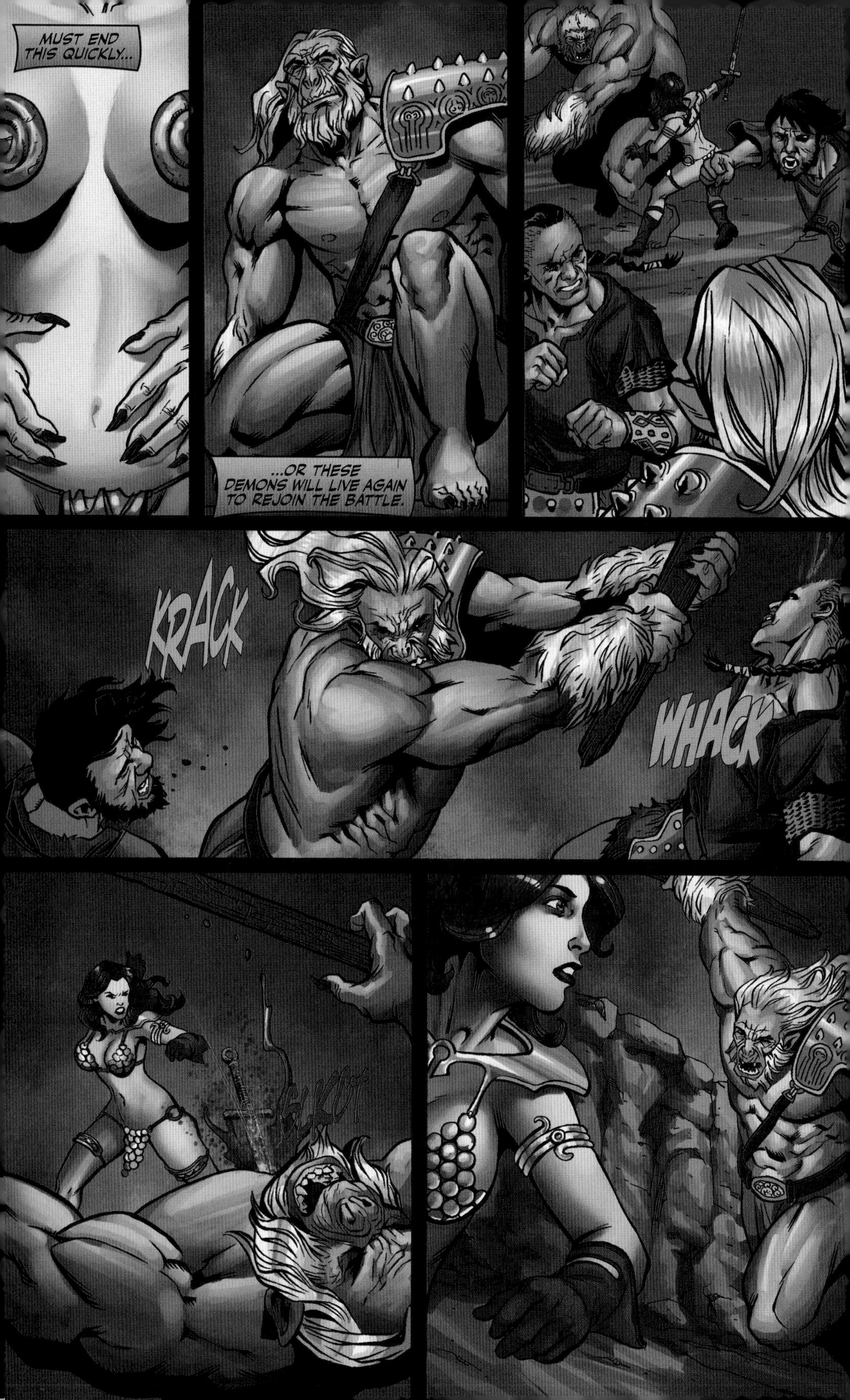
MUST END THIS QUICKLY...
...OR THESE DEMONS WILL LIVE AGAIN TO REJOIN THE BATTLE.
KRACK
WHACK

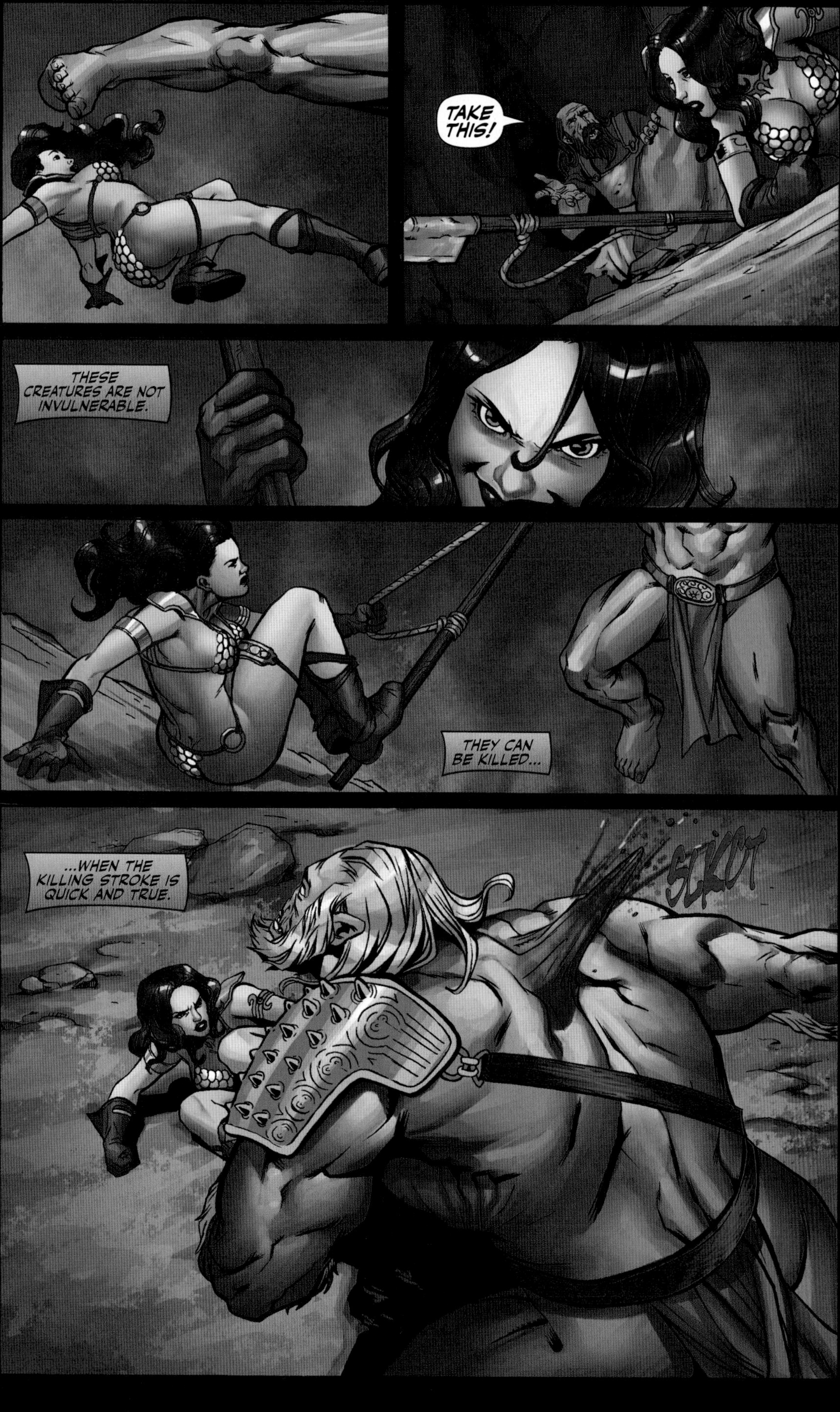
TAKE THIS!
THESE CREATURES ARE NOT INVULNERABLE.
THEY CAN BE KILLED...
...WHEN THE KILLING STROKE IS QUICK AND TRUE.
SCKCT

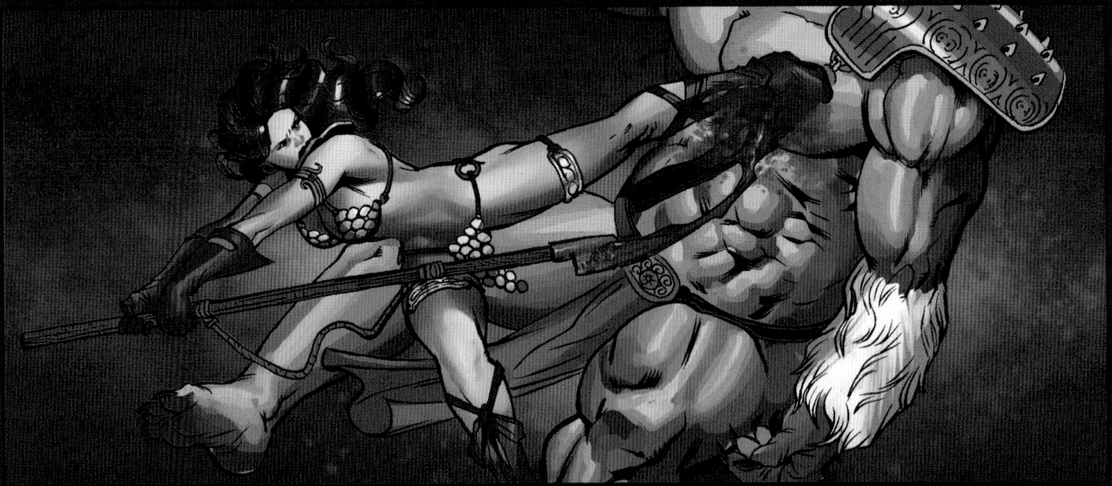

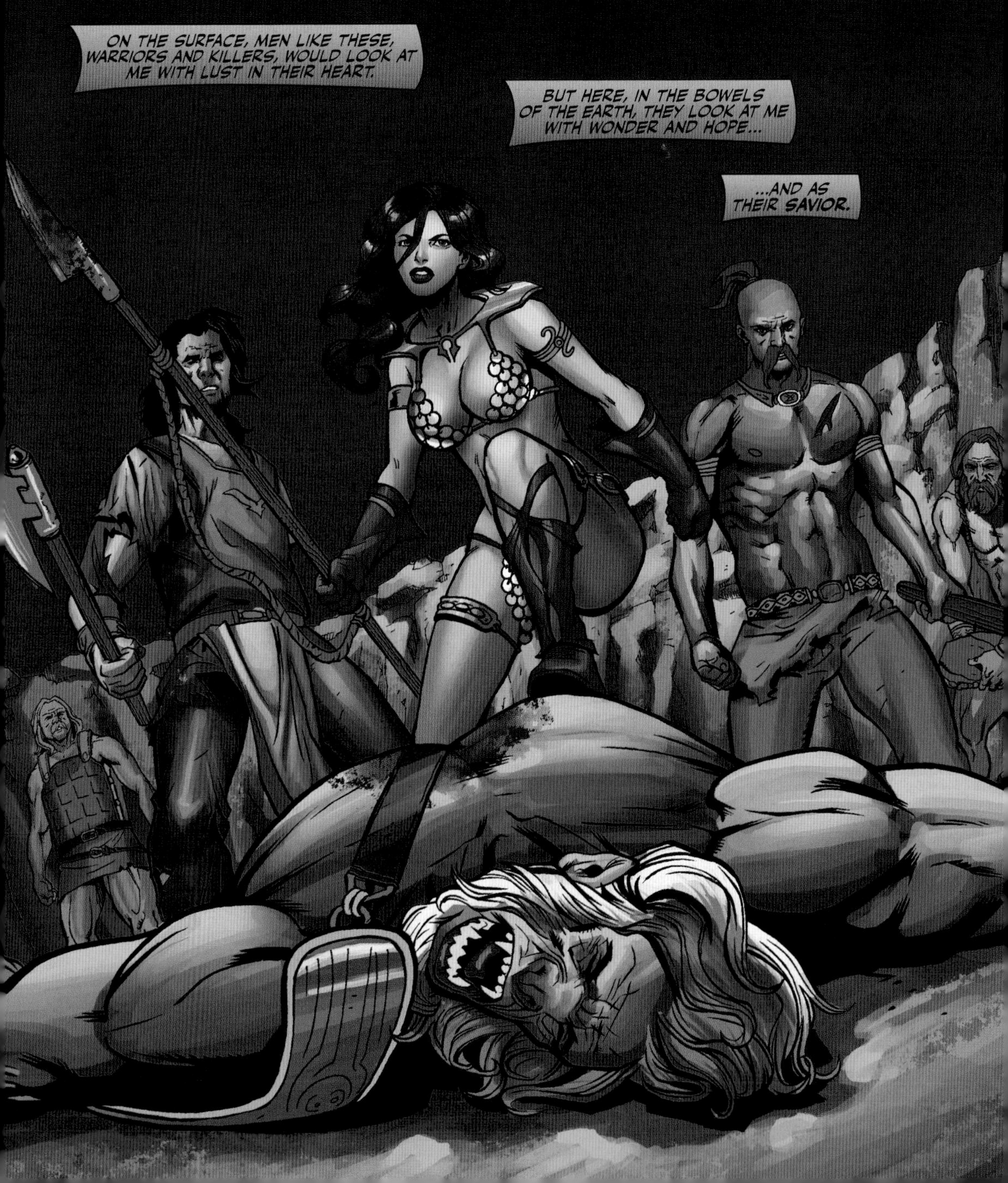
ON THE SURFACE, MEN LIKE THESE, WARRIORS AND KILLERS, WOULD LOOK AT ME WITH LUST IN THEIR HEART.
BUT HERE, IN THE BOWELS OF THE EARTH, THEY LOOK AT ME WITH WONDER AND HOPE...
...AND AS THEIR SAVIOR.

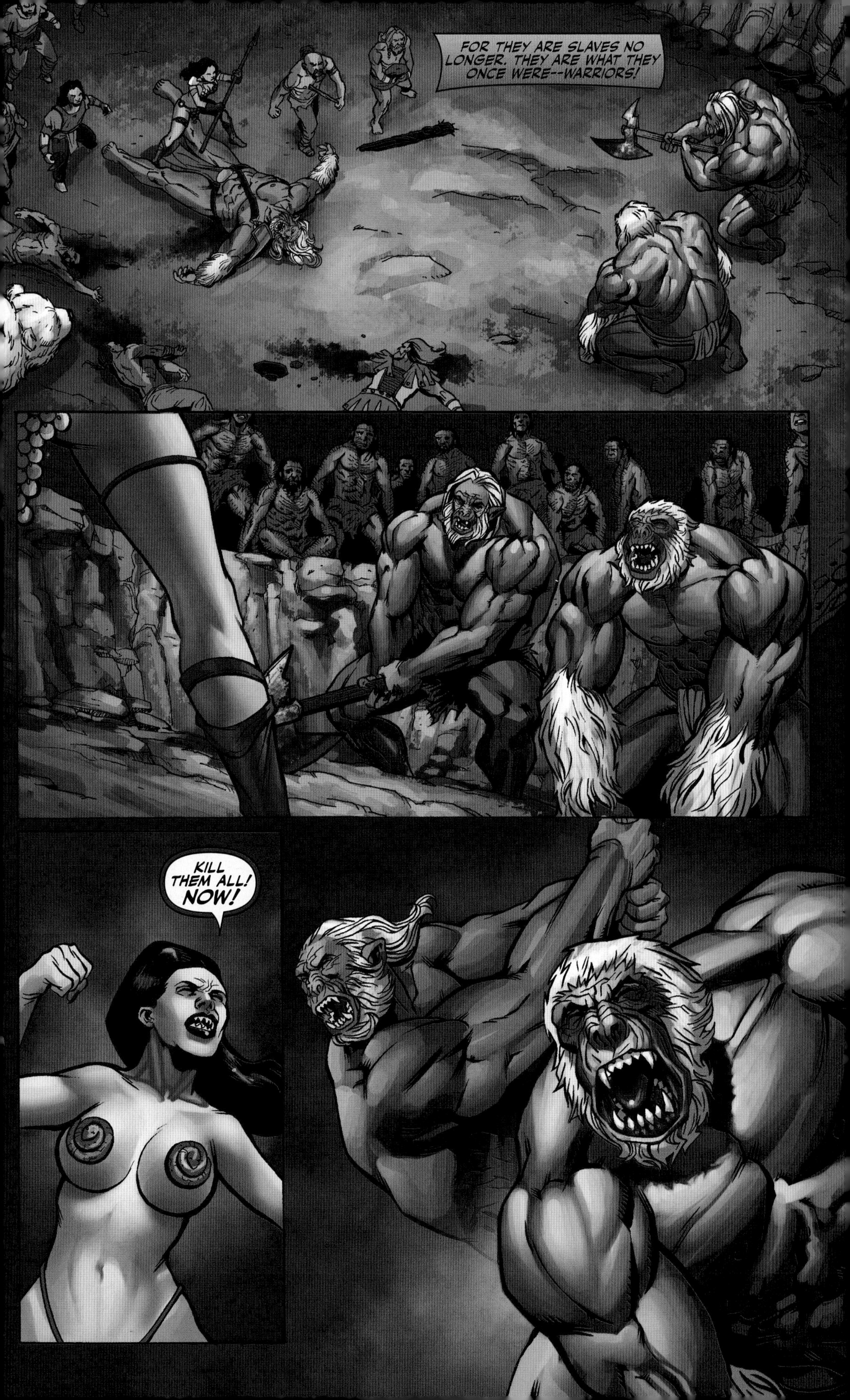
FOR THEY ARE SLAVES NO LONGER. THEY ARE WHAT THEY ONCE WERE--WARRIORS!
KILL THEM ALL! NOW!

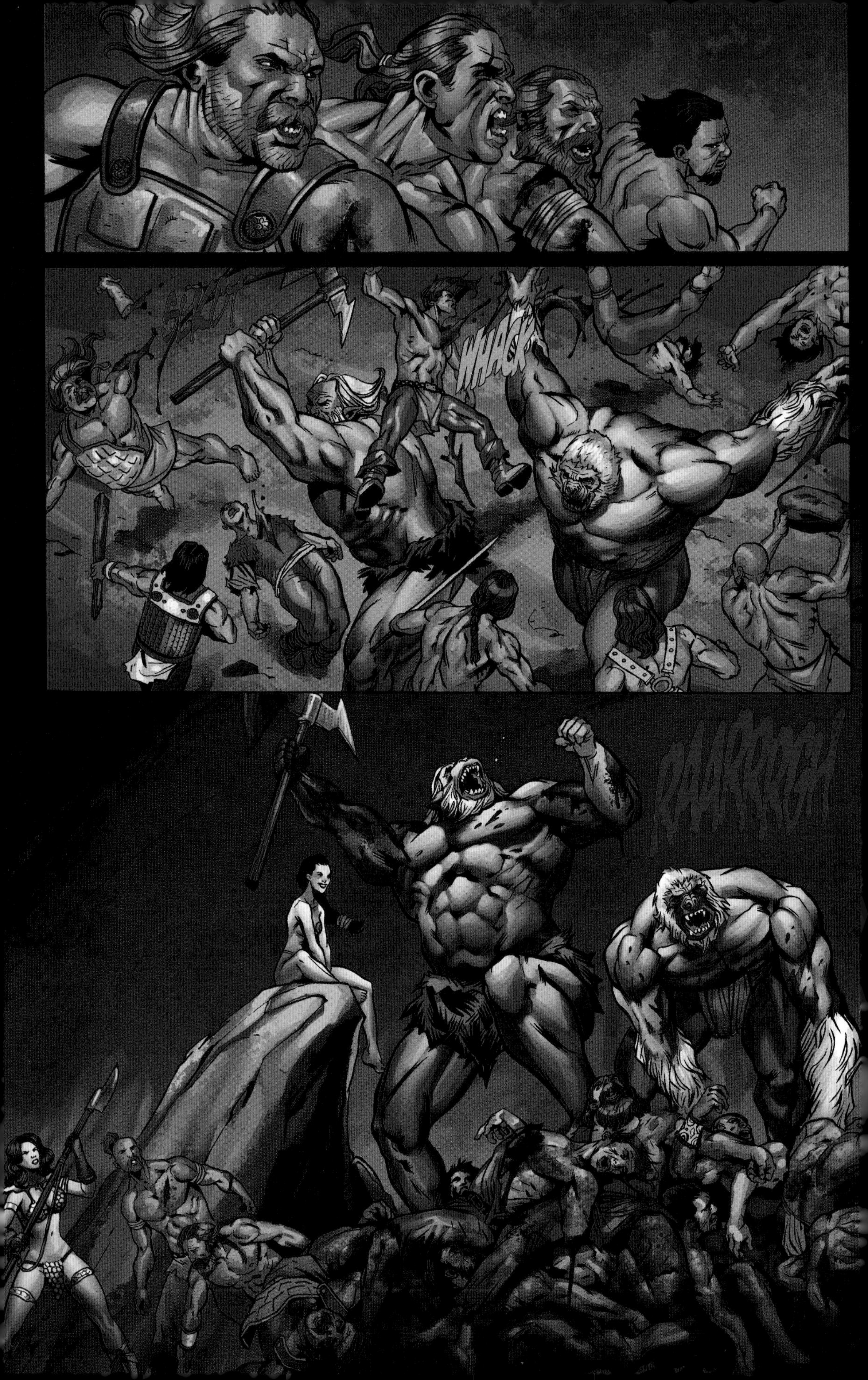
WHACK

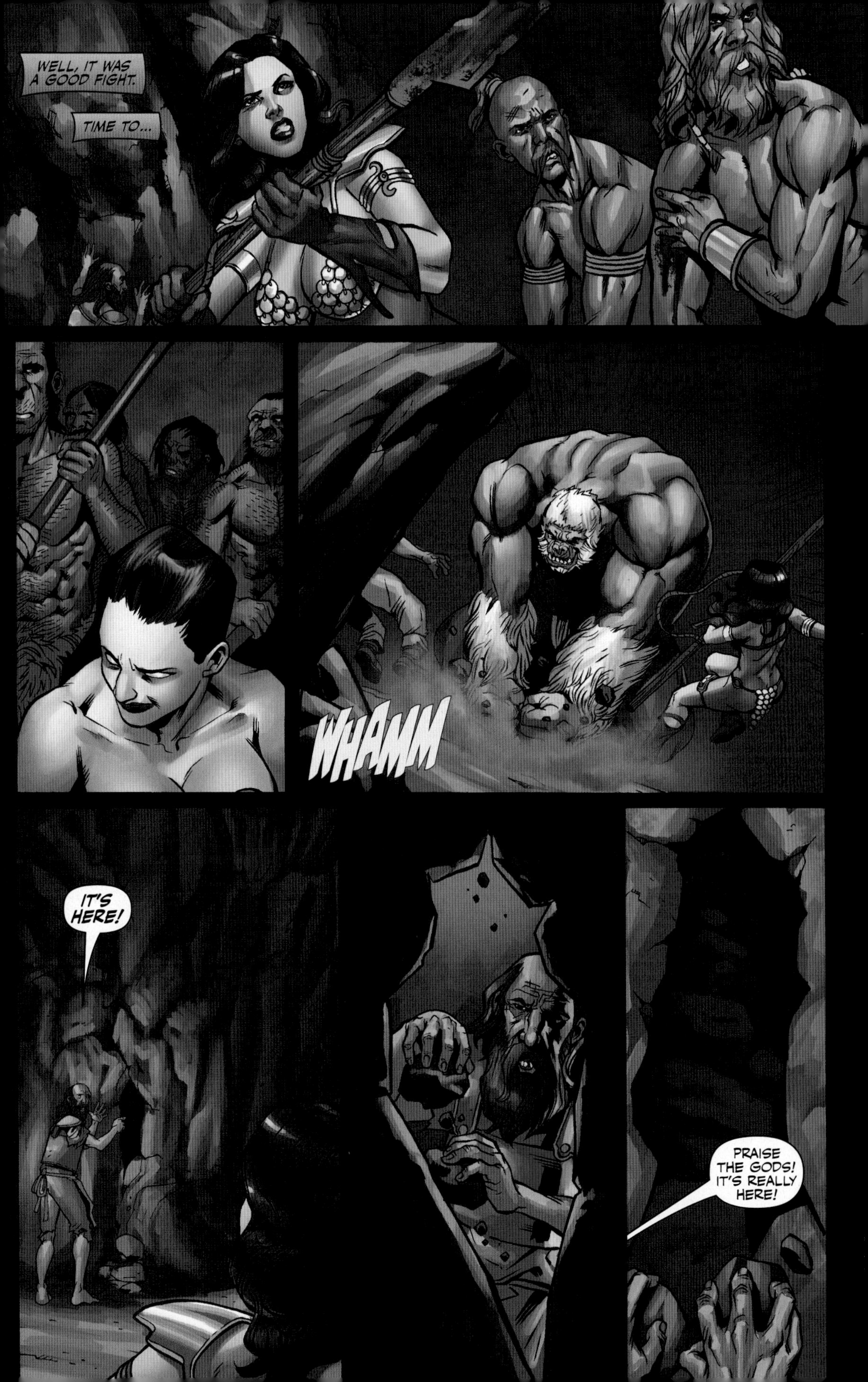
WELL, IT WAS A GOOD FIGHT.
TIME TO...
WHAMM
IT'S HERE!
PRAISE THE GODS! IT'S REALLY HERE!

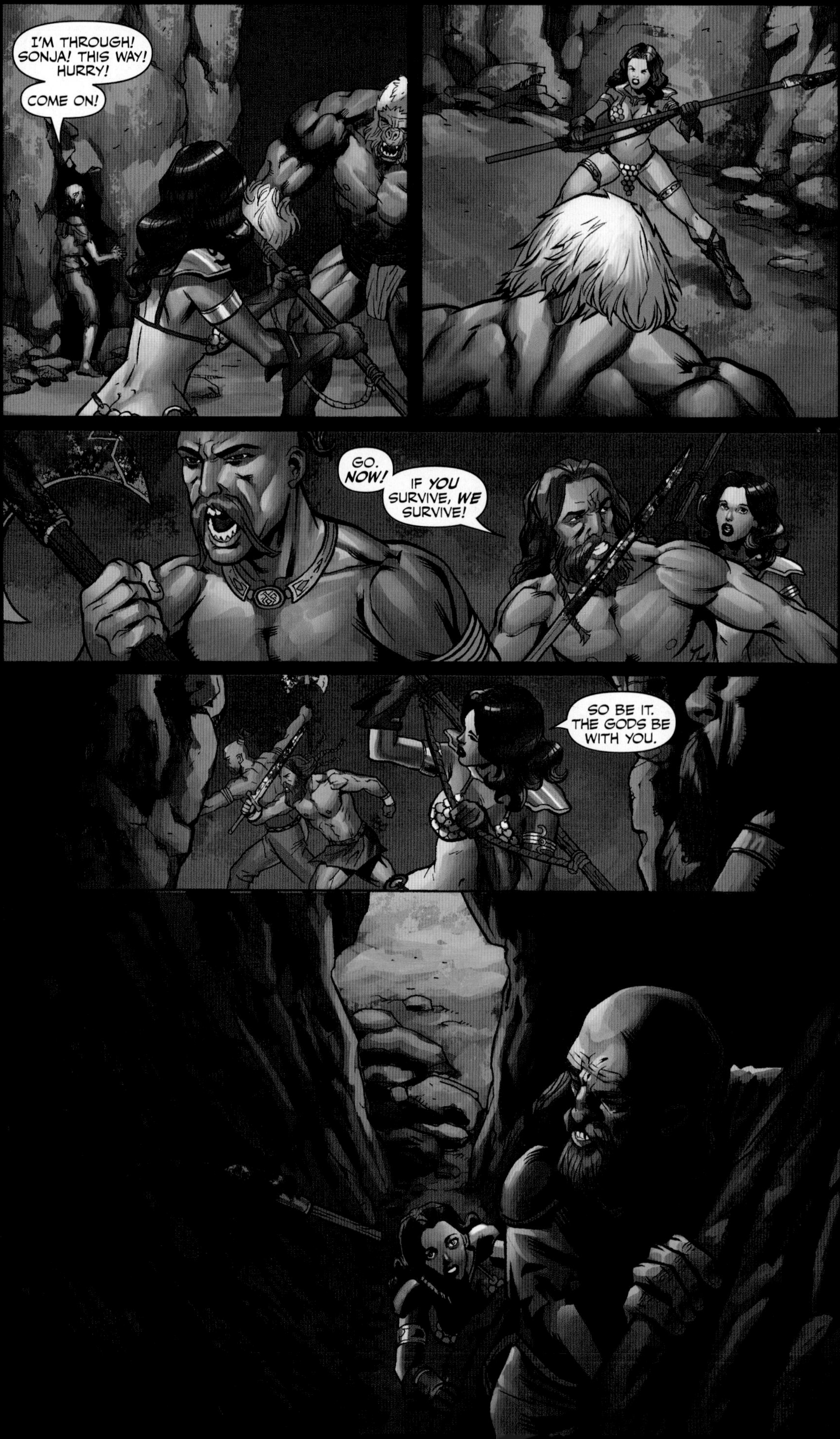
I'M THROUGH! SONJA! THIS WAY! HURRY!
COME ON!
GO. NOW!
IF YOU SURVIVE, WE SURVIVE!
SO BE IT. THE GODS BE WITH YOU.

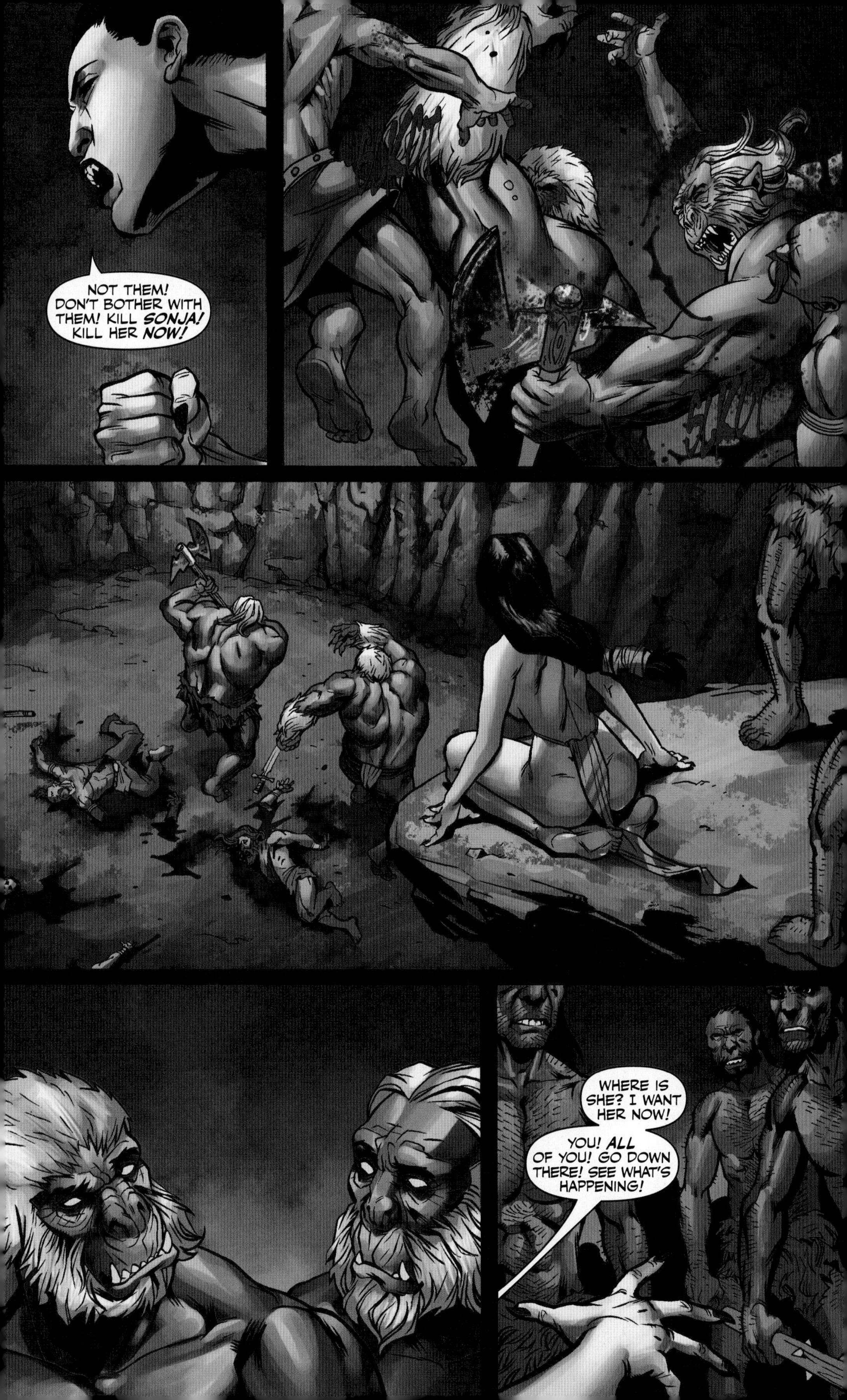
NOT THEM! DON'T BOTHER WITH THEM! KILL SONJA! KILL HER NOW!
WHERE IS SHE? I WANT HER NOW!
YOU! ALL OF YOU! GO DOWN THERE! SEE WHAT'S HAPPENING!

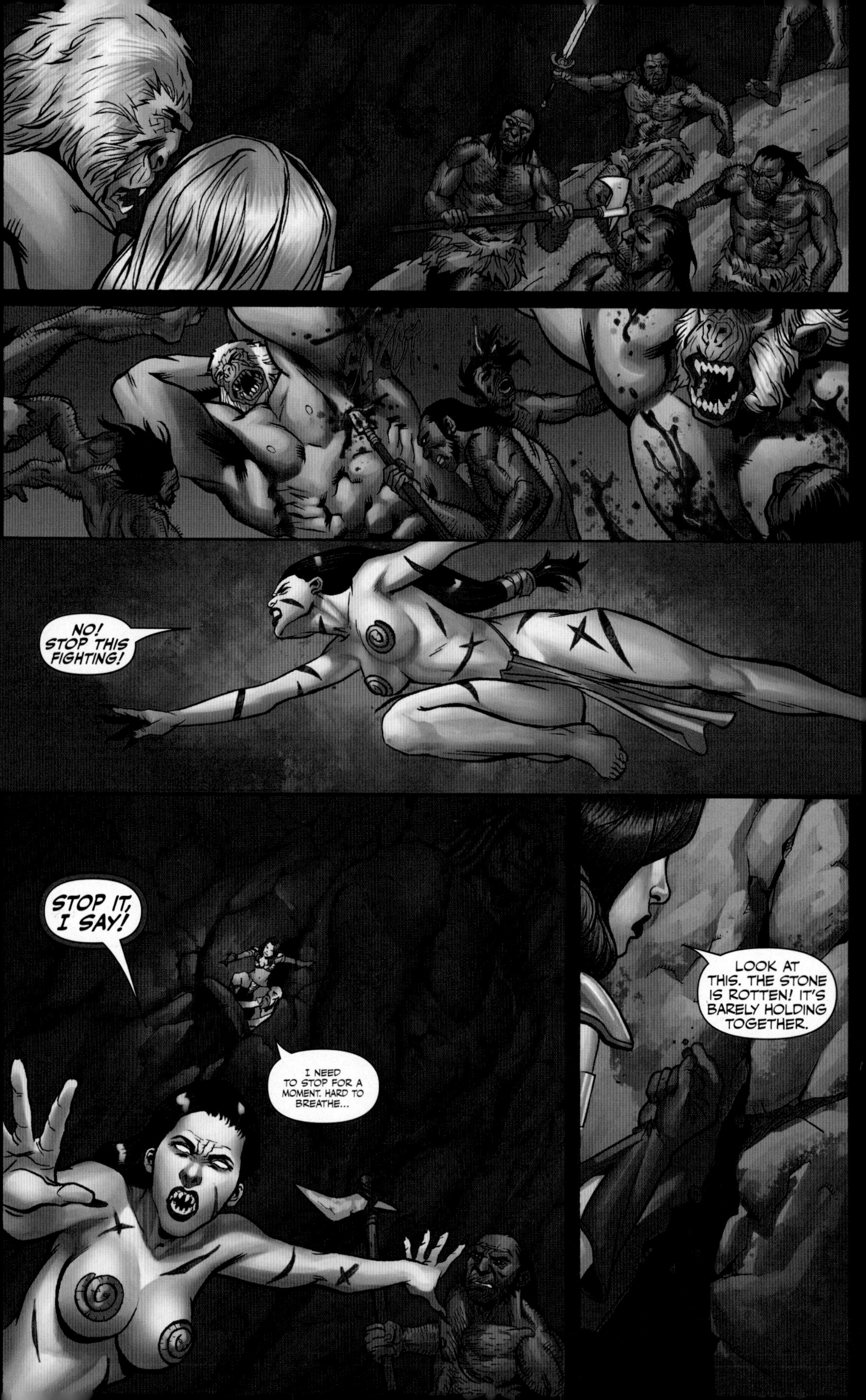

NO! STOP THIS FIGHTING!
STOP IT, I SAY!
I NEED TO STOP FOR A MOMENT. HARD TO BREATHE...
LOOK AT THIS. THE STONE IS ROTTEN! IT'S BARELY HOLDING TOGETHER.

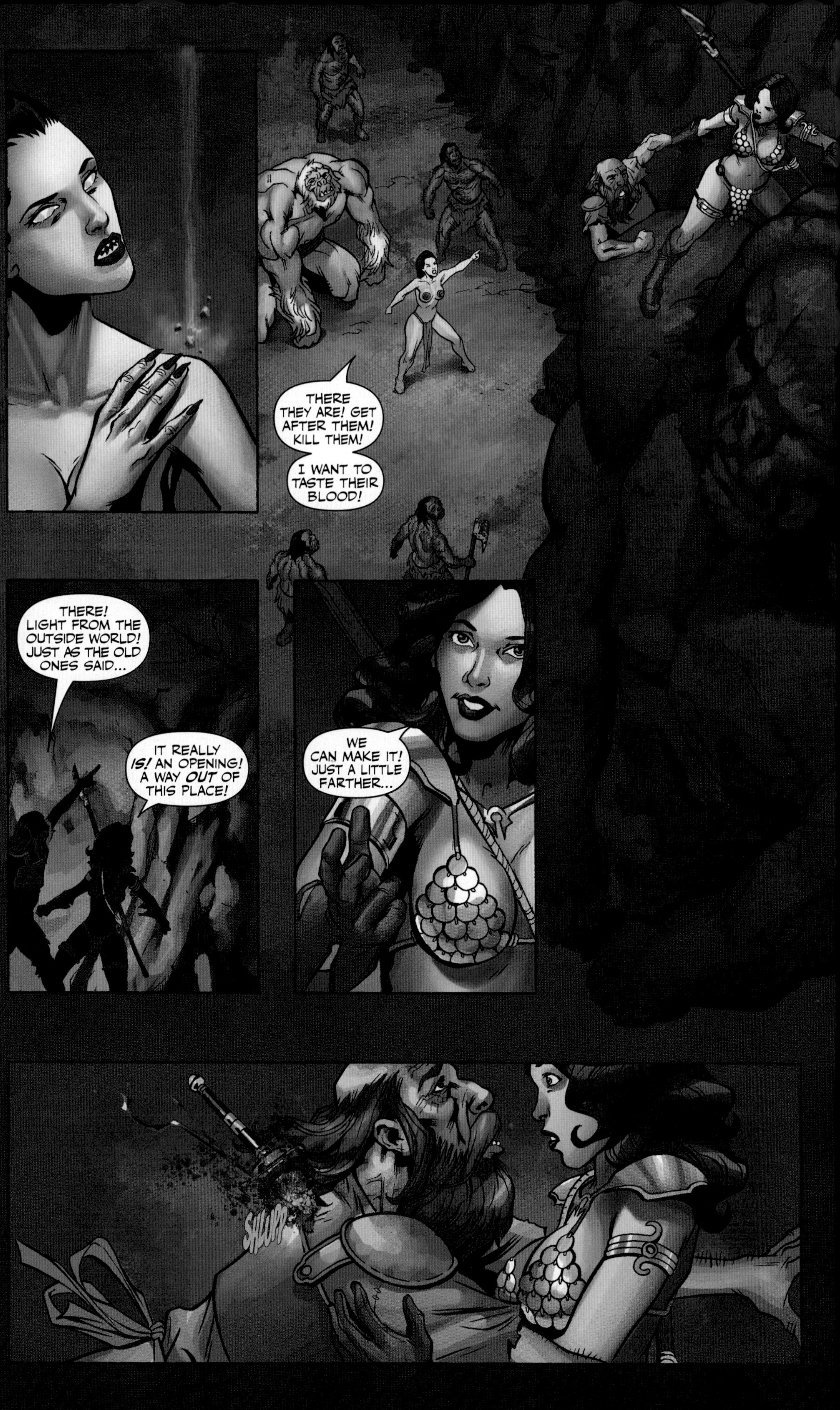
THERE THEY ARE! GET AFTER THEM! KILL THEM!
I WANT TO TASTE THEIR BLOOD!
THERE! LIGHT FROM THE OUTSIDE WORLD! JUST AS THE OLD ONES SAID...
IT REALLY *IS!* AN OPENING! A WAY *OUT* OF THIS PLACE!
WE CAN MAKE IT! JUST A LITTLE FARTHER...
SHLUPP

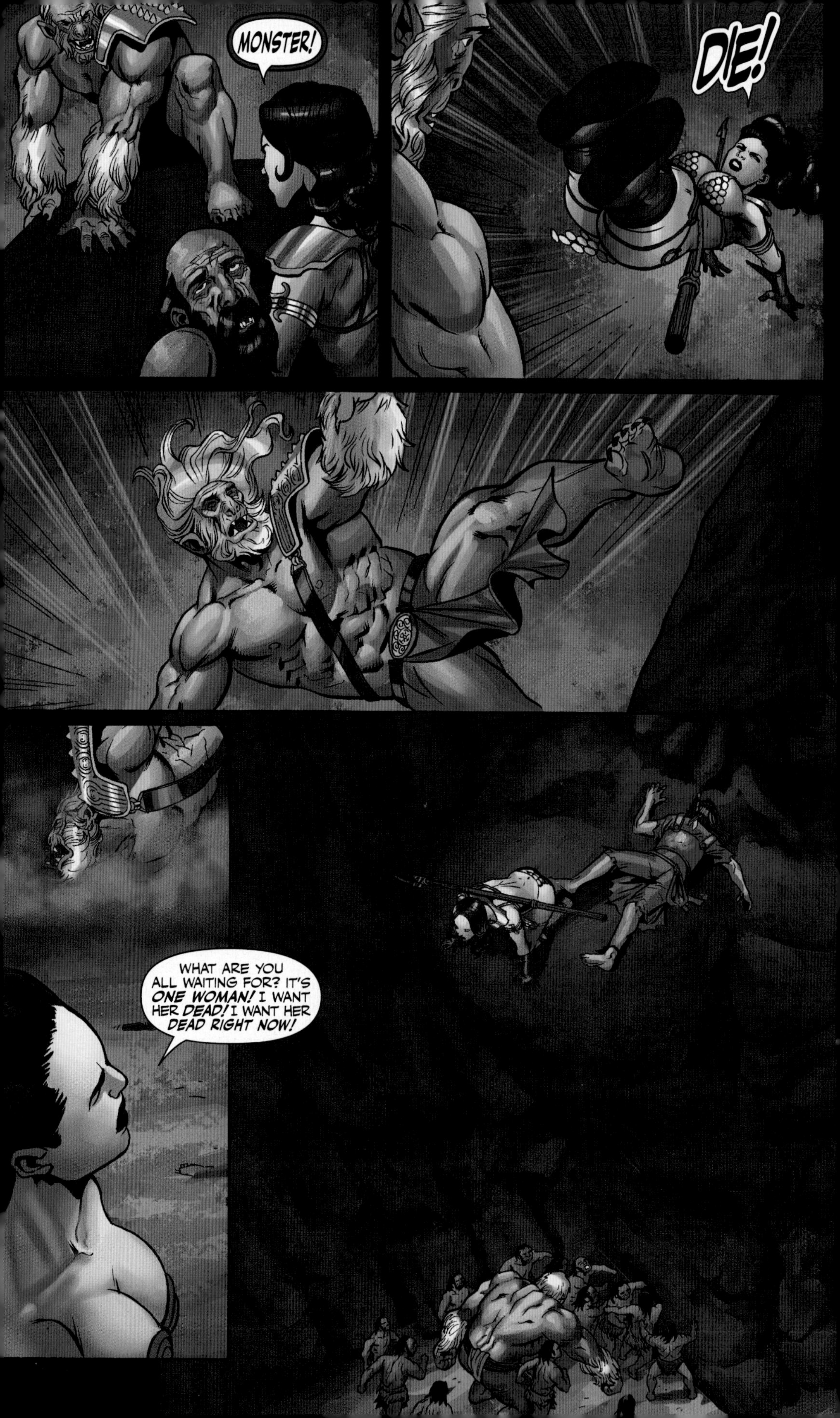
MONSTER!
DIE!
WHAT ARE YOU ALL WAITING FOR? IT'S ONE WOMAN! I WANT HER DEAD! I WANT HER DEAD RIGHT NOW!

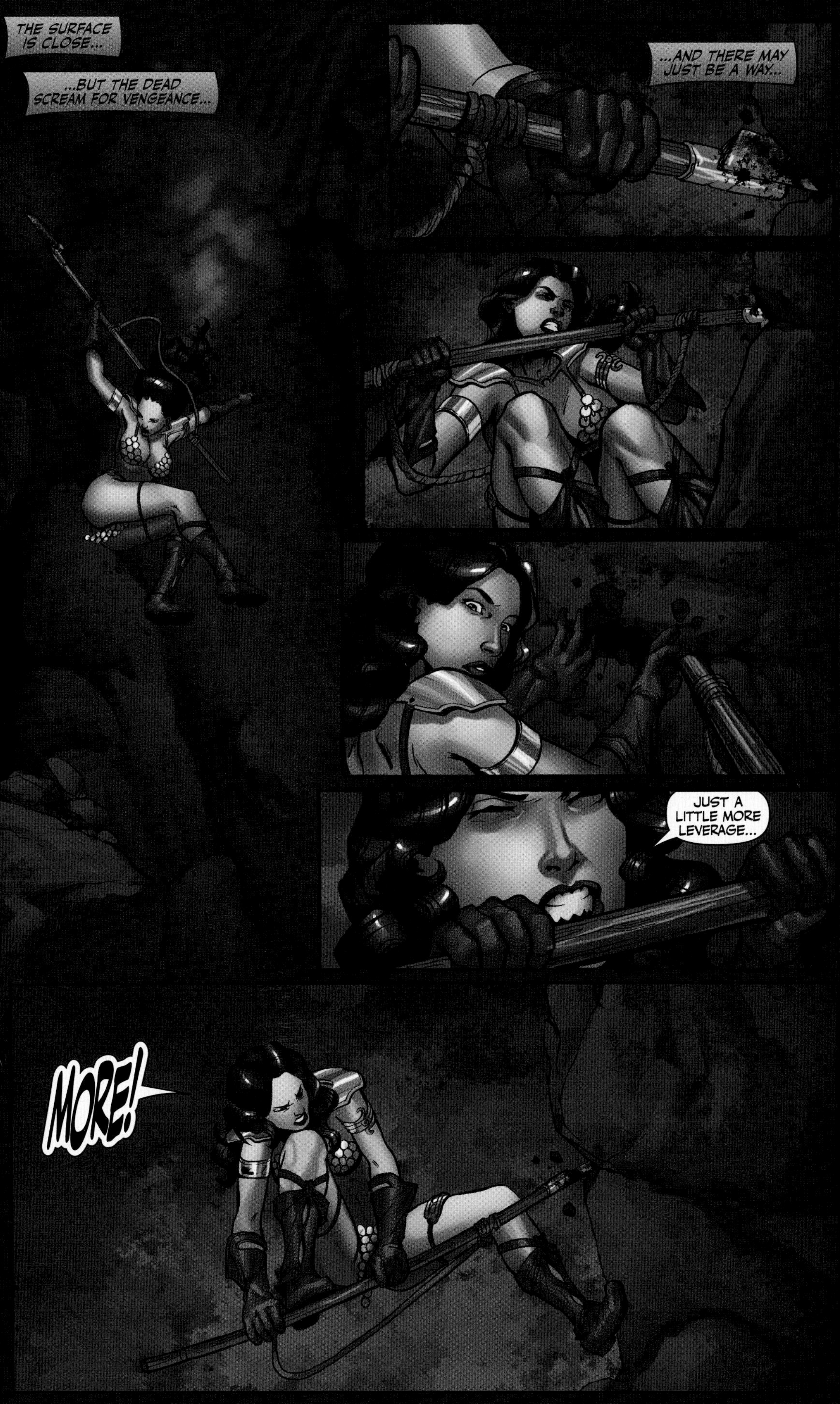
THE SURFACE IS CLOSE...
...BUT THE DEAD SCREAM FOR VENGEANCE...
...AND THERE MAY JUST BE A WAY...
JUST A LITTLE MORE LEVERAGE...
MORE!

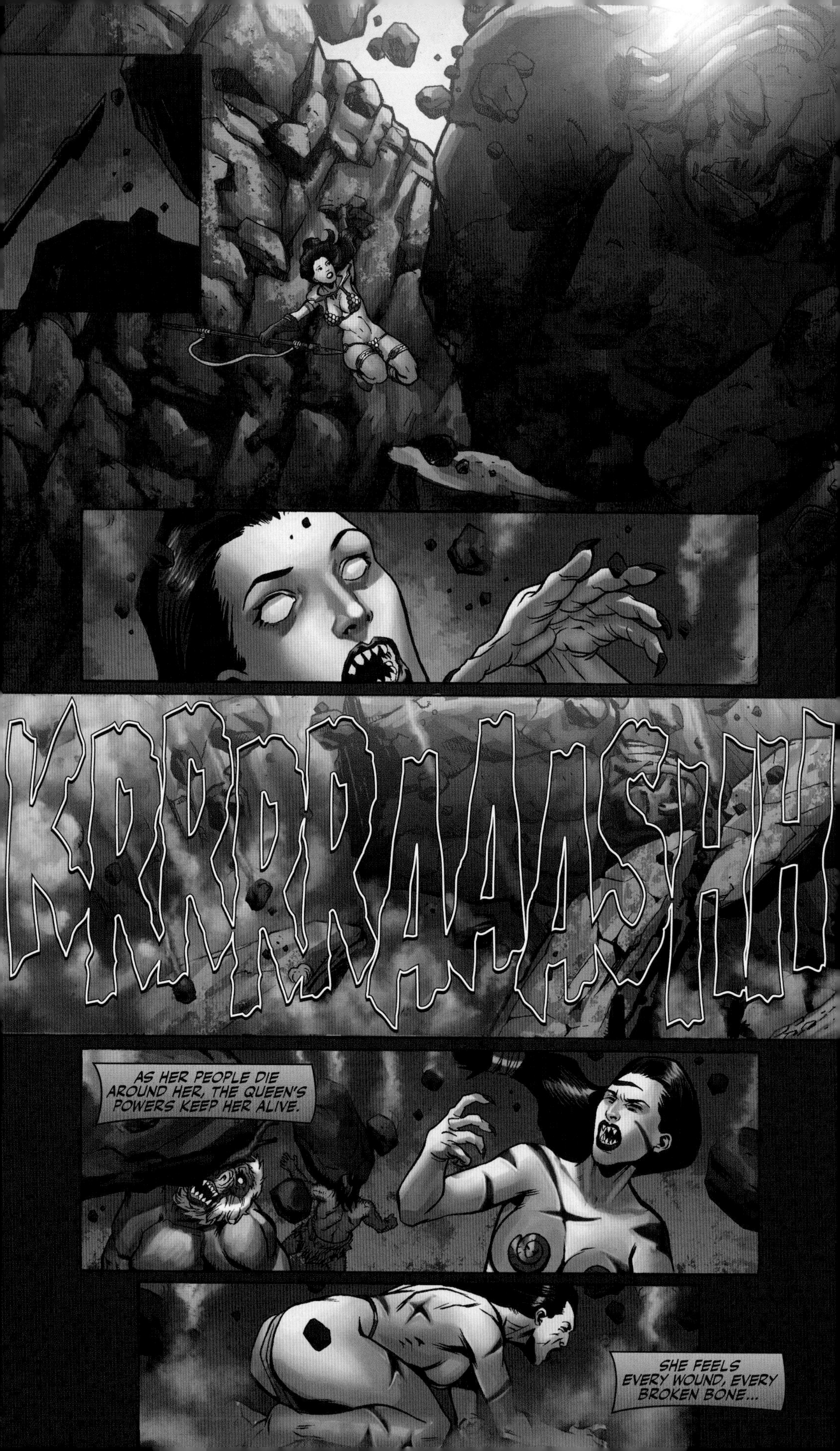
KRRRRAAASHH
AS HER PEOPLE DIE AROUND HER, THE QUEEN'S POWERS KEEP HER ALIVE.
SHE FEELS EVERY WOUND, EVERY BROKEN BONE...

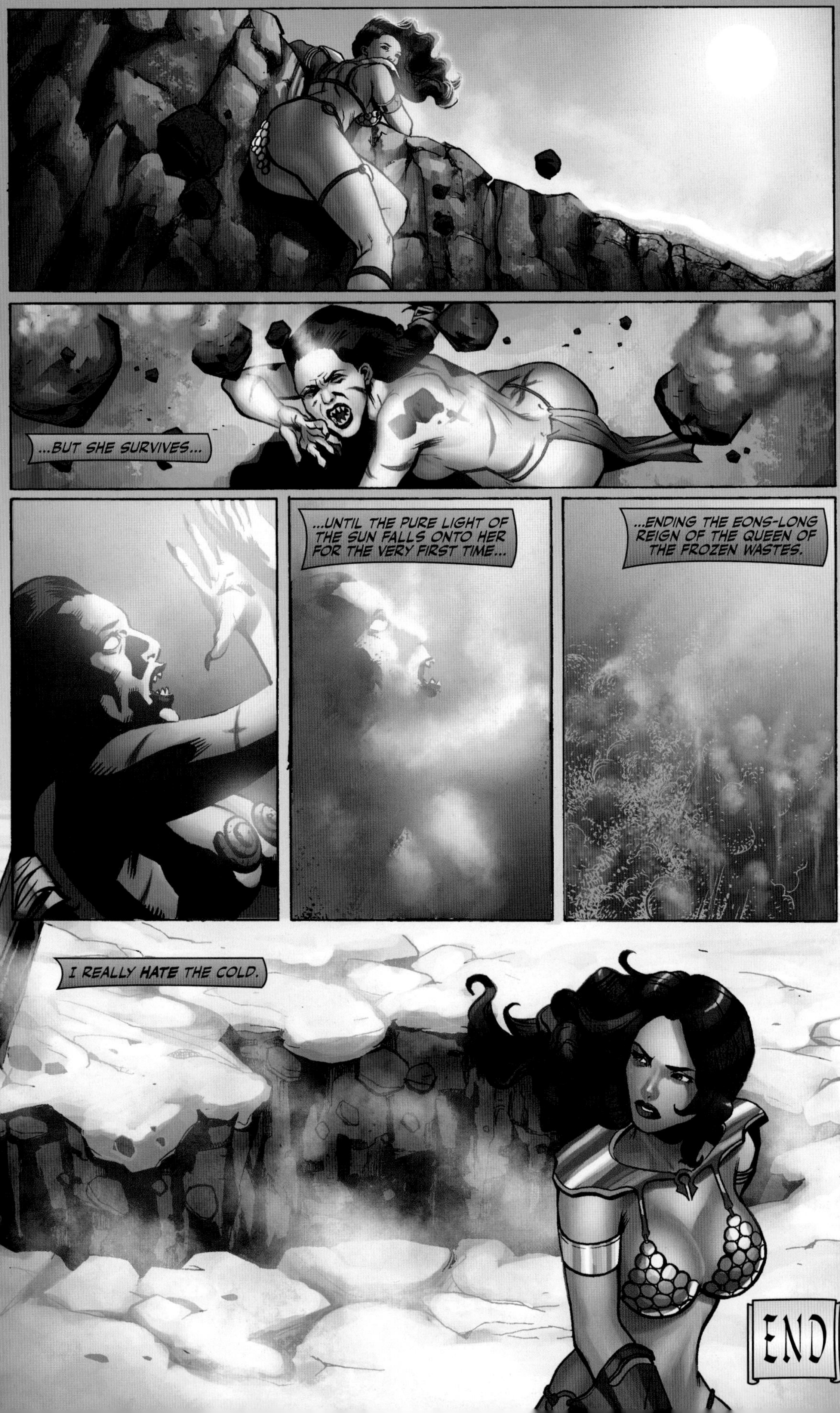
...BUT SHE SURVIVES...
...UNTIL THE PURE LIGHT OF THE SUN FALLS ONTO HER FOR THE VERY FIRST TIME...
...ENDING THE EONS-LONG REIGN OF THE QUEEN OF THE FROZEN WASTES.
I REALLY HATE THE COLD.
END

BONUS MATERIAL

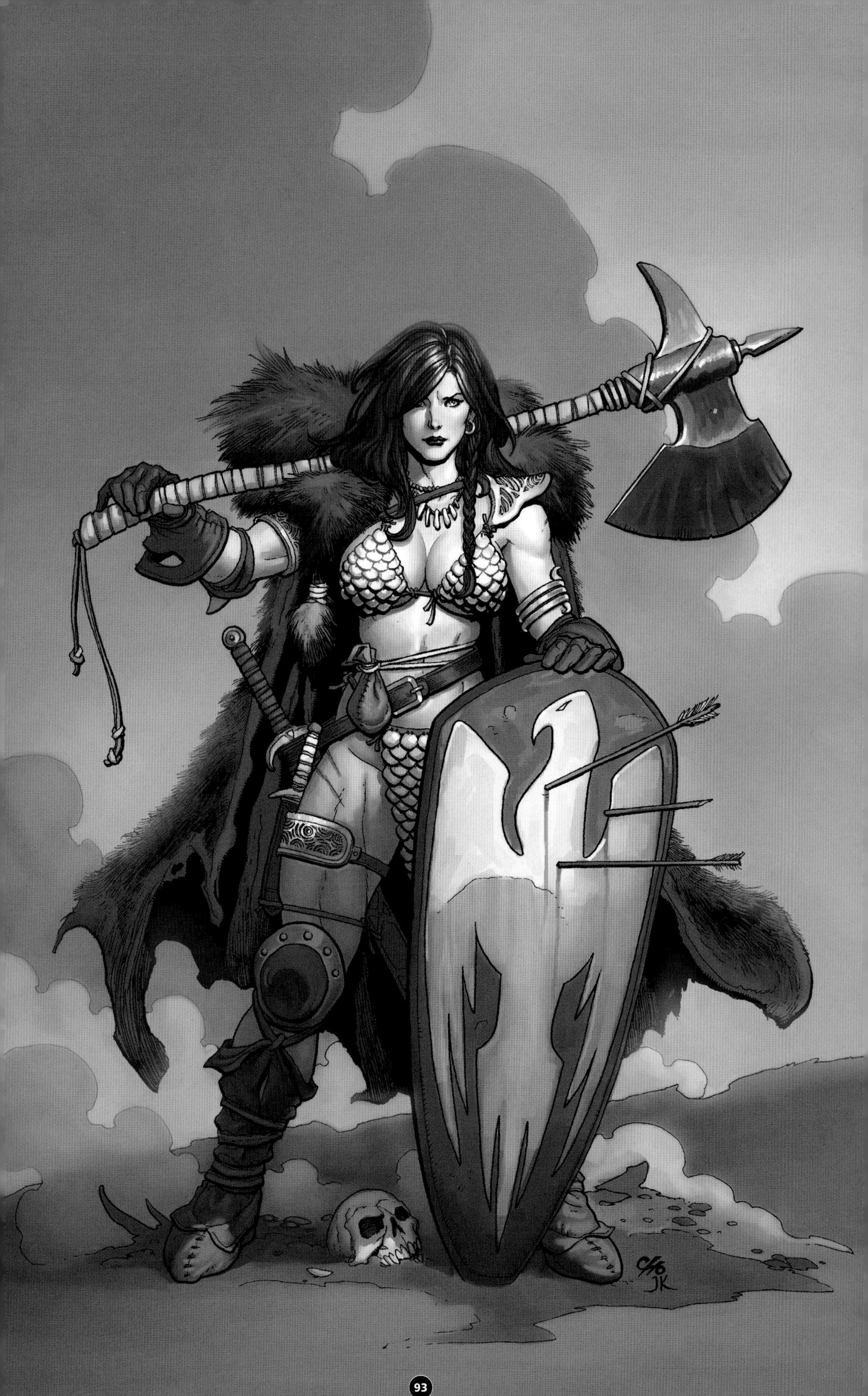

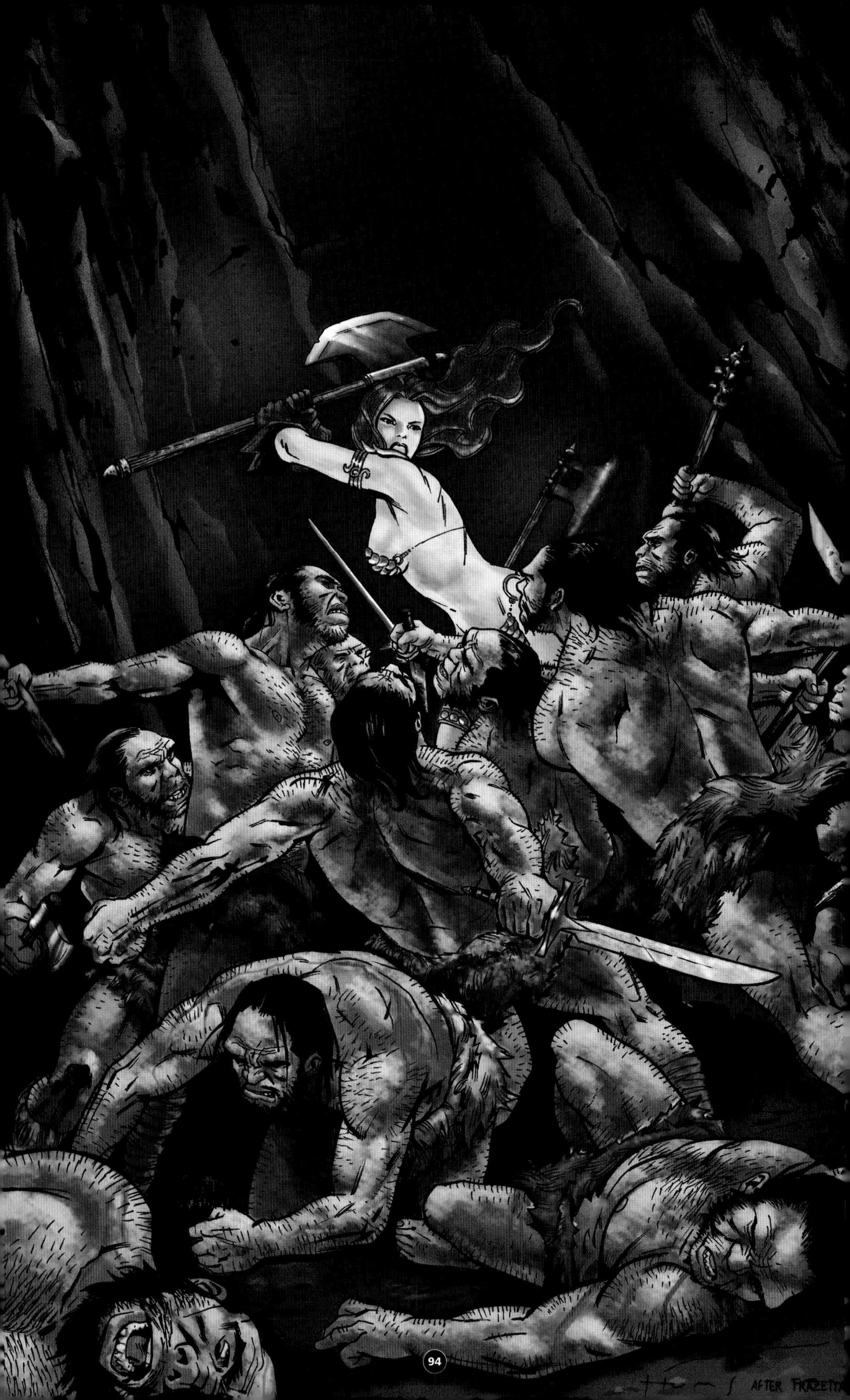
AFTER FRAZETTA

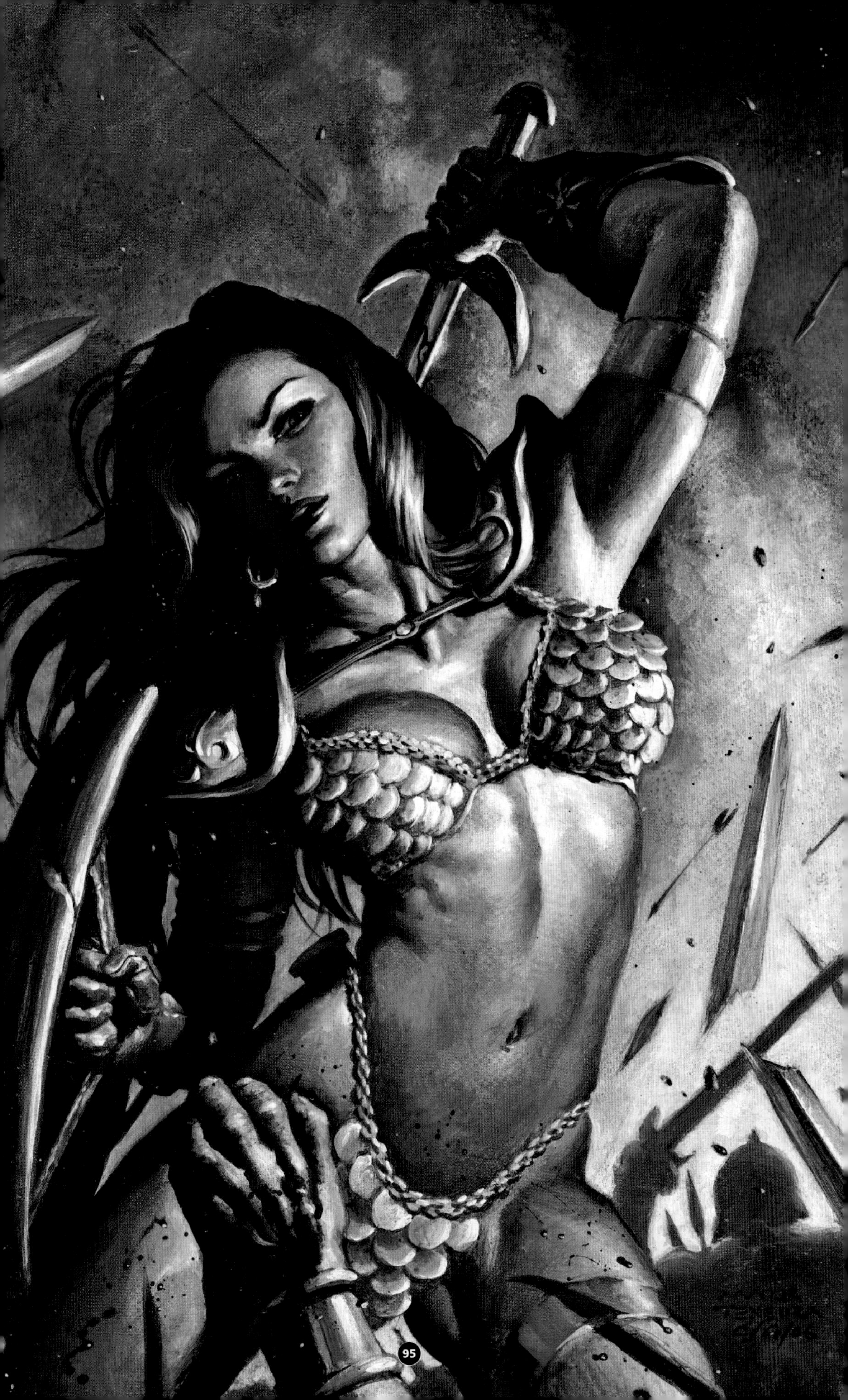

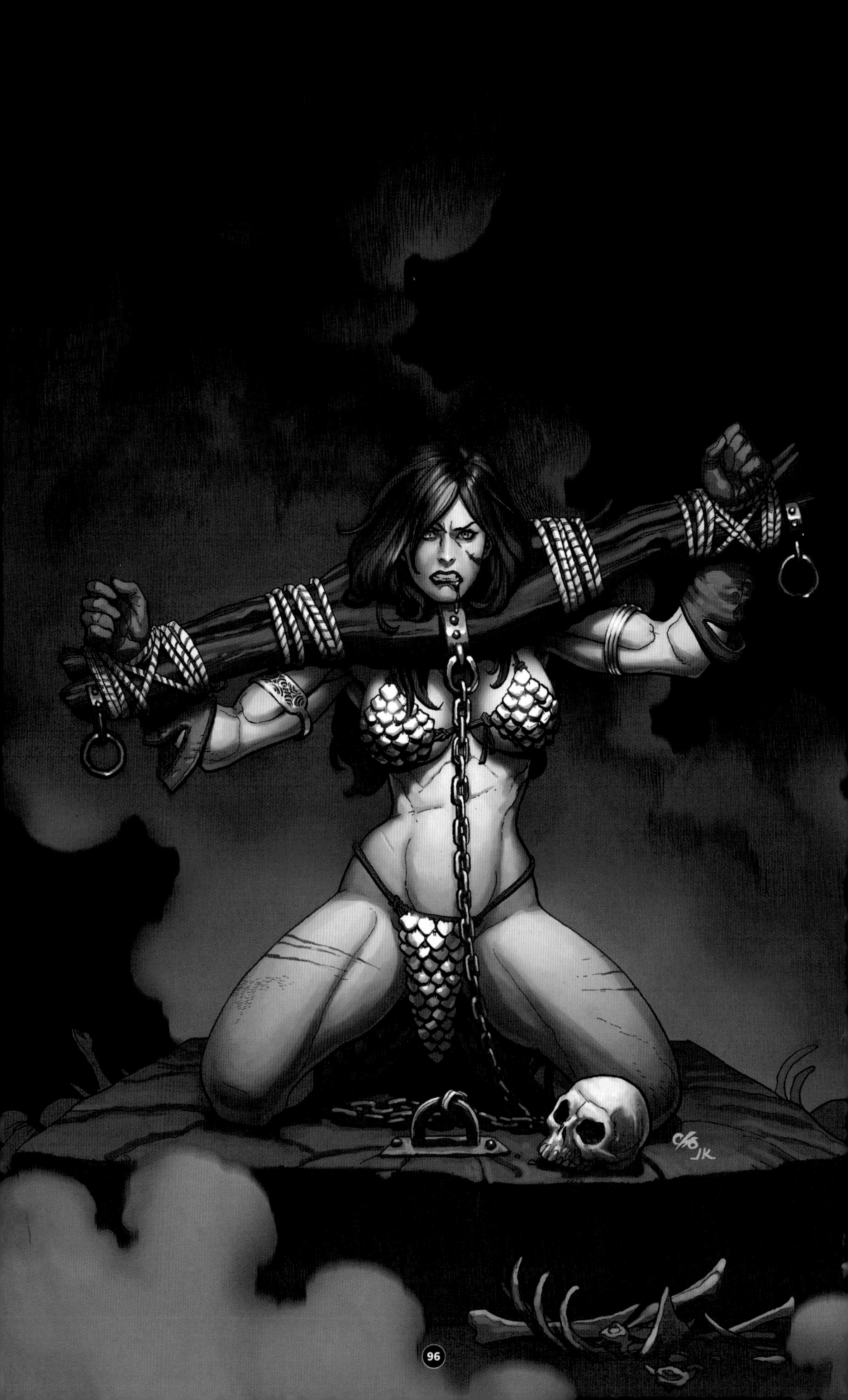

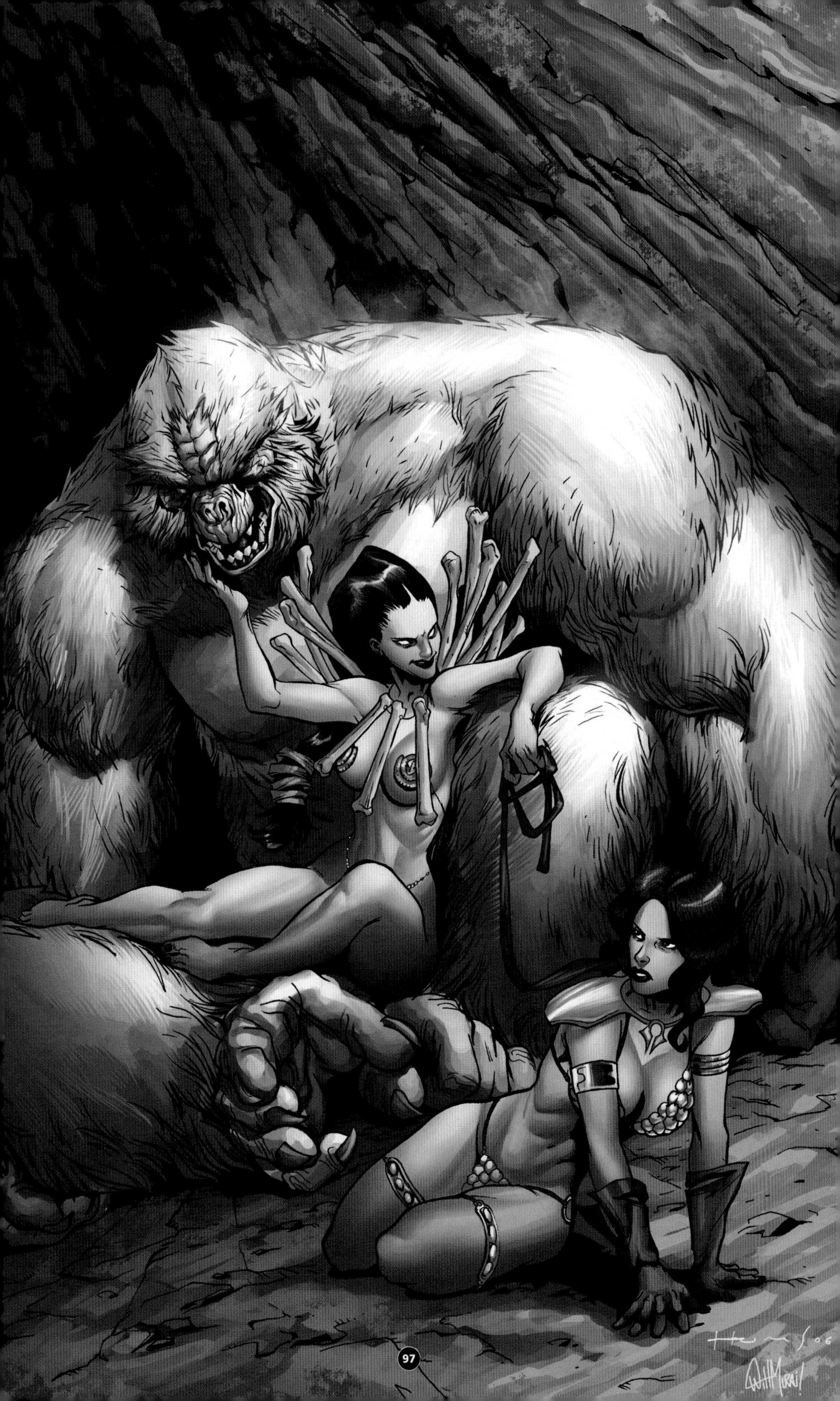

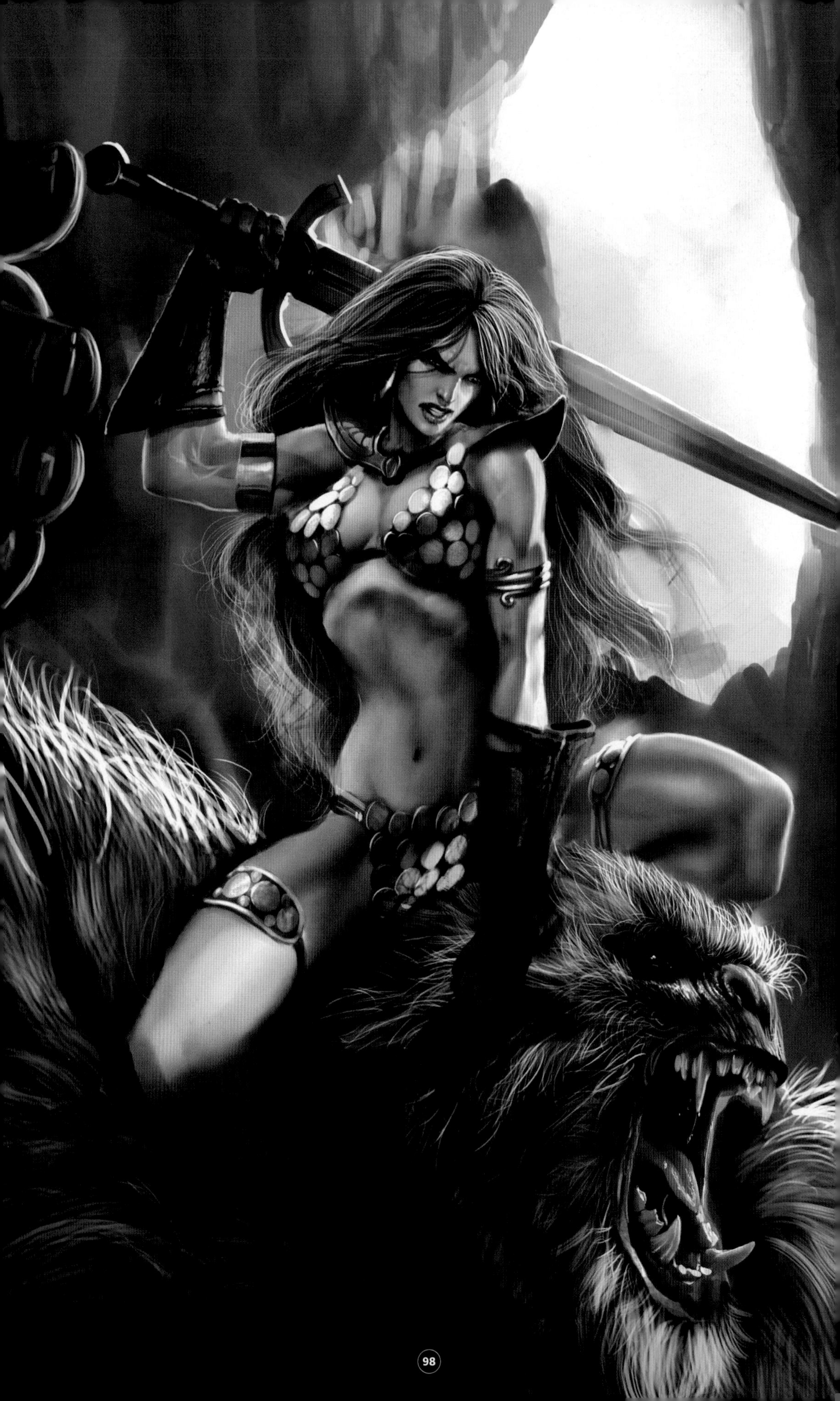

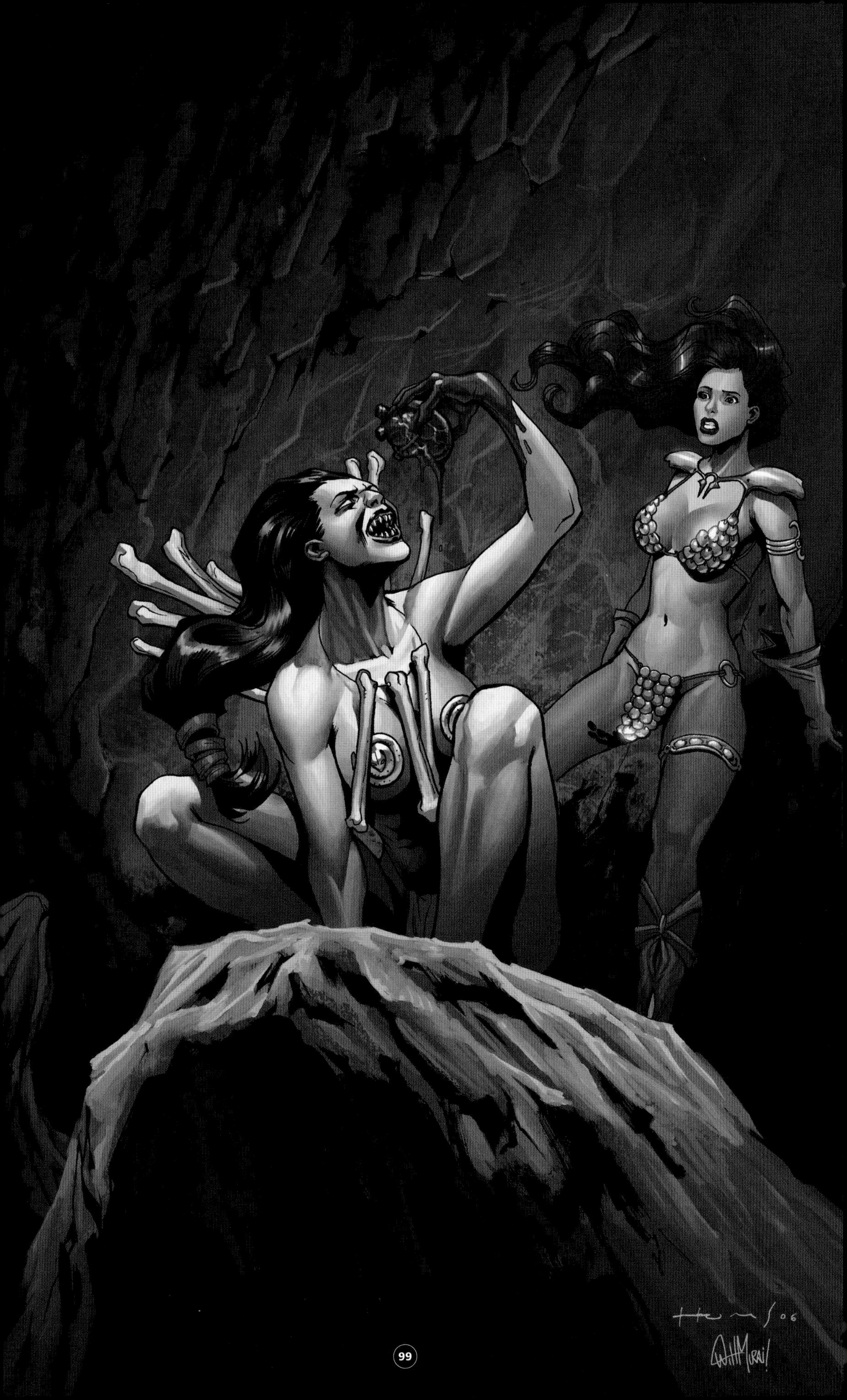

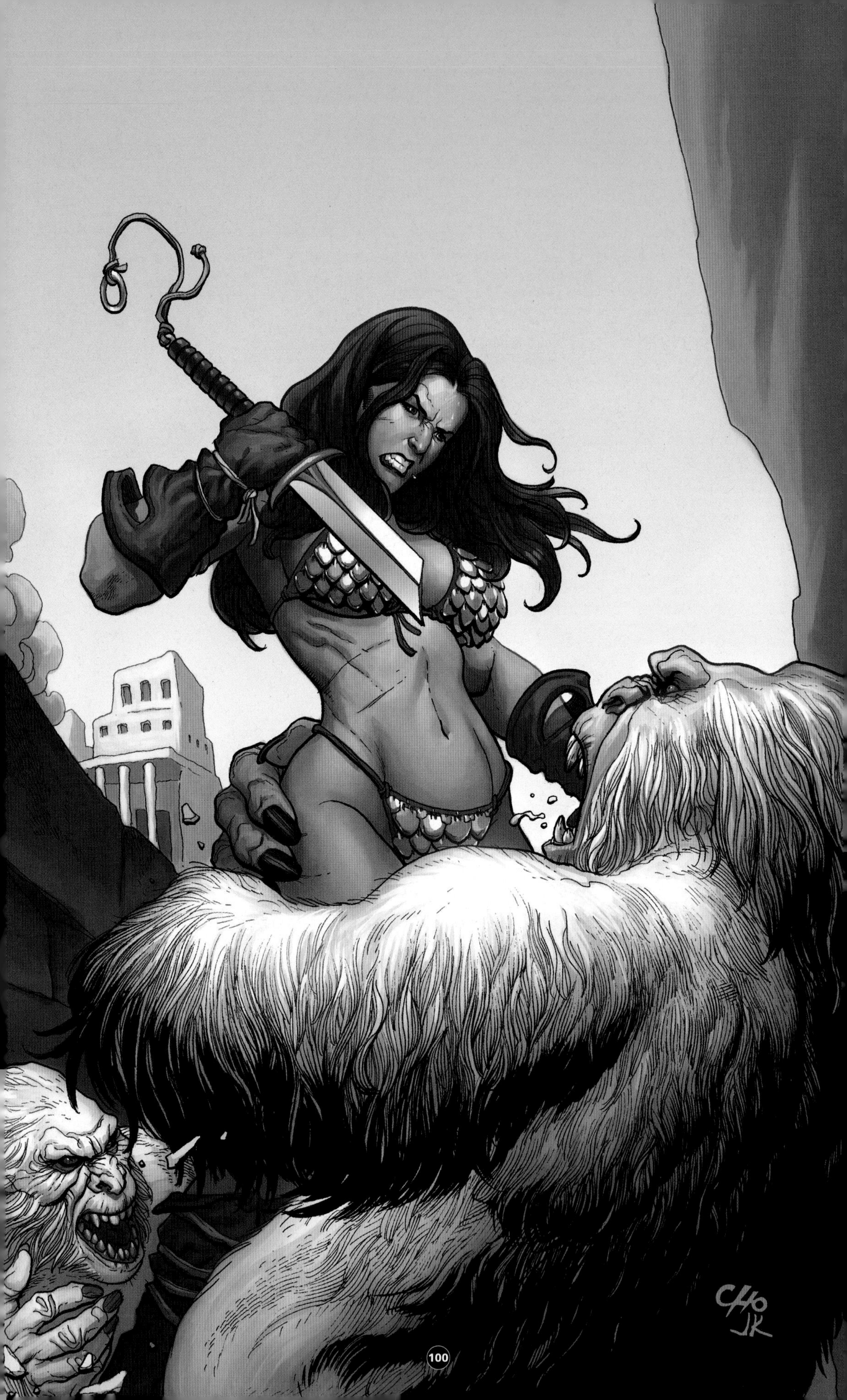
CHO
JK

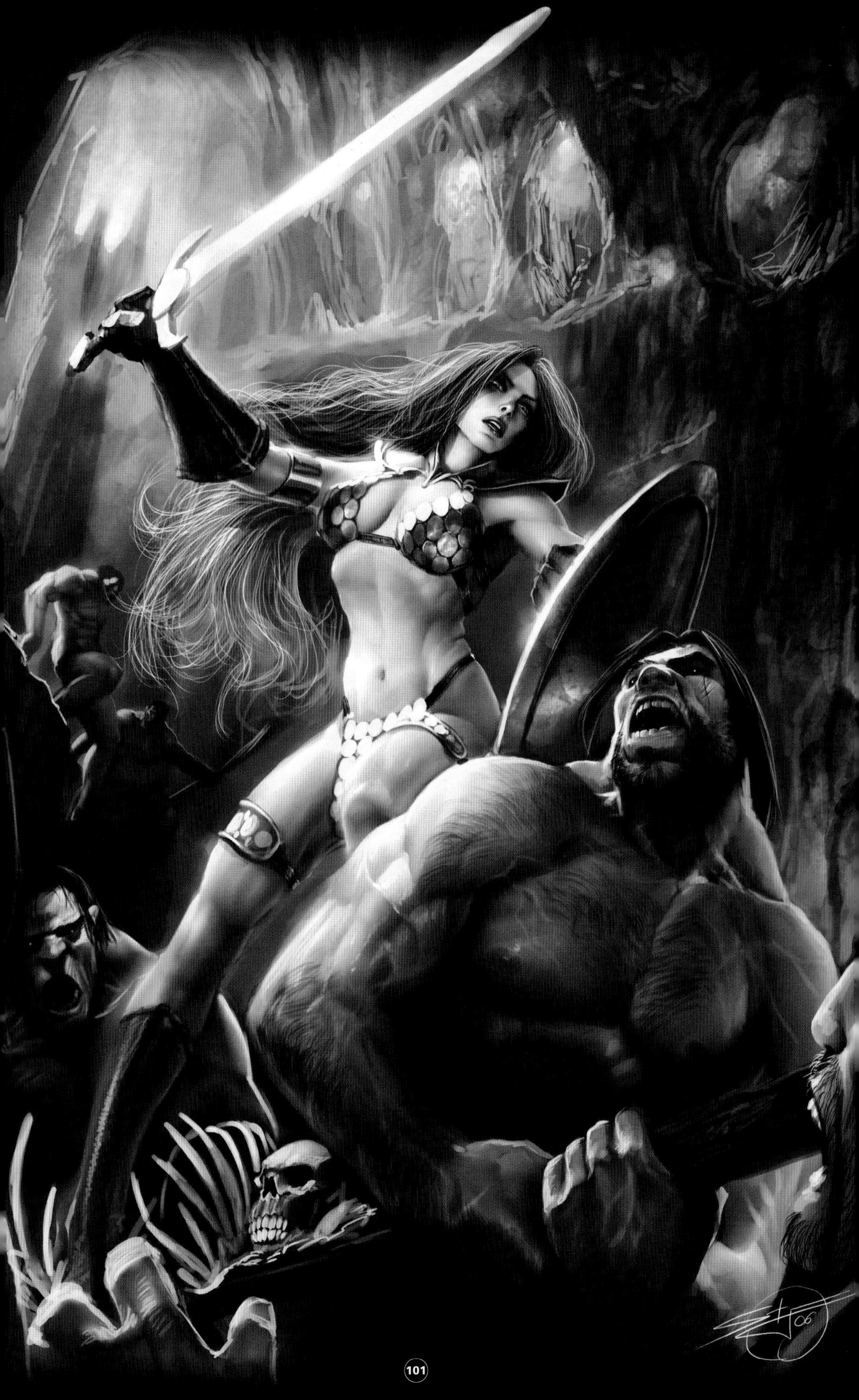

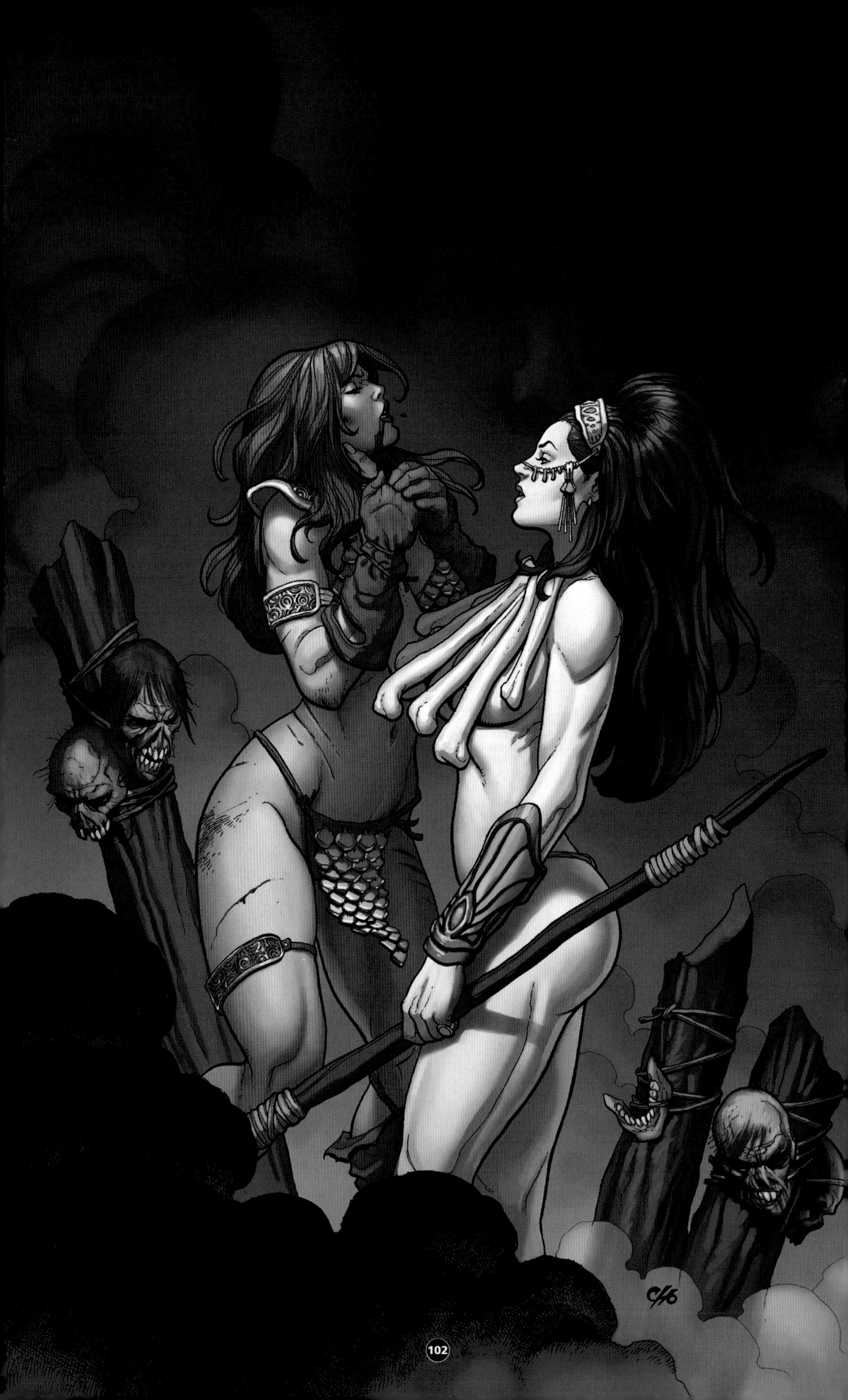

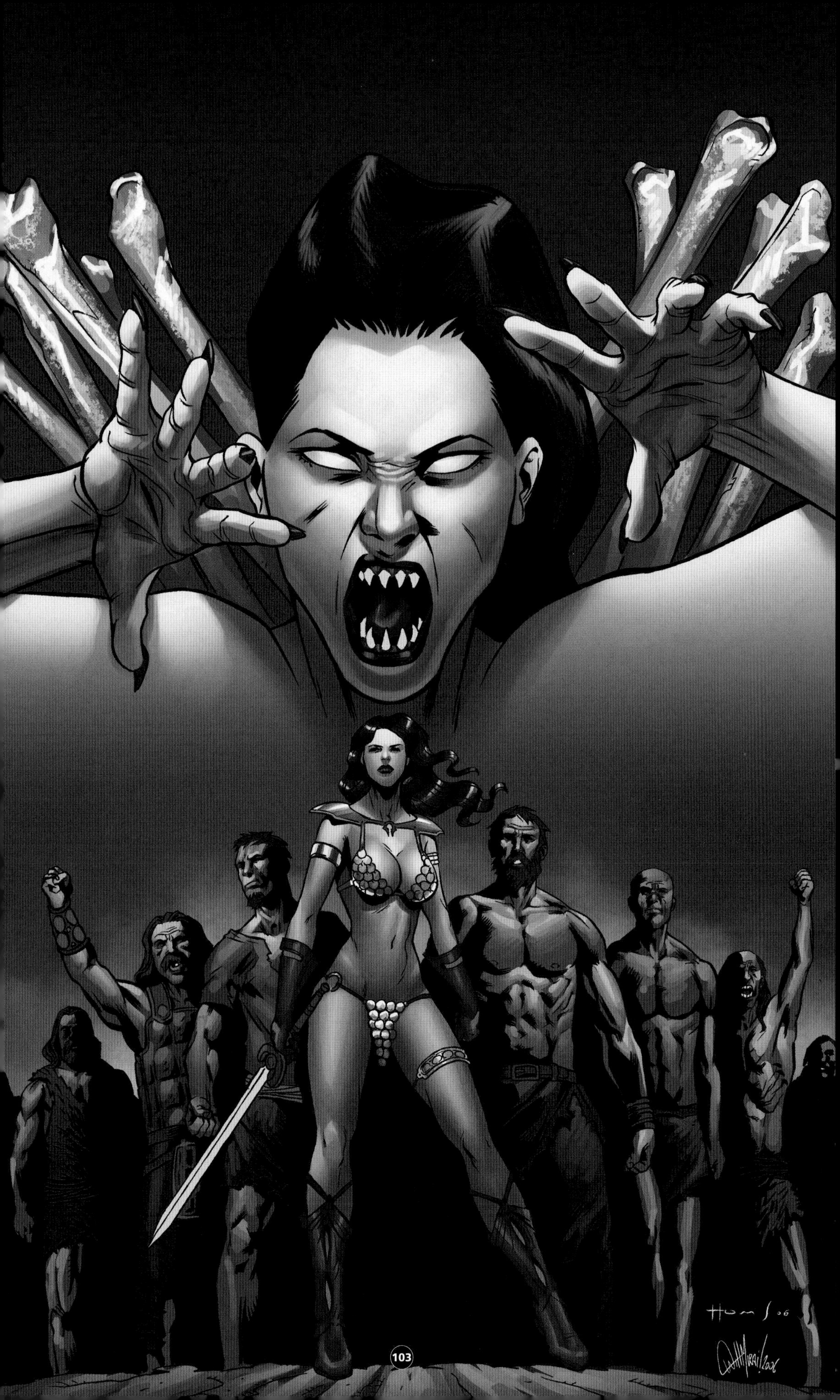

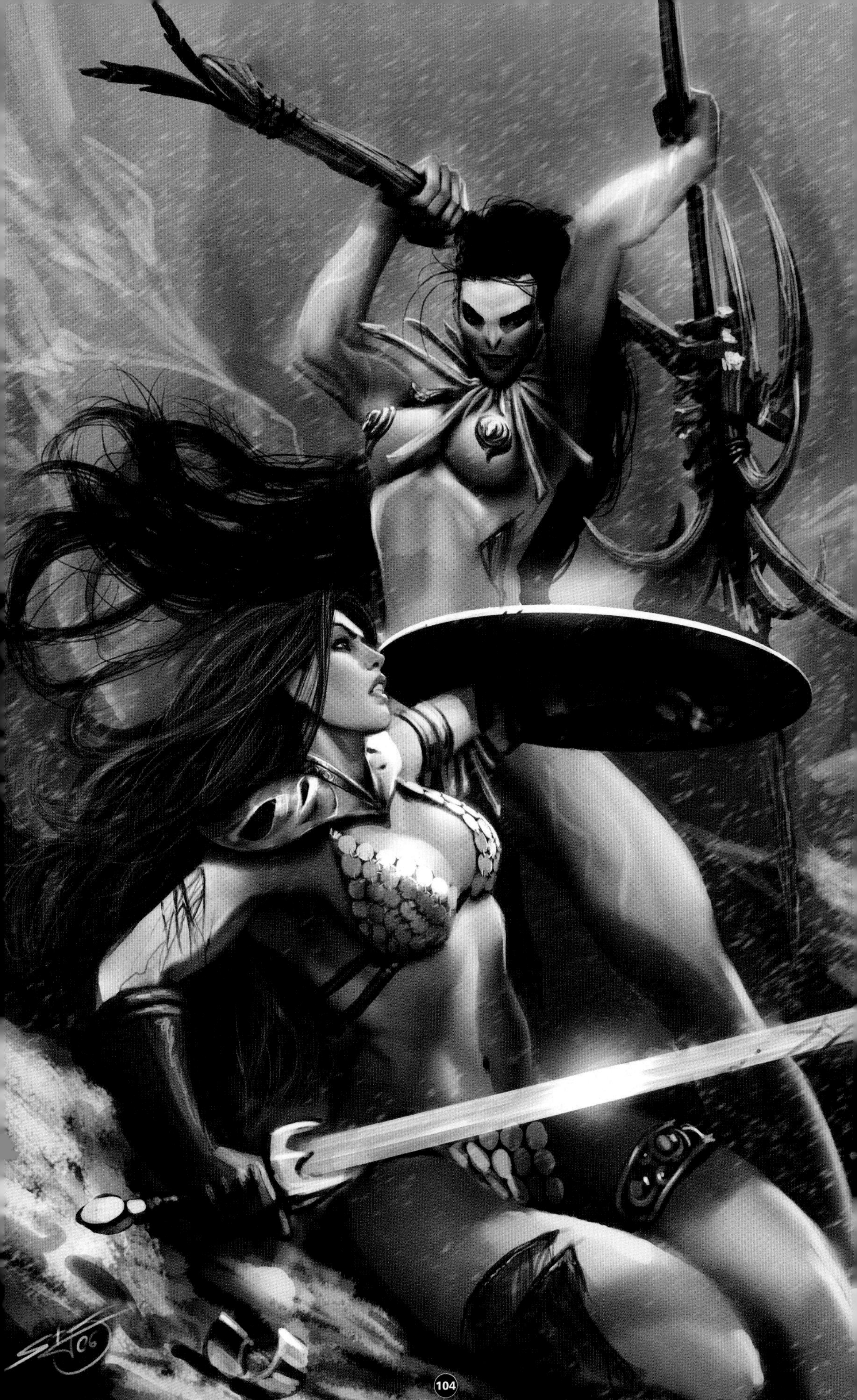

SKETCHBOOK

FRANK CHO
SKETCHBOOK

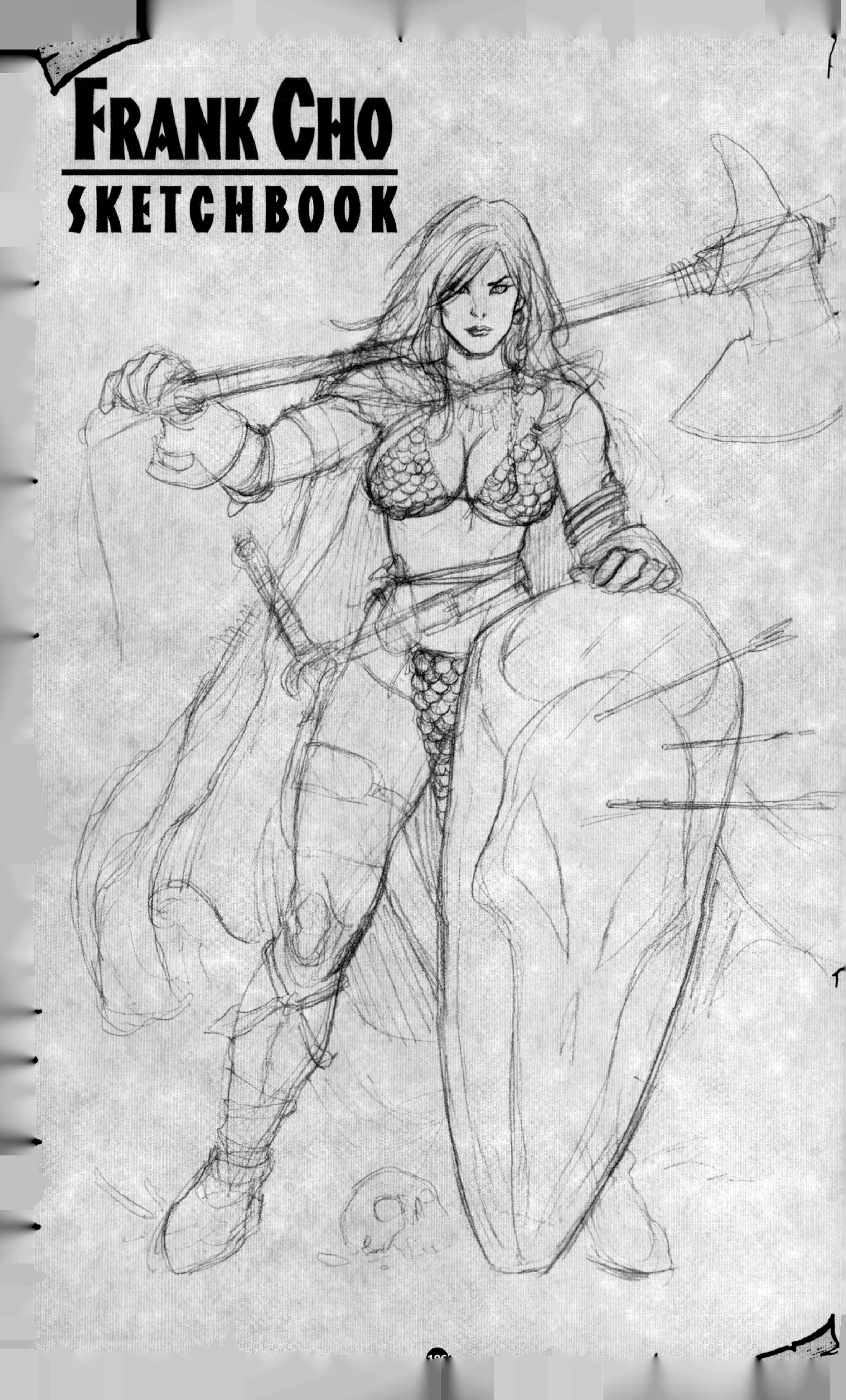

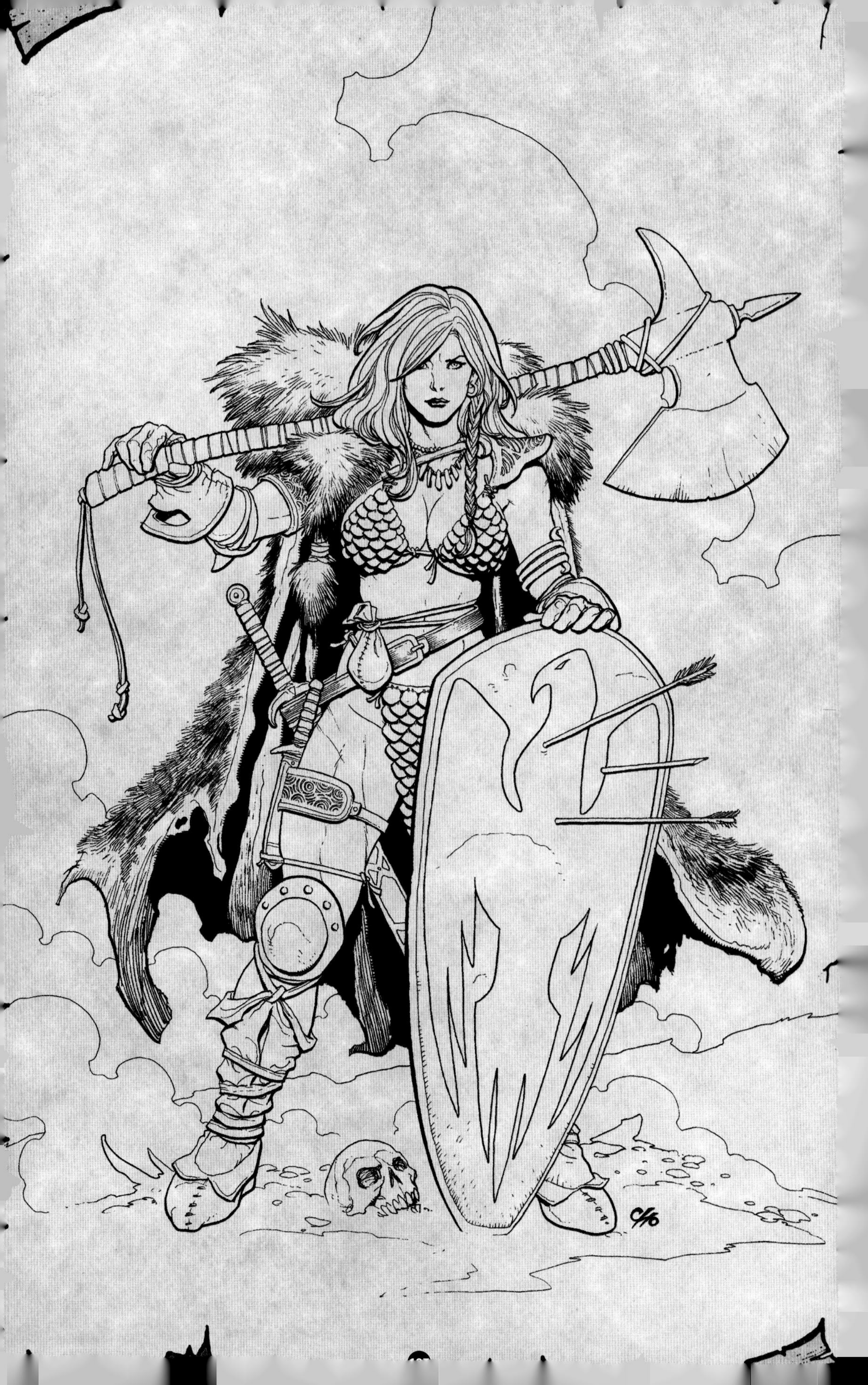

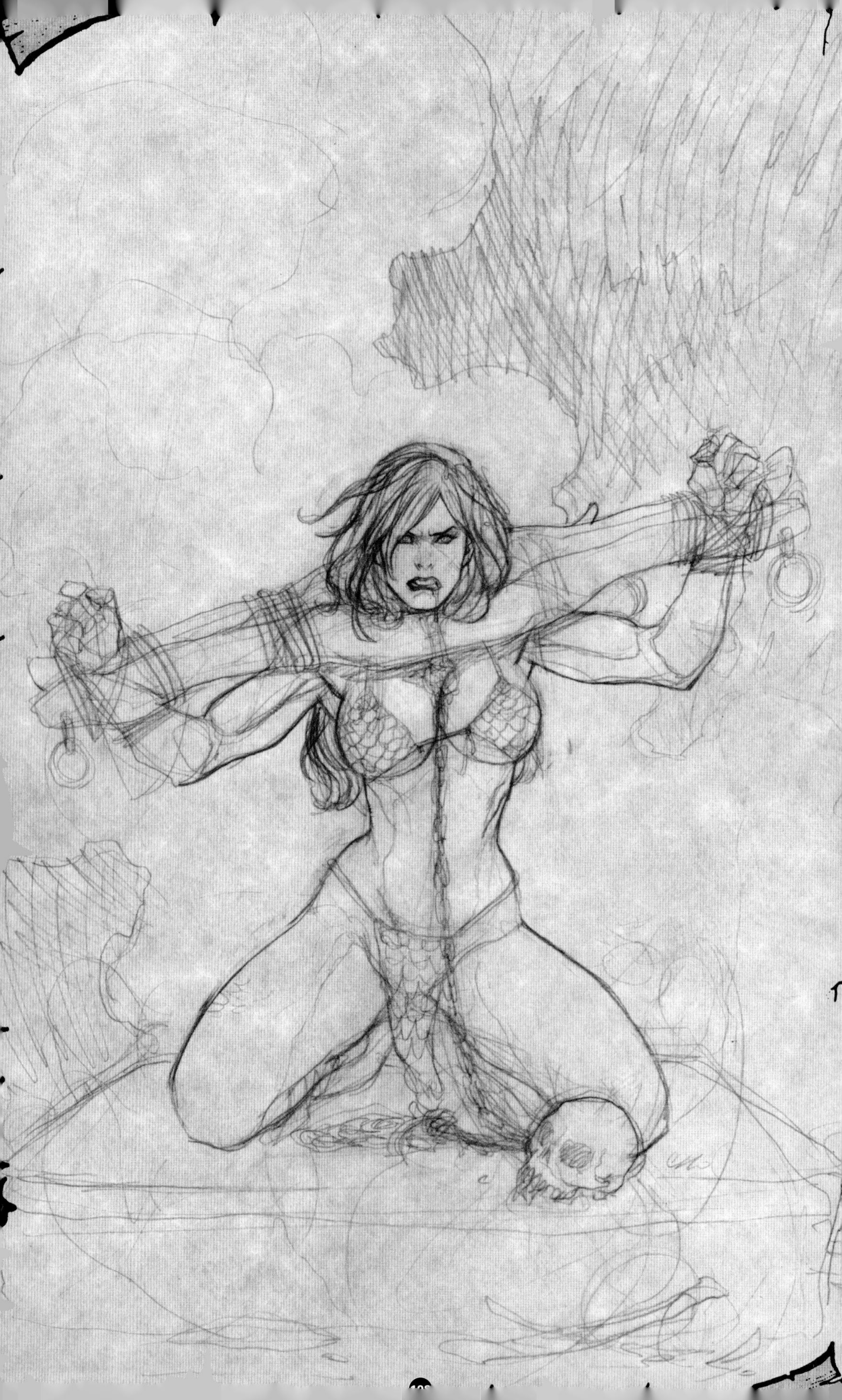

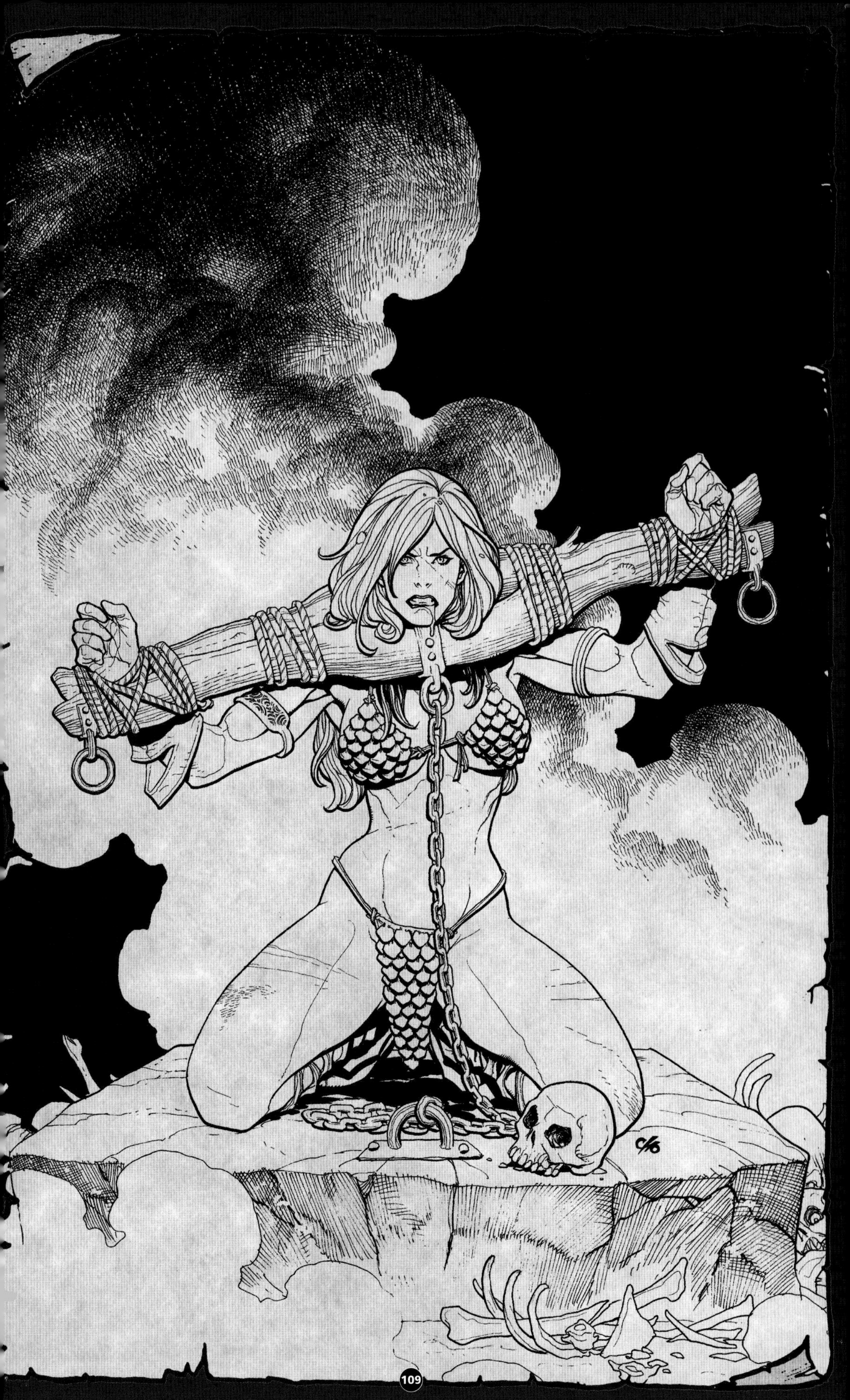

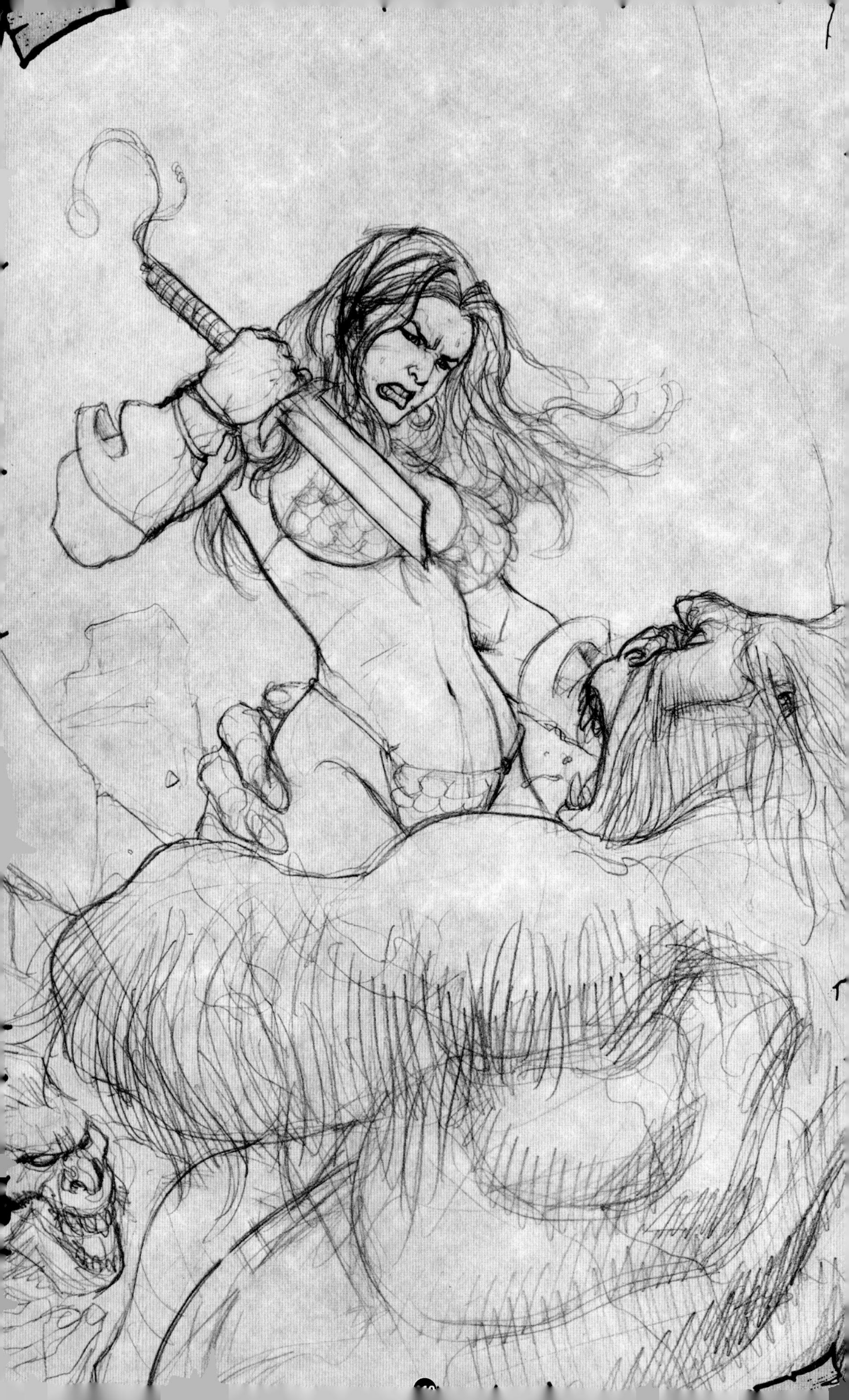

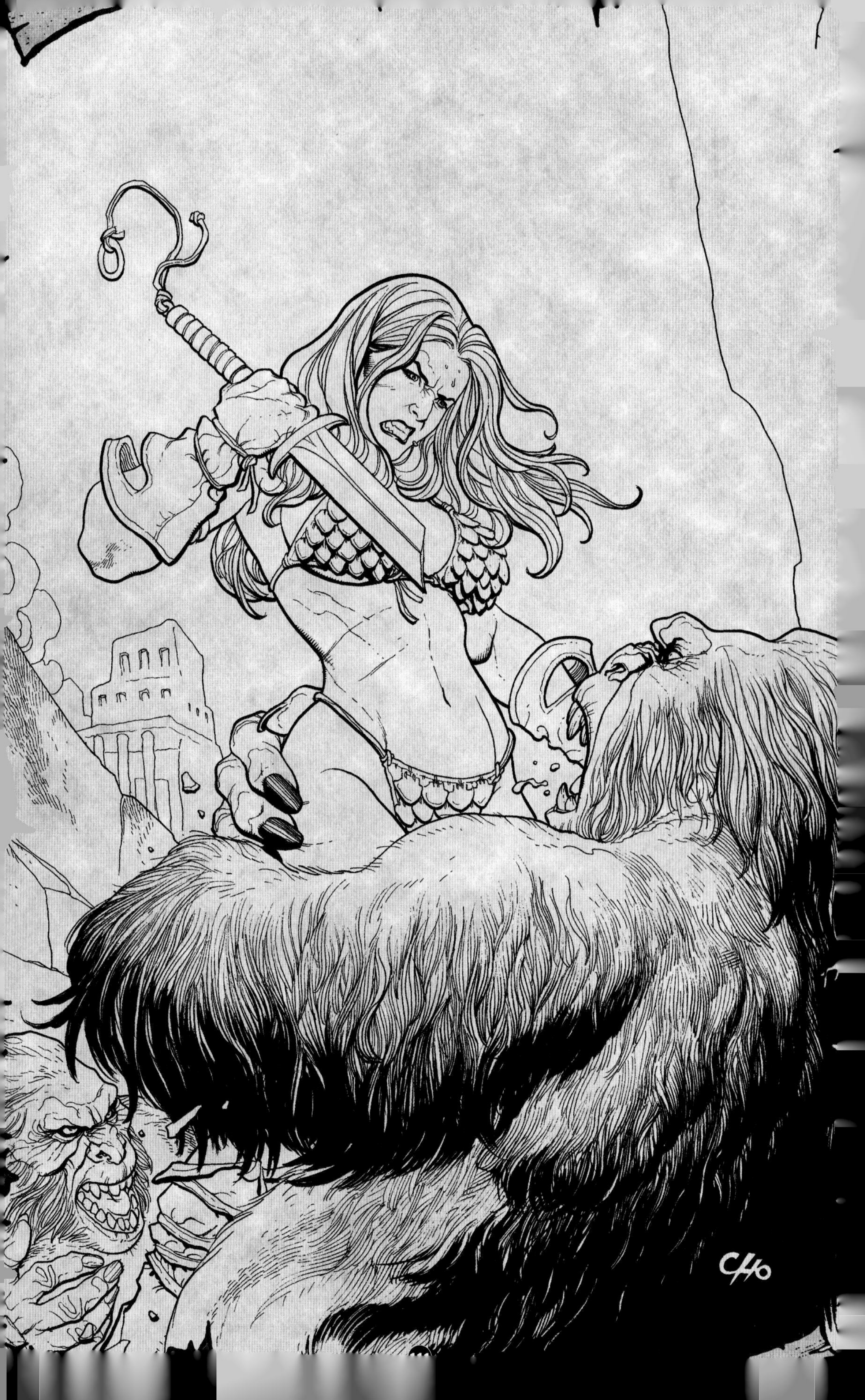
CHO

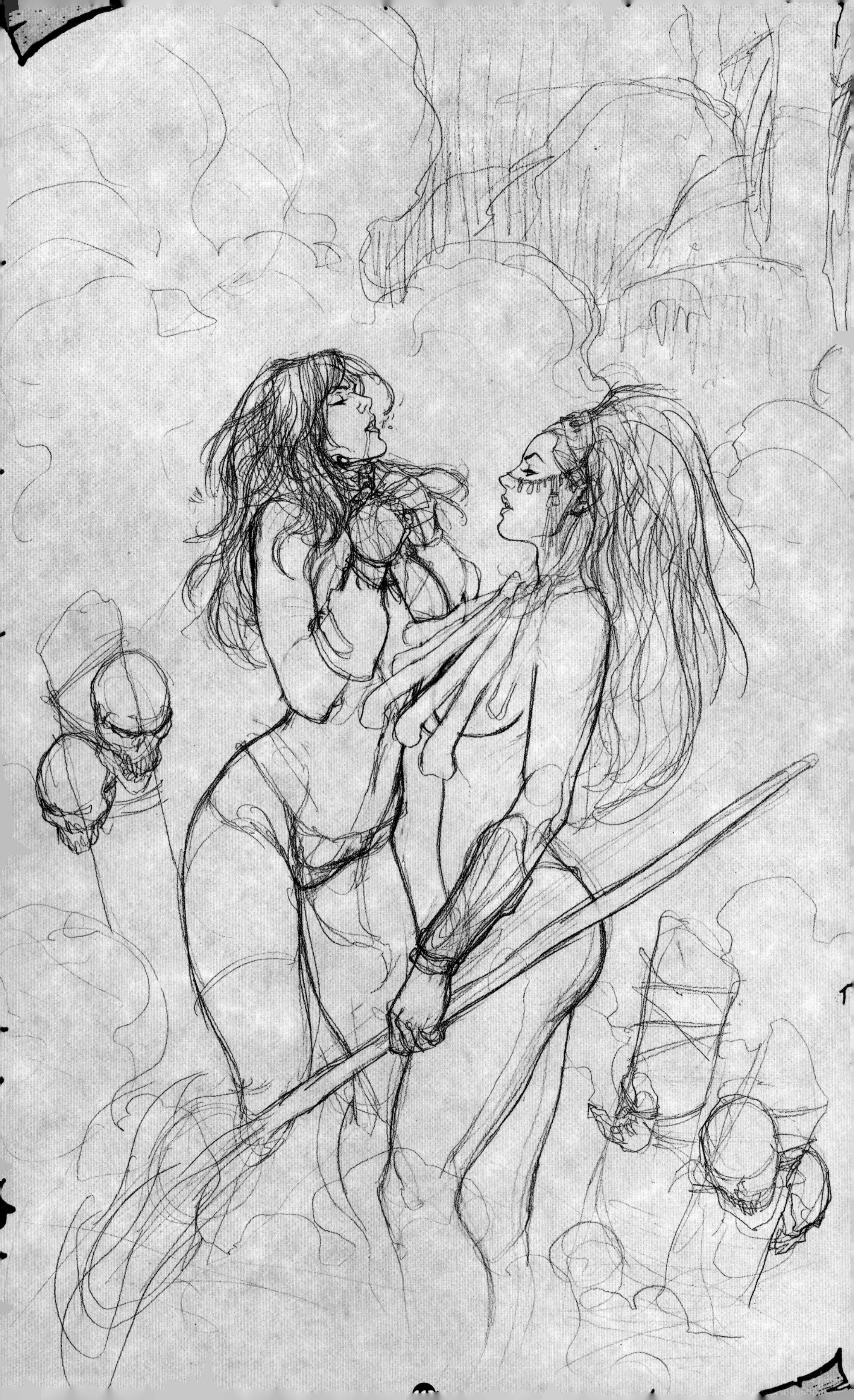

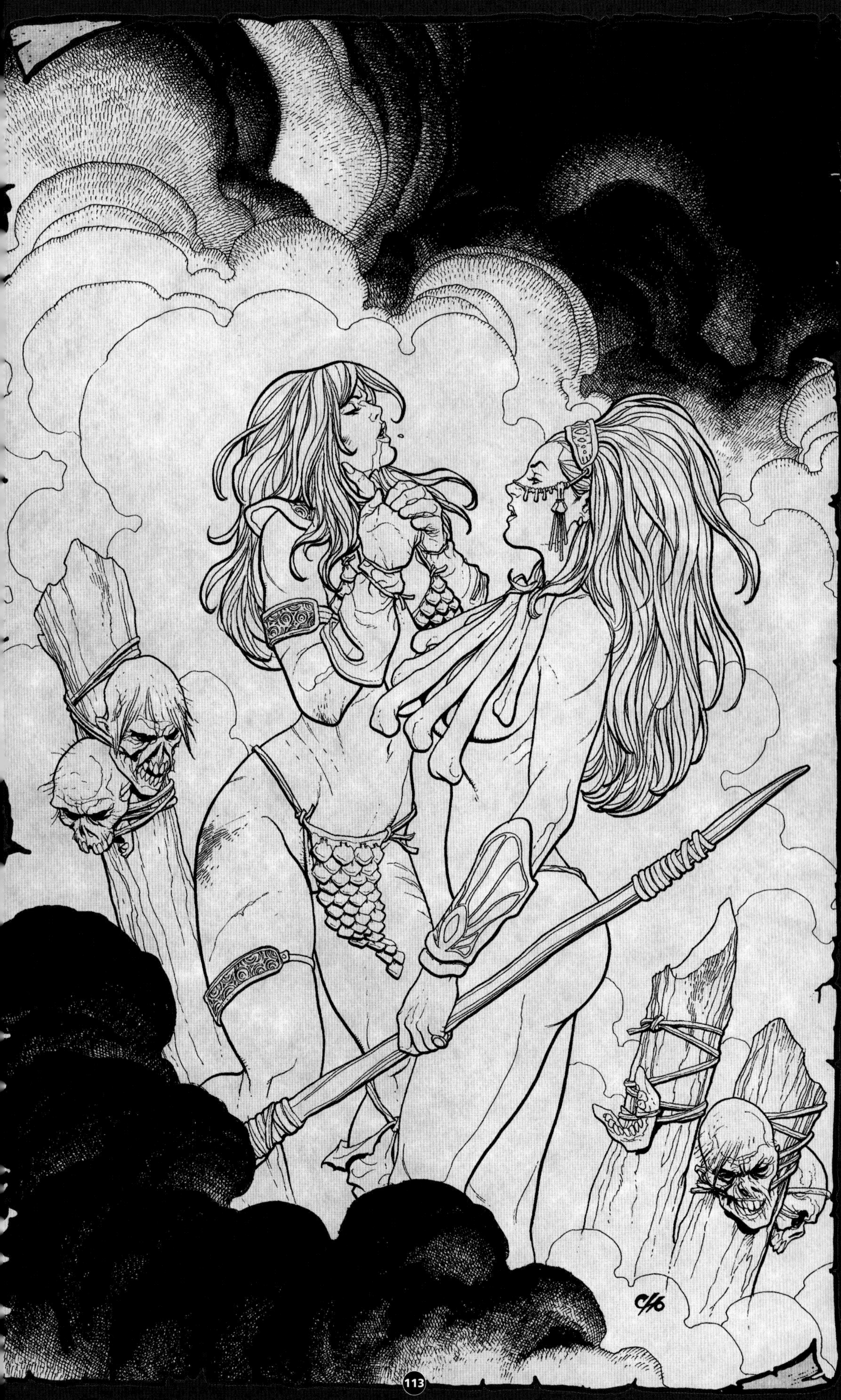

HOMS
SKETCHBOOK

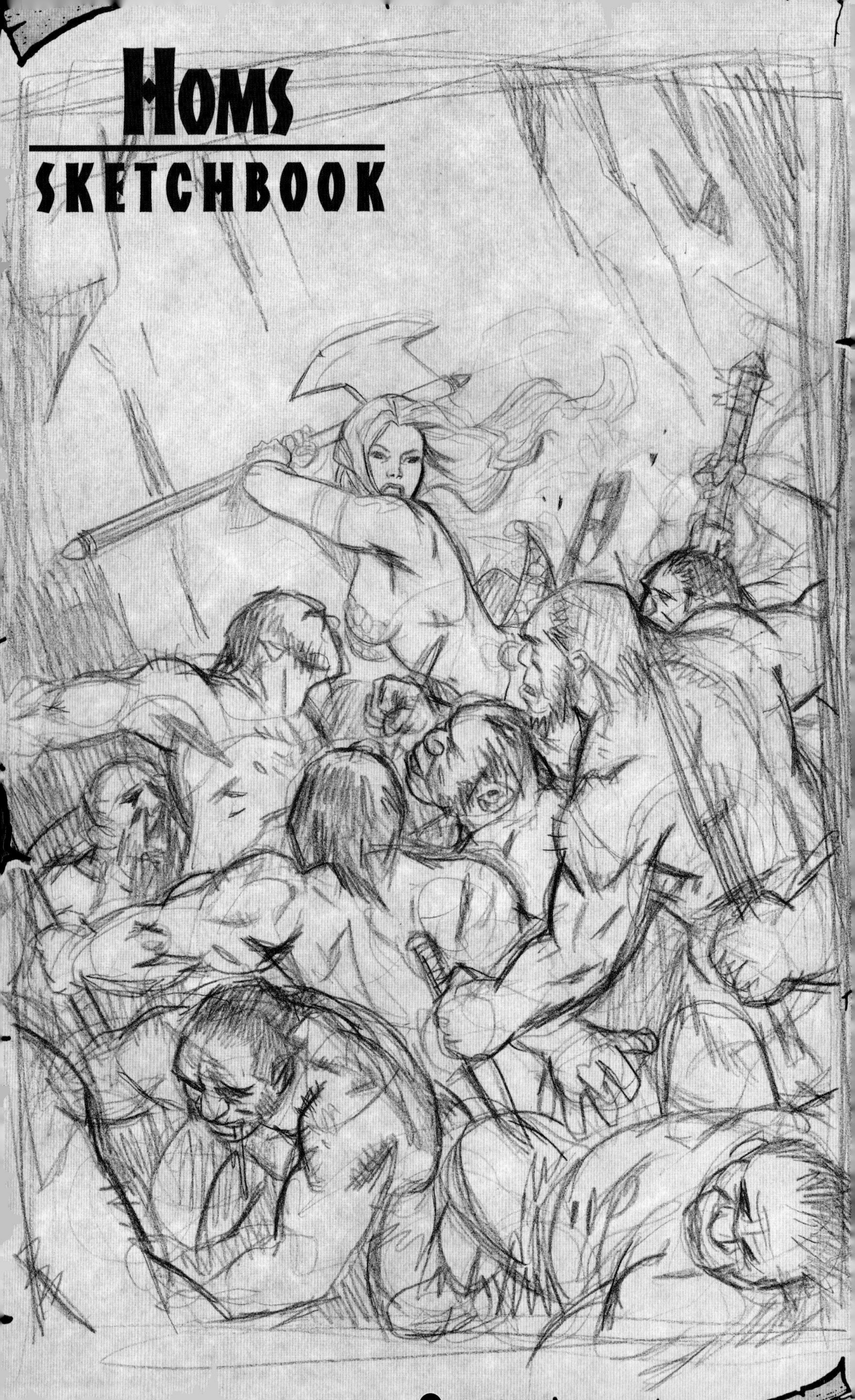

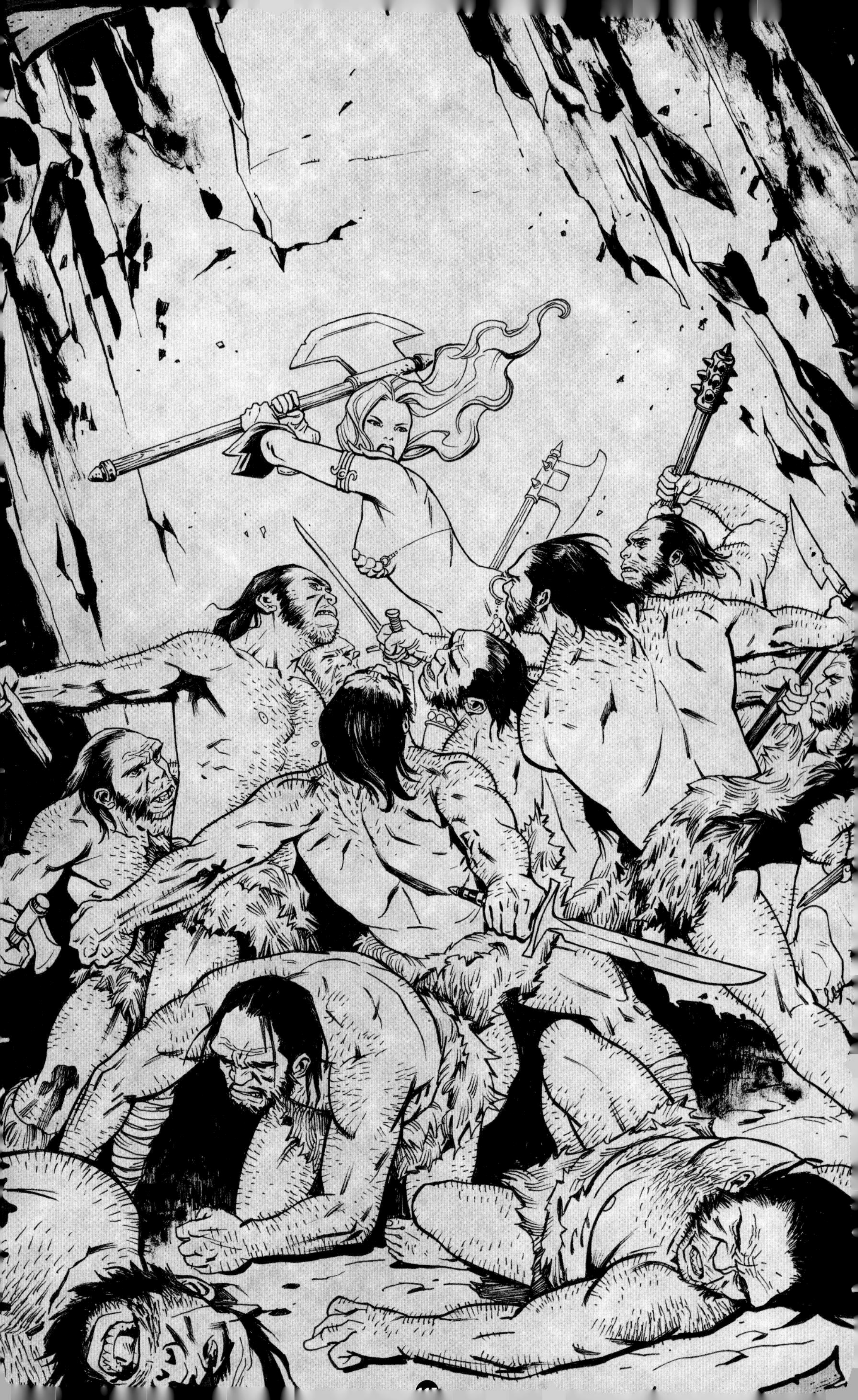

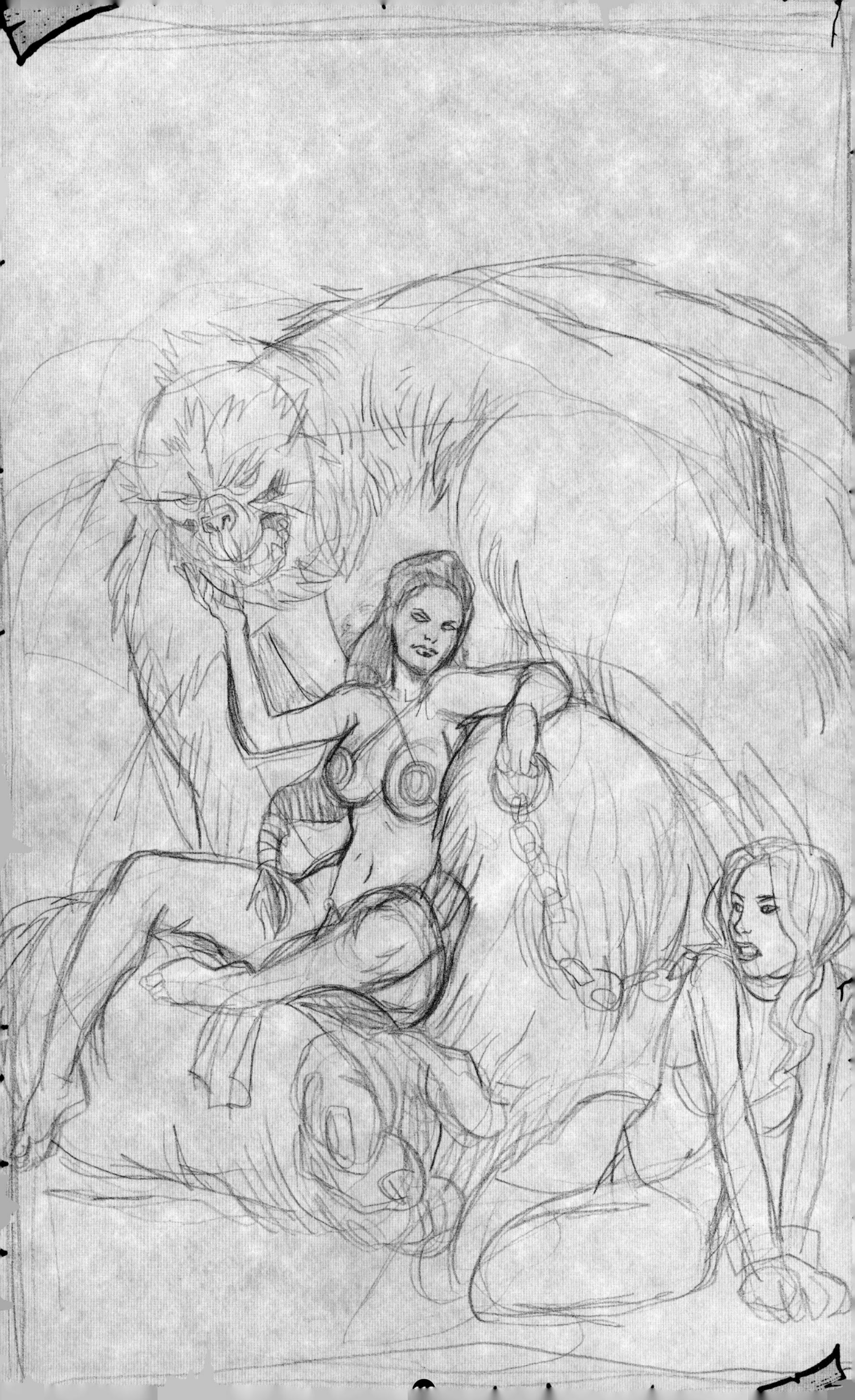

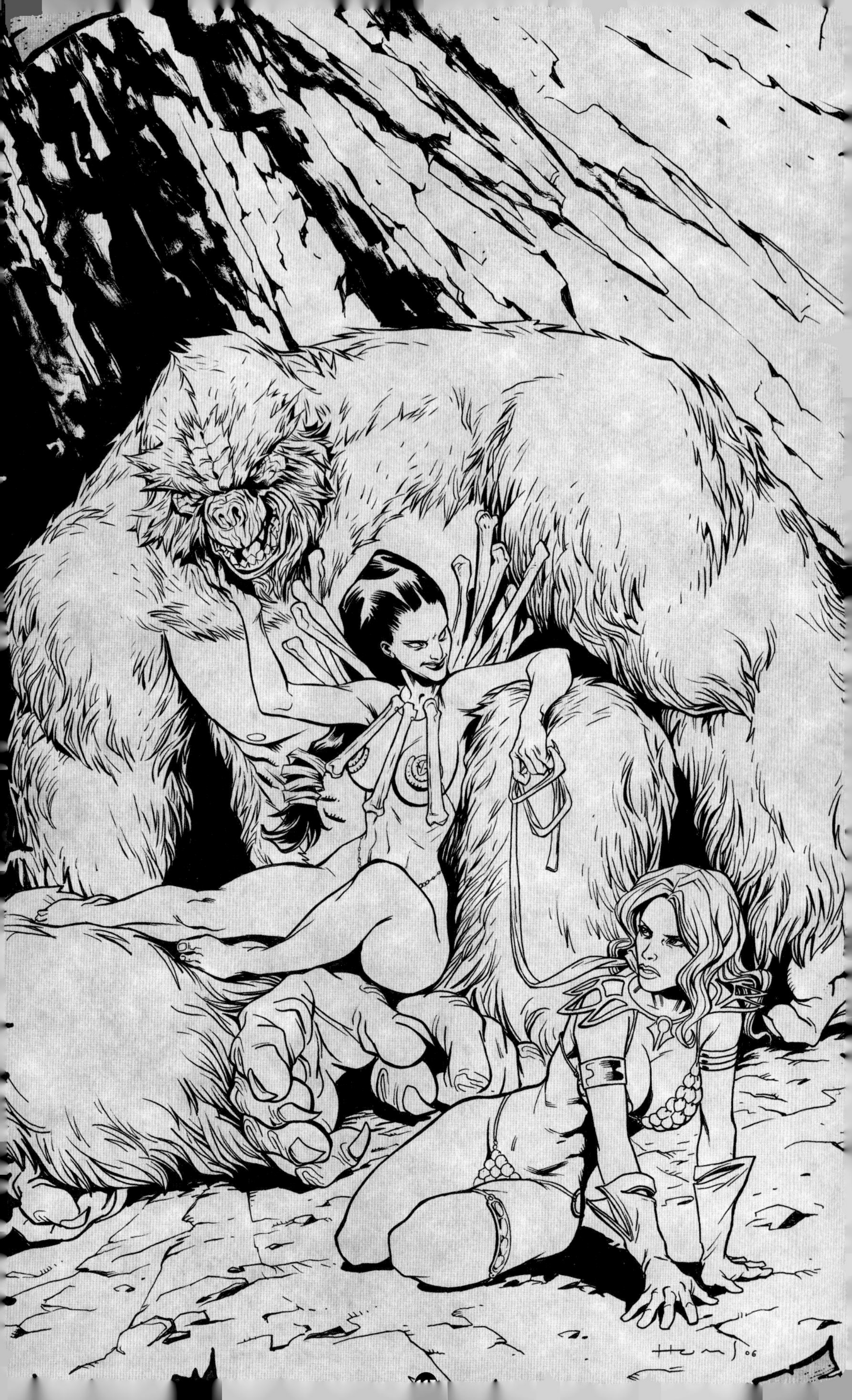

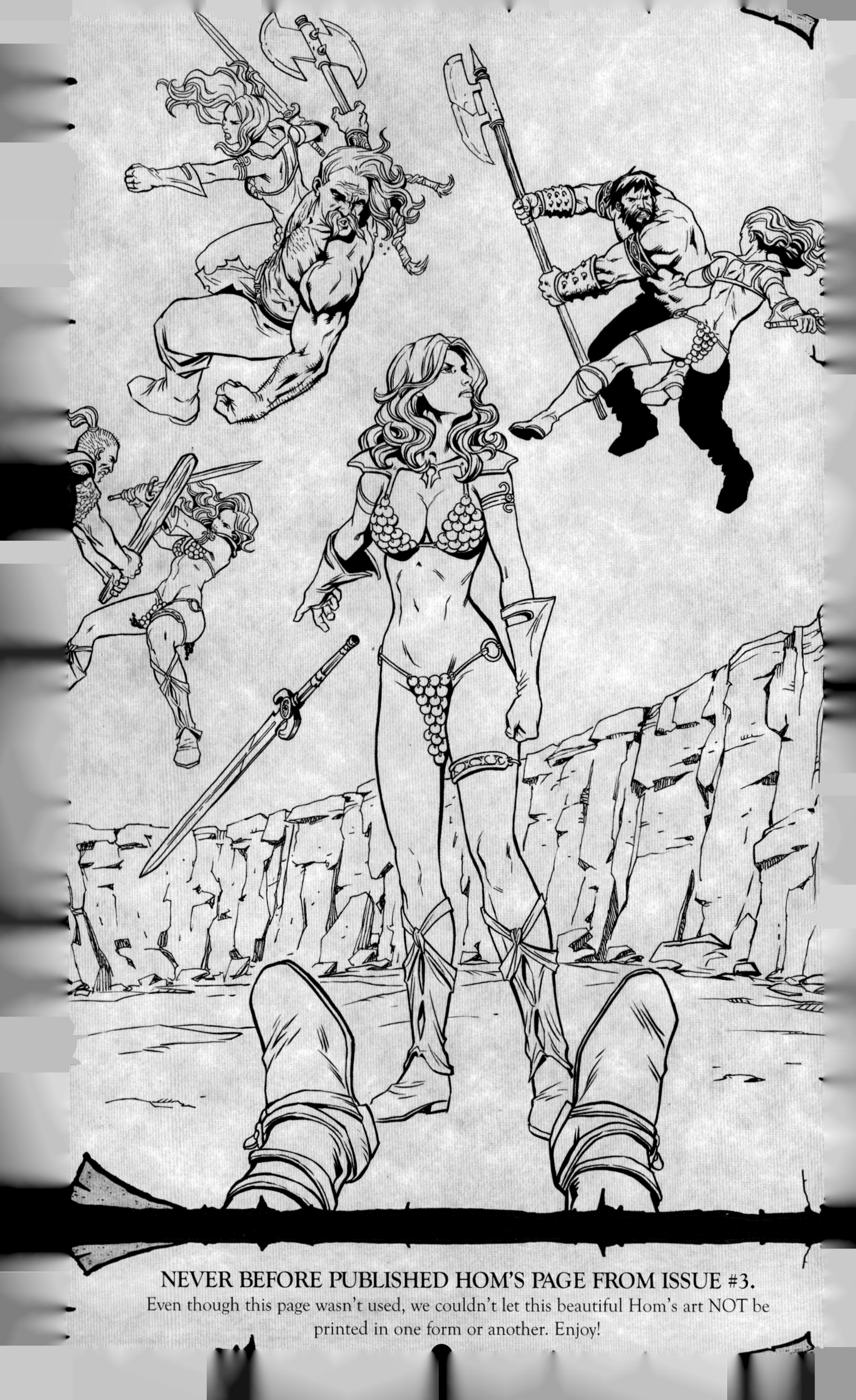

NEVER BEFORE PUBLISHED HOM'S PAGE FROM ISSUE #3.

Even though this page wasn't used, we couldn't let this beautiful Hom's art NOT be printed in one form or another. Enjoy!

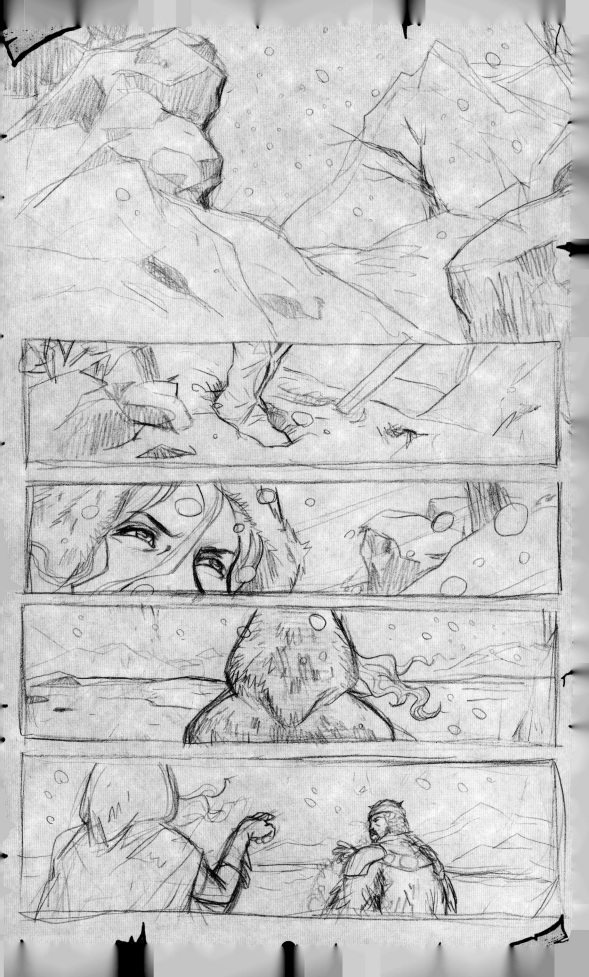

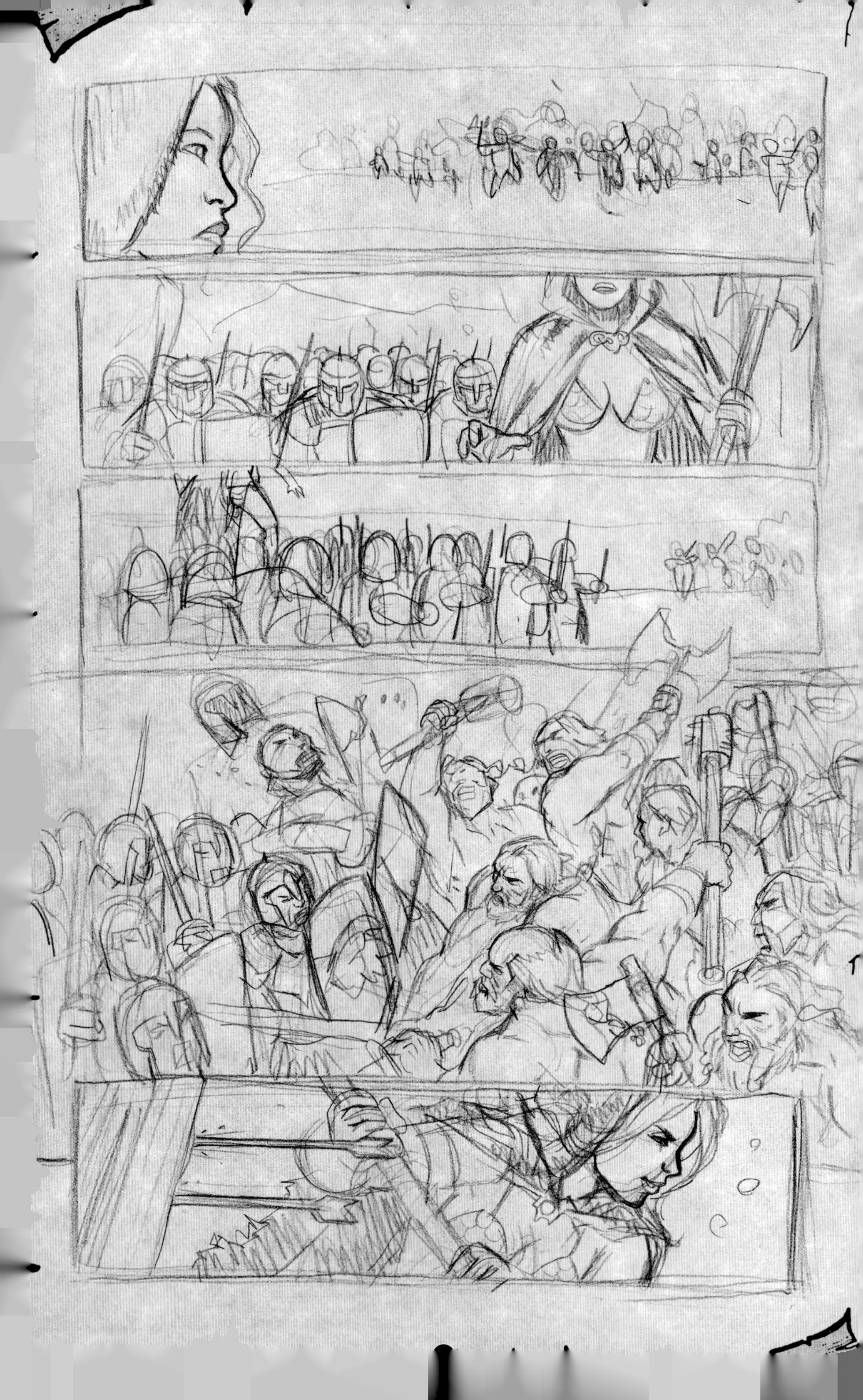

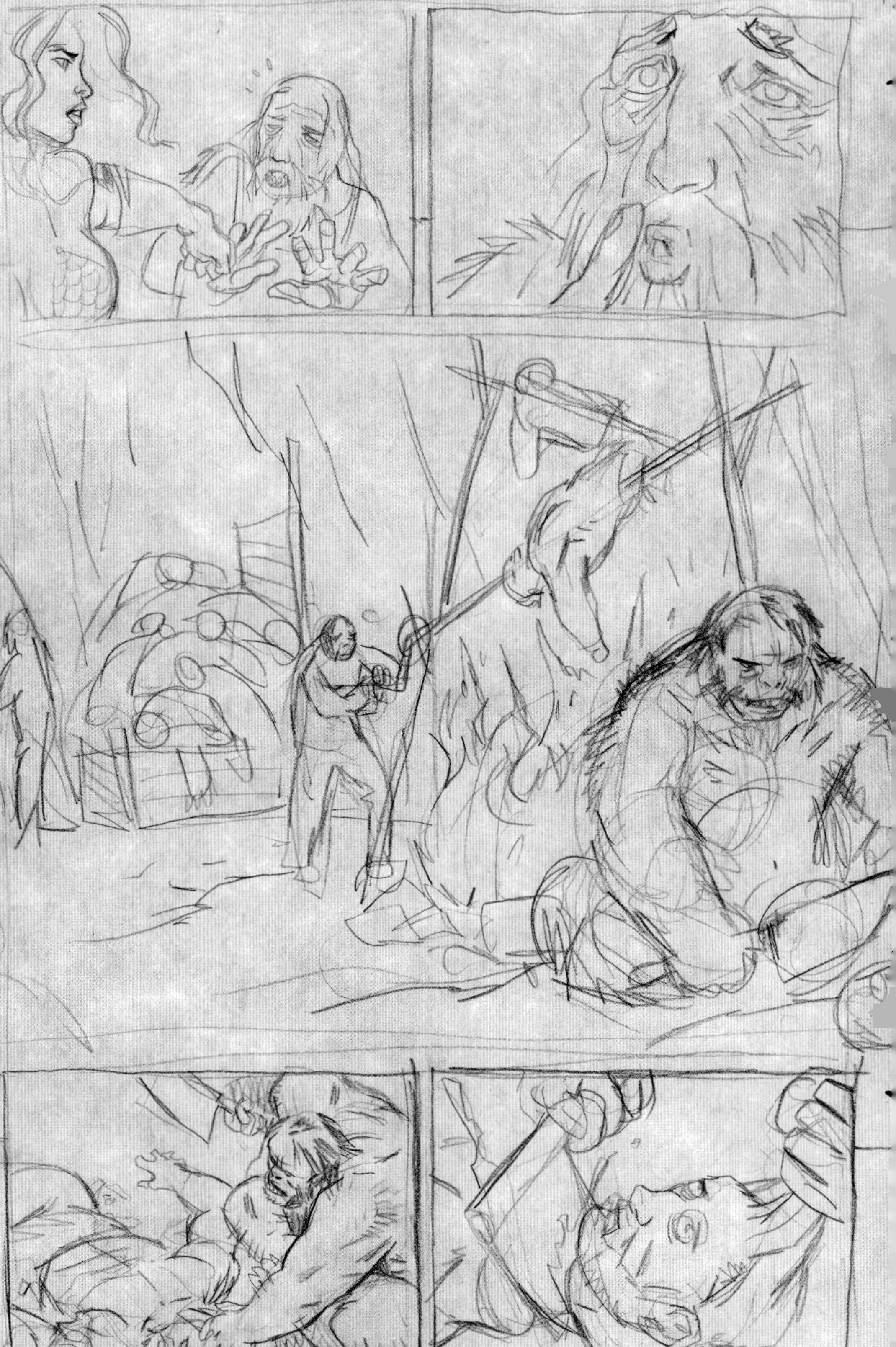

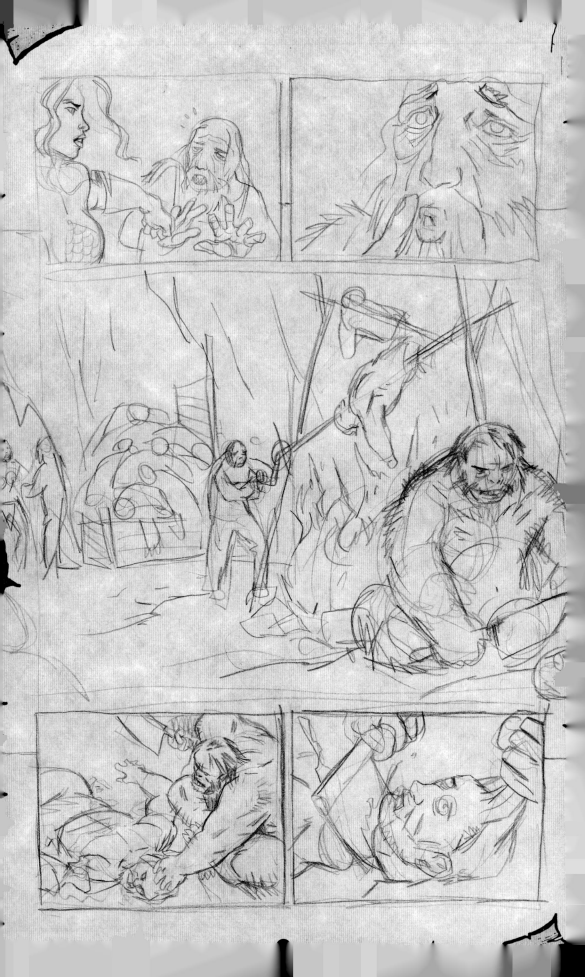

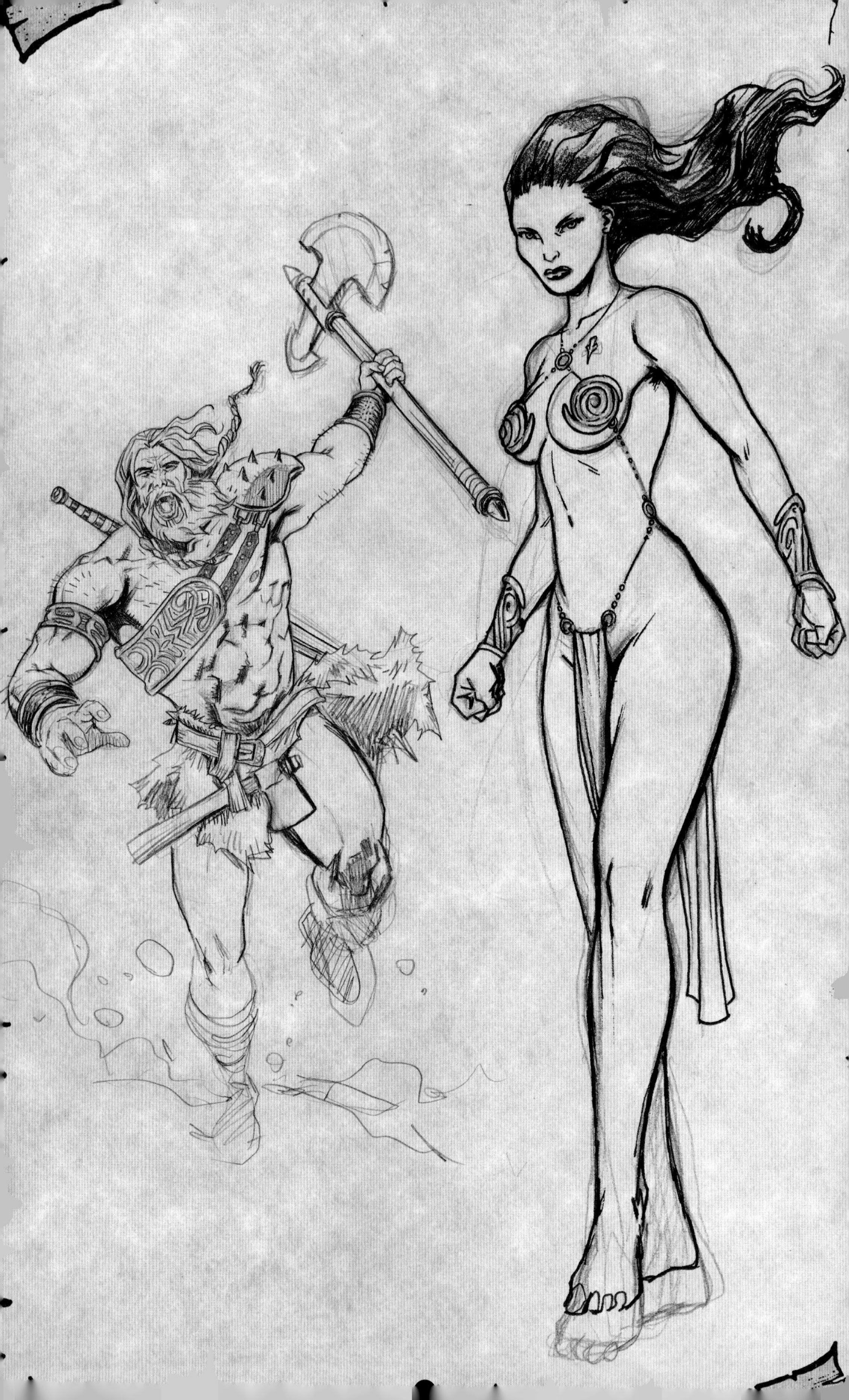

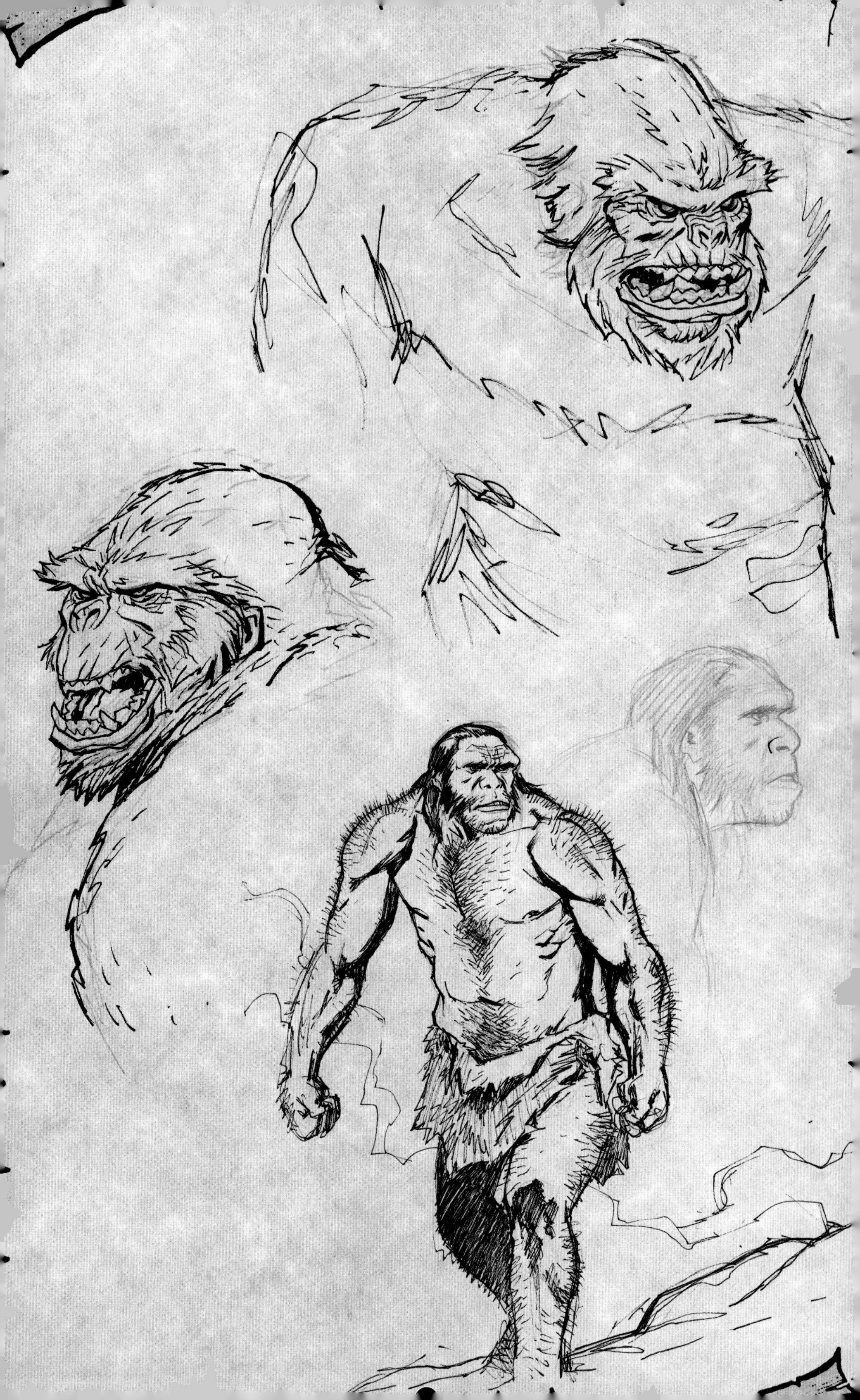

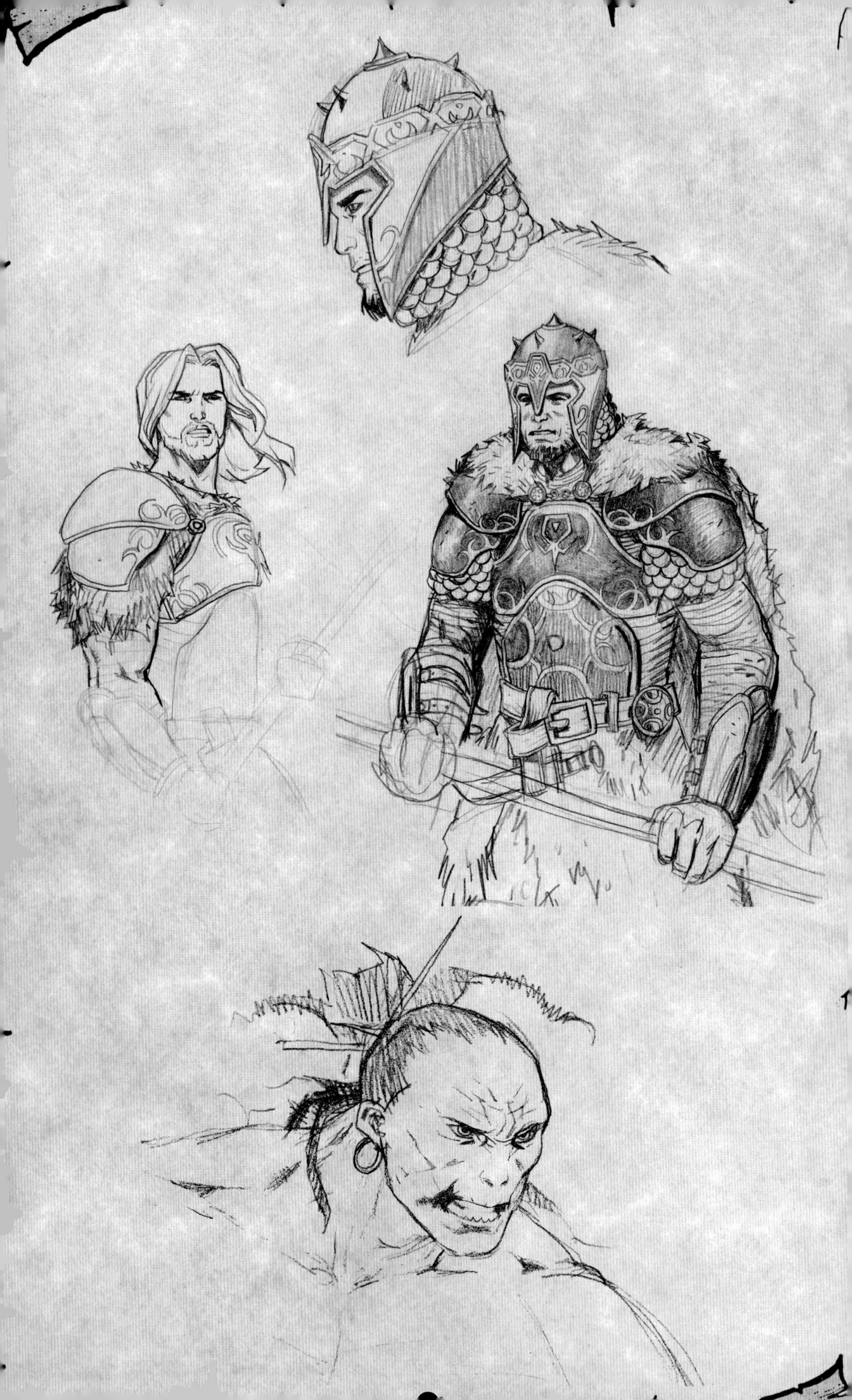

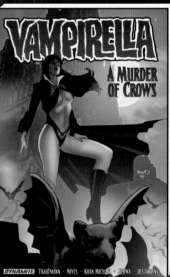

In Stores Now From Dynamite!

VAMPIRELLA VOL. ONE: "CROWN OF WORMS"
written by ERIC TRAUTMANN art by WAGNER REIS & WALTER GEOVANI cover by J. SCOTT CAMPBELL
Collects issues 1-7

VAMPIRELLA VOL. TWO: "A MURDER OF CROWS"
written by ERIC TRAUTMANN & BRANDON JERWA
art by FABIANO NEVES, HEUBERT KHAN MICHAEL & JOHNNY DESJARDINS cover by PAUL RENAUD
Collects issues 8-11

VAMPIRELLA VOL. THREE: "THRONE OF SKULLS"
written by ERIC TRAUTMANN art by JOSE MALAGA & PATRICK BERKENKOTTER cover by PAUL RENAUD
Collects issues 12 through 20 of the hit series!

LOOK FOR THESE DYNAMITE GREATEST HITS!

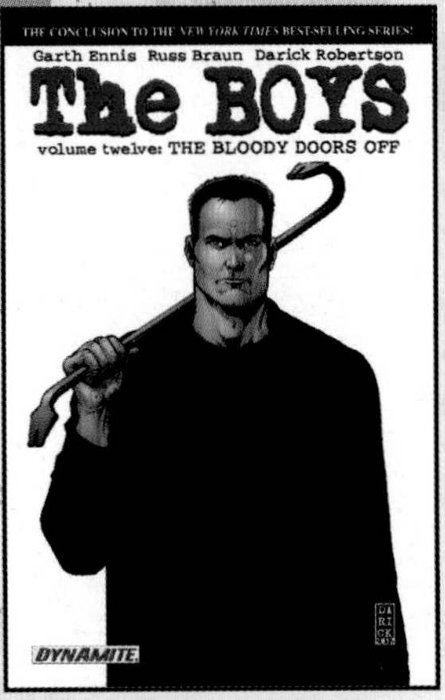
THE CONCLUSION TO THE NEW YORK TIMES BEST-SELLING SERIES!
Garth Ennis Russ Braun Darick Robertson
The BOYS
volume twelve: THE BLOODY DOORS OFF
DYNAMITE

**GARTH ENNIS
THE BOYS & MORE!**

(Garth Ennis') Battlefields V1: The Night Witches
Ennis, Braun

(Garth Ennis') Battlefields V2: Dear Billy
Ennis, Snejbjerg

(Garth Ennis') Battlefields V3: The Tankies
Ennis, Ezquerra

(Garth Ennis') The Complete Battlefields V1
Ennis, Braun, Ezquerra, more

(Garth Ennis') Battlefields V4: Happy Valley
Ennis, Holden

(Garth Ennis') Battlefields V5: The Firefly and His Majesty
Ennis, Ezquerra

(Garth Ennis') Battlefields V6: Motherland
Ennis, Braun

(Garth Ennis') The Complete Battlefields V2
Ennis, Braun, Holden, more

The Boys V1 The Name of the Game
Ennis, Robertson

The Boys V2 Get Some
Ennis, Robertson, Snejbjerg

The Boys V3 Good For The Soul
Ennis, Robertson

The Boys V4 We Gotta Go Now
Ennis, Robertson

The Boys V5 Herogasm
Ennis, McCrea

The Boys V6 The Self-Preservation Society
Ennis, Robertson, Ezquerra

The Boys V7 The Innocents
Ennis, Robertson, Braun

The Boys V8 Highland Laddie
Ennis, McCrea

The Boys V9 The Big Ride
Ennis, Braun

The Boys V10: Butcher, Baker, Candlestickmaker
Ennis, Robertson

The Boys V11 Over the Hill With the Swords of a Thousand Men
Ennis, Braun

The Boys Definitive Edition V1
Ennis, Robertson

The Boys Definitive Edition V2
Ennis, Robertson

The Boys Definitive Edition V3
Ennis, Robertson, more

The Boys Definitive Edition V4
Ennis, Robertson, more

Dan Dare Omnibus
Ennis, Erskine

Jennifer Blood V1 A Woman's Work Is Never Done
Ennis, Batista, Baal, more

Jennifer Blood V2 Beautiful People
Ewing, Baal, more

Just A Pilgrim
Ennis, Ezquerra

The Ninjettes
Ewing, Casallos

Seven Brothers Omnibus
Ennis, Diggle, Kang, more

The Shadow V1 The Fire of Creation
Ennis, Campbell

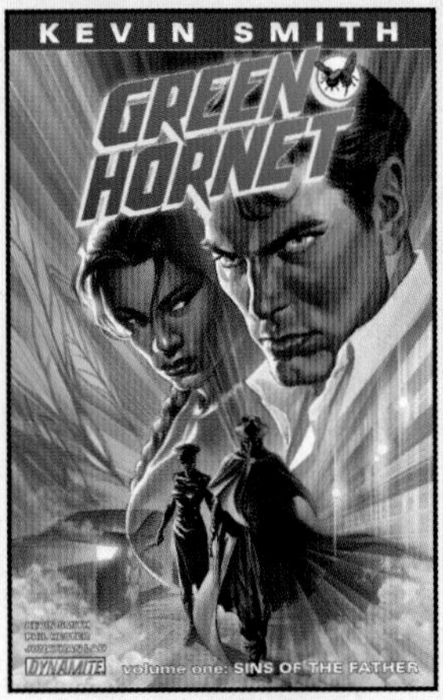
KEVIN SMITH
GREEN HORNET
DYNAMITE volume one: SINS OF THE FATHER

**GREEN HORNET
KEVIN SMITH & MORE!**

(Kevin Smith's) Green Hornet V1 Sins of the Father
Smith, Hester, Lau

(Kevin Smith's) Green Hornet V2 Wearing 'o the Green
Smith, Hester, Lau

Green Hornet V3 Idols
Hester, Lau

Green Hornet V4 Red Hand
Hester, Smith, Vitorino, more

Green Hornet: Blood Ties
Parks, Desjardins

The Green Hornet: Year One V1 The Sting of Justice
Wagner, Campbell

The Green Hornet: Year One V2 The Biggest of All Game
Wagner, Campbell

The Green Hornet Parallel Lives
Nitz, Raynor

The Green Hornet Golden Age Re-Mastered
Various

Kato V1 Not My Father's Daughter
Parks, Garza, Bernard

Kato V2 Living in America
Parks, Bernard

Kato Origins V1 Way of the Ninja
Nitz, Worley

Kato Origins V2 The Hellfire Club
Nitz, Worley

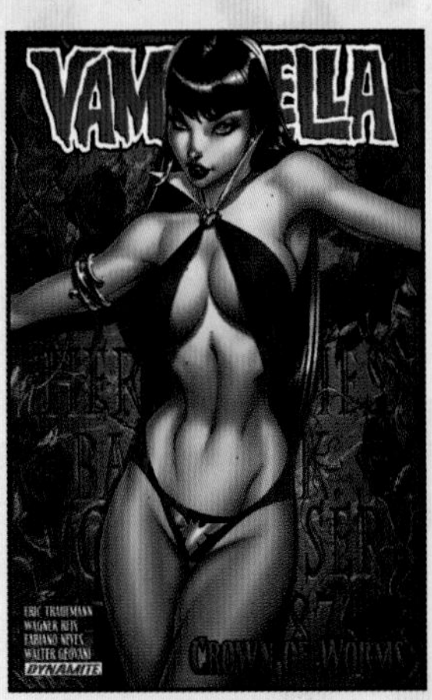
VAMPIRELLA
CROWN OF WORMS
DYNAMITE

VAMPIRELLA!

Vampirella Masters Series V1 Grant Morrison & Mark Millar
Morrison, Millar, more

Vampirella Masters Series V2 Warren Ellis
Ellis, Conner Palmiotti, more

Vampi Omnibus V1
Conway, Lau

Vampirella Masters Series V3 Mark Millar
Millar, Mayhew

Vampirella Masters Series V4 Visionaries
Moore, Busiek, Loeb, more

Vampirella Masters Series V5 Kurt Busiek
Busiek, Sniegoski, more

Vampirella Masters Series V6 James Robinson
Robinson, Jusko, more

Vampirella Archives V1
Various

Vampirella Archives V2
Various

Vampirella Archives V3
Various

Vampirella Archives V4
Various

Vampirella Archives V5
Various

Vampirella V1 Crown of Worms
Trautman, Reis, Geovani

Vampirella V2 A Murder of Crows
Trautman, Neves, more

Vampirella V3 Throne of Skulls
Trautman, Malaga, more

Vampirella And The Scarlet Legion
Harris, Malaga

Vampirella vs. Dracula
Harris, Rodriguez

RED SONJA!

Adventures of Red Sonja V1
Thomas, Thorne, More

Adventures of Red Sonja V2
Thomas, Thorne, More

Adventures of Red Sonja V3
Thomas, Thorne, More

Queen Sonja V1
Ortega, Rubi

Queen Sonja V2 The Red Queen
Nelson, Herbert

Queen Sonja V3 Coming of Age
Lieberman, Rubi

Queen Sonja V4 Son of Set
Nelson, Salazar

Red Sonja She-Devil With a Sword V1
Oeming, Carey, Rubi

Red Sonja She-Devil With a Sword V2: Arrowsmiths
Oeming, Rubi, more

Red Sonja She-Devil With a Sword V3: The Rise of Kulan Gath
Oeming, Rubi, more

Red Sonja She-Devil With a Sword V4: Animals & More
Oeming, Homs, more

Red Sonja She-Devil With a Sword V5: World On Fire
Oeming, Reed, Homs

Red Sonja She-Devil With a Sword V6: Death
Marz, Ortega, Reed, more

Red Sonja She-Devil With a Sword V7: Born Again
Reed, Geovani

Red Sonja She-Devil With a Sword V8: Blood Dynasty
Reed, Geovani

Red Sonja She-Devil With a Sword V9: War Season
Trautmann, Geovani, more

Red Sonja She-Devil With a Sword V10: Machines of Empire
Trautmann, Geovani, more

Red Sonja She-Devil With a Sword Omnibus V1
Oeming, Carey, Rubi, more

Red Sonja She-Devil With a Sword Omnibus V2
Oeming, Reed, Homs, more

Red Sonja She-Devil With a Sword Omnibus V3
Reed, Geovani

Red Sonja vs. Thulsa Doom V1
David, Lieberman, Conrad

Savage Red Sonja: Queen of the Frozen Wastes
Cho, Murray, Homs

Red Sonja: Travels
Marz, Ortega, Thomas, more

Sword of Red Sonja: Doom of the Gods (Red Sonja vs. Thulsa Doom 2)
Lieberman, Antonio

Red Sonja: Wrath of the Gods
Lieberman, Geovani

Red Sonja: Revenge of the Gods
Lieberman, Sampere

Savage Tales of Red Sonja
Marz, Gage, Ortega, more

ART BOOKS!

The Art of Howard Chaykin
The Art of Painted Comics
The Art of Ramona Fradon
The Art of Red Sonja
The Art of Vampirella
The Dynamite Art of Alex Ross
George Pérez: Storyteller
The Romita Legacy